The Other Mother

The Other Mother

by Mary Zenorini Silverzweig

1817

HARPER & ROW, PUBLISHERS, New York
Cambridge, Philadelphia, San Francisco,
London, Mexico City, São Paulo, Sydney

To Stan with Love

and to

Leslie, Amy, and Jennifer

who have been so patient with me

FIRST EDITION

Designed by C. Linda Dingler

Library of Congress Cataloging in Publication Data

Silverzweig, Mary Zenorini.
  The other mother.
    1. Silverzweig, Mary Zenorini. 2. Stepmother—United States. 3. Divorced fathers—United States. 4. Custody of children—United States. I. Title.
HQ759.92.S53 1982   306.8'7   81–47677
                        AACR2
ISBN 0–06–038014–4

---

82 83 84 85 86 10 9 8 7 6 5 4 3 2 1

1

I first met Stan's three little girls on a day considerably more suited to roaming the moors in search of the hound of the Baskervilles than shopping at Bloomingdale's, although unless one lives in England there are few better things to do on a misty, foggy, rainy Saturday in late December. This trip to Bloomie's, however, was no regular shopping trip. Only two days after Christmas, there were no purchases to be made or packages to exchange. It was intrigue and adventure, and the weather suited the plot to perfection.

On Friday night Stan had said to me, "I'll pick up the girls early tomorrow and you can meet us in Hackensack, at Bloomingdale's. Leslie says she needs school clothes, so you can help us shop, and we can have lunch together, at least. And then I'll get them to Dad's. They'll spend the night there." We were to meet his father and stepmother for dinner in my formal introduction to the family. He had even arranged for a sitter, so it sounded as if he had it all very neatly planned.

"Do you think it's wise? After all, you haven't told Roberta about us yet, and maybe the kids need more time to get used to the whole idea of you and her splitting up."

Just as much, and perhaps more to the point, I needed time to get used to Stanley before I had to get used to his offspring. These weeks of just the two of us were the most delightful I had ever spent. He was wooing me with great fervor, and having quickly convinced me to marry him when his divorce became final, he was now devoting his energy to getting my consent to his moving in with me. So far I'd held out, but I was weakening.

"They won't say anything to her—they'll just think we ran into each other. Don't worry."

"If they're as smart as you say, maybe we should wait a while . . ." Like forever, I felt like saying.

"Probably, but I don't want to wait any longer." He had moved out of his and Roberta's house a month before and had been spending his nights in hotels or camping in the woods. Weekends he was taking the girls to hotels or to his relatives. "I want to be able to spend our weekends together. Don't worry, it'll work out. I'm really excited about your meeting them, Mary. They are beautiful little girls." He paused. "I miss them terribly. And the only thing I worry about sometimes is that I won't be as good a father now. And they really need me more than ever." He looked wistful, and more than a little sad. He couldn't admit, and maybe didn't yet realize, that the worry was really a growing sense of guilt at "abandoning" his children.

"That's not true, and you know it." I reached for his hand across the expanse of couch in my living room where we had been sitting, reading, each leaning up against an arm. "You'll be as good a father as ever—better, because you're happier, and that will make a difference to them. And you may not see them as much, but when you do, it's concentrated quality time."

"I guess so. And I was traveling so much with my work that maybe I wasn't with them as much as I think." He went back to the *New Republic* and I to Agatha Christie. A few minutes later, he dropped the magazine to his chest so there was nothing blocking his view of me.

"You're really excited about meeting the girls, aren't you? And having them spend weekends with us? I know you want kids of your own, but mine really need someone like you. You'll get along great."

I didn't answer. What could I say? That I wasn't looking forward to, much less excited by, the prospect of meeting these three little dears of his? Hardly. That I wished he'd never been married, or at least had never had kids? Again, hardly. All I really wanted was for us to spend our weekends cozily together instead of having him off with them, or eventually them with us. But I was silent, and he took my silence for assent.

I had fallen in love with Stan, and at this early stage in our relationship I was doing half unconsciously what I thought he expected and desired of me, being the kind of woman that he seemed to want and need. But in relation to the children and my feelings toward them, I was fully aware that Stan needed to believe the idea of having his three little girls around was indeed a pleasure, not an inconvenience. My intuition told me that to let my own ambivalence ever progress to a point which would force him to make a choice between me and his children would be disastrous.

It took me a while to find out that it probably wouldn't have mattered whatever I said, that he would have heard what he wanted to hear anyway, and done what he wanted to do. But after twenty-eight years of being alone and lonely, of searching for the man I'd daydreamed of since I was ten, of sorting, appraising, and rejecting men of various shapes, persuasions, and types, I felt that I had finally found the missing piece to the puzzle of my personality. Stan was any number of things that I was not and never could be, yet he had made me realize in a very short time I was much more the kind of person I wanted to be than I had ever imagined. I didn't want to lose him now that I had found him, and I couldn't bring myself to cross him, for fear that he would change his mind about all the good things he thought I was.

So in his quiet, persuasive manner, Stan finally convinced me that there was no harm in a brief interlude in Toddler's and Pre-teen's, and to myself I rationalized that the longer I delayed the meeting, the more difficult it was going to be.

I arrived at Bloomingdale's half an hour past the appointed time, postponing the inevitable. After wasting even more time wandering through post-Christmas sales, I pulled myself together and mounted the escalator to the Children's Department on the second floor. I was a little nervous, and a lot reluctant. I had no idea what I was getting into, and in the end, that was probably my salvation.

Observing the scene in Girls, 3–6X from afar my first instinct was to run away. Two frazzled, harried-looking saleswomen were trying to wait on at least six customers. I saw Stan standing at a counter in front of a pile of clothes, a straggly, brown-haired urchin crying soulfully at his knee and stamping her foot. A boy child dressed in torn jeans and a dirty T-shirt was charging about like Teddy Roosevelt, emitting Tarzan-like whoops, playing "attack" with two other equally noisy youngsters. A waif of a girl, feigning maturity yet looking lost and unhappy, was absent-mindedly thumbing through every rack in sight, occasionally calling, "How about this, Dad?" Stan would just as absentmindedly nod his head and gaze about, also lost, also unhappy.

I didn't need Sherlock Holmes to deduce that the two girls were Stan's daughters, Jennifer, nearly four, and Leslie, who had just passed her tenth birthday. They looked pathetic and fretful. I felt slightly nauseous facing this flesh-and-blood reality.

Always before, the girls had been fragments of conversation, relegated, in my mind at least, to a subordinate position in the pressing business of meshing our two adult lives into one, changing life-styles and roles, making new demands, meeting new responsibilities. They had just been "great kids," "terrific," "smart," "special." The little I had heard had in no way prepared me for what I saw. Where were the ribbons, the ruffles, and the winsomely styled hair? The two children who were going to be "mine" part-time looked more like orphans who had run away from The Home, and been in hiding ever since.

I was trying to decide whether to stay or go. At least he doesn't have boys, I thought with relief, staring at the ragged little boy now making absurd faces and crawling around on his hands and knees, black hair in his eyes.

"*Amy.*" Stan's voice, aimed in the general direction of the child on all fours, held not quite patience but not anger either—at

4

most, moderate exasperation. That wild, undisciplined creature was no boy at all . . . it was, in fact, my third weekend "daughter."

My heart plummeted, and my stomach churned harder. I felt duped, cheated, and furious. How could he have done this to me? Why hadn't he told me what his children were really like? There was a split second in which I began to turn away, knowing that to stay was a terrible mistake, but Stan saw me. His face lit up in greeting and he raised his hand. It was too late.

That day began one of the most difficult, demanding, exasperating, frustrating, lonely, and rewarding experiences of my life. That day I had motherhood thrust upon me in Children's Wear at Bloomingdale's by Stanley, who wanted me to help him with his darlings. And by salespeople, who assumed I shared responsibility for the creation of this crying, fingering, insubordinate trio, and looked on me with scorn for not controlling them. And by the girls themselves, who were desperately reaching, searching for something, but weren't quite sure what it was.

It should have been the dawning of a glorious age in my life, three little girls looking, as I was, for love and encouragement to come of age. It was a challenge to test my mettle. In a sense I was a sculptor and they were clay, and I should have seen this as the most marvelous opportunity to help them grow and learn. I should have been relieved that my newfound stepchildren would rejoice in whatever little attention and love I might care to bestow on them. The fix was in—I couldn't lose. Instead, as I watched them on that first disastrous day, I convinced myself if I could just get through the next few hours I would somehow never have to deal with them again.

The day was an embarrassment, an ordeal, a trap, several hours that felt like several years, and no escape, since I wasn't ready to relinquish the new life I was choosing for myself, not yet having tested it. It was an initiation into the foot-stamping tantrums of a three-year-old, the irrational behavior of a hyperactive five-year-old, the disrespectful precocity of a ten-year-old Jewish American Princess. I wouldn't have believed three young girls could get the better of me, but they managed it nicely while scarcely trying.

Stan had introduced us as casually as he could, given the relief he felt that I had come, that I hadn't let him down. Leslie glanced away from the blouse rack long enough to run her eyes from my head to my toes in cool appraisal, then turned away with a noncommittal "Hi." Amy bombarded me with a string of questions—"How old are you?"—"Where do you live?"—"How long have you known my dad?"—"Where do you work?"—and zoomed away without waiting for a single answer. Jennifer just gazed upward with woeful, luminous eyes.

"Madam, would you *please* take your child off there? Don't you realize that it's dangerous?" Inwardly I cursed Stanley for setting Jennifer on a flat glass shelf over a dress rack, then casually walking off to find Amy, who had disappeared.

"Amy, Amy, Amy, where are you?" I panicked when she didn't answer his call. Then we heard a blood-curdling shriek from the shoe department on the other side of the floor, and my face began to burn. The sensation traveled down my neck and through my breast, and settled in a fiery lump in my stomach. People all around were looking at me and Stan and at each other, and in the direction of that unbelievable voice. Everybody knew it belonged to us. When we got to the source, Amy jumped out of a huge toy box like a human jack-in-the-box and ran away again. Mortified beyond description, I prayed I would not meet anyone I knew, and tried to pretend I wasn't with Stanley.

"Can I buy that dress? I want that sweater! Oh, what a pretty blouse." As Stan went off to retrieve his middle daughter, I turned to help Leslie, who certainly needed something other than the too-short jeans and thin T-shirt she was wearing. They all did: unkempt, unclean, dressed like ragamuffins, or street children. I found my heart going out to each of them in spite of myself, and I began to take some pleasure in transforming cinder children into Cinderellas. By the time they were reasonably outfitted, they were bored, crabby, and hungry. I remembered how tired and irritable my mother would get after shopping with me and my two sisters, one older, one younger. Now I knew why.

Praying that lunch would bring relief, I suggested we go to Holly's, across the highway; we managed to leave the store with Amy hiding only twice more, once in Toys and once in Handbags, and the three of them touching everything they passed as they walked by, including an occasional customer. My patience, already micro-thin, finally cracked. "Shouldn't you tell them not to touch things like that? What if . . . can't you . . . control them?" My voice was also thin.

"They're okay. They're really enjoying themselves. And I can tell they like you. Look at Amy. Isn't she cute?"

Amy had picked up a brightly colored Vera scarf from a table in the center of the aisle, and began to do a Dance of the Seven Veils, a three-and-a-half-foot-tall belly dancer. She did not look cute to me, and had she been my child, I'd have had her in a straitjacket a long time ago. I couldn't fathom Stan's placidity. He watched her thoughtfully, but he seemed unperturbed.

"Amy . . ." Stanley startled me by finally asserting himself. "Amy, put that down, and let's go." Still, there was nothing in his voice but gentle patience, and I don't think Amy even heard him. We walked past her, she still wrapped in the scarf, peering up at us sullenly through her bangs. As we turned at the door, she dropped the scarf and came tearing after us, like a little torpedo.

That dreadful day moved along with an uneaten hamburger, two unfinished hot dogs, three undrunk Coca-Colas, french fries with too much ketchup or not enough. The waitress was exasperated because I didn't seem to know what "my" children liked to eat. She was right. I'd never seen them before in my life. How was I to know they hated mustard on their hot dogs and preferred Seven-Up?

And then it was the bathroom. A barroom voice pleaded, "Hey, Dad, I got to pee." (Shut up, Amy, please.)

"I'll take her, Daddy." Leslie was being capable and officious, showing me she had her unruly sister very much under control.

"I'll go, Leslie, you don't have to." It was a brave offer on my part, and no one, least of all me, was sure if I could handle it. But Leslie, sensing acutely that there was more between her father and me than we had purported, decided to let me take whatever risk and punishment I sought out.

"Me, too," piped up Jennifer.

Damn, I thought, because she was getting cranky, and "No" or "I don't want to" was all she'd been saying for the last hour. I couldn't renege on my offer, so gingerly I led—or tried to lead— the two of them to the ladies' room. Amy ripped out in front, and I managed to catch up with her only because she paused in front of a florid, gray-haired man who was eating a very large strawberry sundae.

"Gee, that looks good," she said, and audibly smacked her lips. "Can I taste it?"

I grabbed her arm and pulled her along, leaving the gentleman sputtering into his ice cream. His wife gave me a look of undisguised dismay and, I do believe, pity. Jennifer was beginning to whimper.

Naturally Amy locked herself in one of the booths in the restroom and refused to come out.

"I'm not ready." She resisted all my weary reasoning.

And of course Jenny's little cries turned into a tantrum.

"Mommy, Mommy, Daddy, Daddy, Leslie, Leslie."

At first the cries were low, but persistent. The lady washing her hands at the sink peeked first at me, then Jennifer, through the mirror. Then the little voice rose and the feet began to stamp, and I once again began to think of running away. I couldn't quiet Jenny, and couldn't get Amy to budge. After an eternity, Leslie appeared, ignoring me, with an "Oh, Jennifer, what's the matter?" and a hug for her sister, which calmed Jennifer almost immediately. She merely called to Amy, "Hurry up, Daddy wants to go to Grandpa's," but that was all that Amy needed. I was obviously, in her eyes, extraneous and impotent.

Stan met us at the exit, after once again retrieving Amy, who had darted off to tell the same astonished sundae eater, "Nice talking to you." As Stan pulled her out the door he said to me over his shoulder, "Isn't it great the way she can relate to strangers?" Amy was smiling at herself, pleased that her intrusion had drawn a response.

It was time for us to go our separate ways for a few hours—and possibly, I was beginning to think, forever. The first phase of my ordeal was over. All that was left for me that day was to have dinner with Stan's father and stepmother.

"Say goodbye, kids. Maybe you'll see Mary again."

"Oh yes, yes, yeah." A chorus of concurrence, which they did or didn't feel (it was hard for me to tell). Then Amy bellowed, "I have a surprise for you."

"What's that?" I asked.

Her tough little arms reached up toward my neck, and she planted a smack firmly on my cheek. From the silence, and the look on Stan's face, I could tell they all were as astonished as I was.

That wet, noisy kiss did as much to disrupt my equanimity as anything else that had happened. It touched me, and even interrupted my preparation of a little speech in which I was going to tell Stan calmly that I refused to have anything to do with his three little darlings, and take the consequences, whatever they were.

And though Amy's kiss turned my mind around for a moment, a quick review of the situation reaffirmed my conviction that I wasn't going to be able to accept the reality of his kids, that our backgrounds were too different, that we wouldn't be able to make it work.

Stan was ten years my senior, a Jewish/agnostic radical in contrast to my Catholic Republicanism, unstructured and freewheeling in contrast to my often irrationally imposed self-discipline. He was an idealist, a romantic, always expecting and believing in the best side of people. I was a realist and very cynical, always slightly wary, always half expecting the worst. In a relationship that had become really close only in the past month, we were already beginning to change each other in subtle ways, each playing the role of Pygmalion, and trying to do it unobtrusively.

But he had been married for seventeen years, and I had been single all of my adult life, and after several hours with his children, I wasn't sure whether the differences weren't insurmountable, our courtship too intense, our decision to marry too hasty. And maybe it wouldn't be the end of the world for me if it didn't work out. After all, he *had* made me feel incredibly competent, talented, attractive, and special without asking anything in exchange. If he thought that well of me, wasn't it possible someone else (without children) just as intelligent and interesting as he was could make me feel just as good about myself?

At the moment I was pretty certain that the biggest problem in calling everything off would be my embarrassment. I could hear my mother saying, "I just *knew* you wouldn't go through with it. What's the matter with you, anyway?" My parents had kept our relationship quiet so that they wouldn't have to tell anybody that their daughter had been taken advantage of, was too immature to know what she was doing, or was just plain promiscuous. They were, I felt, expecting it to break up.

As I drove to New York City to keep my dinner date with my prospective in-laws, the windshield wipers swept rhythmically back and forth in the cold rain, saying with each swipe, "You're crazy, you're crazy," and the lights from the cars reflected each shiny, wet, red, flashing mile after mile of "Warning, Danger Ahead." As I had expected, Stan was late, so I was later on purpose. His family was early, waiting for us uncomfortably in the foyer of the Seafare of the Aegean.

Harry, Stan's father, had seen his beloved wife Rosila die painfully of cancer five years before, and although he had married her younger sister Rachel, in formal Orthodox Jewish tradition, he had never stopped mourning Rosila. (Rachel had finally insisted that he take the picture of Rose's tombstone off their dresser, but aside from that she simply lived with his grief.) Now Harry's oldest son—the joy of his life, the success of the family, what had he done? Stanley was not only getting divorced—abandoning his wife, deserting his children—he was, of all things, taking up with a gentile woman—a shiksa—and that approached the unforgivable.

I sat through dinner, listening to tales of Bobbi and Stan, how sad it was, what dear sweet little girls his grandchildren were, and how much in need they were of attention. I was certain that the attention he thought they needed was probably quite different from that which I perceived they deserved.

"You know, Mary, Bobbi is a very good person. She was always very good to me and my Rose, and all my children. So maybe she wasn't always the best mother, but—eeh!" And Harry gave an eloquent little shrug. "Who are we to judge? Terrible, this is all just terrible. My poor little granddaughters. What's to become of them?" He shook his head from side to side, then cupped it in his hands. "Shmielila," Harry said to his son, "I hope you know what you are doing."

"Yeah, Dad, I know. Believe me there are lots of things you don't know anything about, but if you did, you'd understand." Stan's tone had an edge to it that I'd never heard before, slightly bitter.

"Like what?" Harry was relentless. I wanted to talk about something else. Anything else. I kicked the table leg by mistake, trying for Stanley's shin, but he had, thank God, already begun to change the conversation.

"Look, Dad, I didn't come here to talk about Roberta or why I'm getting a divorce. We came here so you could meet Mary and get to know her better. You and Mom always told me I was crazy to marry Bobbi in the first place, and neither one of you ever had anything good to say about her. Well, you were right. She was a lousy wife, and a lousy mother, so let's just drop it. Why don't we order? I'm starving." And he turned his attention to the menu.

Rachel, the second senior Mrs. Silverzweig, was very much impressed by the Seafare of the Aegean.

"This is such a beautiful restaurant. Have you ever been here before?" She was a little round woman, with flat graying hair and penetrating gray eyes.

"Yes." I nodded, and smiled at Stanley. "This is the first place he took me out to dinner." He squeezed my hand under the table.

"I came here once many years ago, with my dear wife, Rose,"
Harry began to reminisce. "Such a beautiful woman. How she
loved eating in fancy restaurants." Harry sighed with sadness
and discontent. "Such a loss, such a loss. Did you ever come
here with Bobbi, Stanley?" I snatched my hand out of Stanley's,
irrationally transferring my displeasure at my prospective father-
in-law to my prospective husband. Why did Harry have to keep
bringing up Roberta? "Dad, *please.*" Stan's voice had much more
authority and firmness than it did with his own children.

The evening passed more slowly than I would have liked, but
on the whole it was less unpleasant than I had expected. I was
nervous about the impression I was making on my new family,
probably without cause, and it was with relief I heard Harry
say, "Rachel, it's time we go home. I have to open the store
early."

(The store, a little superette, used to be called Harry and Rose's
Dairy. After she died, he had painted out the "and Rose," so
the sign now read "Harry   's Dairy.")

Stan and I rode back to my house in Mount Tabor, New Jersey,
quiet at first, snaking our way through the midnight of the city.

"How are you holding up?" Stan broke the silence with his
concern.

"It's been quite a day." An understatement, if I ever heard
one.

"The kids were crazy about you. I could tell. I think everything
is going to be fine."

How could you tell? I wondered. By the way Amy hid? Or
the tantrums Jenny threw? Or the way Leslie said *"I'll* take care
of it" when Jenny needed help, letting me know in no uncertain
terms that she was running things, and I was incompetent to
handle her or her sisters?

Now was the time to tell him, tell him that the sweetness
wasn't worth the pain.

"They sure are something else. Do they always behave so . . ."
I was groping for the right word.

"Lively? Yup. They're so intelligent and inquisitive. Wasn't

Amy cute, talking to that man in Holly's? She always makes friends wherever she goes. And Jenny's so good—although she did seem a little sad to me today."

"You mean they *always* run around like that, and look like that, and talk like that?" My horror must have been obvious in my voice.

"What do you mean? What's the matter?" He sounded genuinely perplexed.

"What's the matter? Weren't you embarrassed? How could you let them act that way in public? Or look like that? It was awful." Thinking back and reliving those hours began to nourish the anger and frustration that I felt at being thrown into a lion's den after having been told it was full of kittens. "I don't understand it and I don't think I can handle it." There. It was out.

"Mary, I don't understand *you*. They weren't any different than usual. That's the way they are. They're just children. What's wrong with it?" He was hurt; I had done the forbidden and criticized his three perfections. But he hadn't heard what I had really said.

I didn't want to push him too far; I knew that he was going through some difficult months. For Stanley to make a conscious decision to hurt someone, no matter how much he had been hurt himself, was totally out of character for him. And the fact that intellectually he knew the divorce meant everyone was going to be better off in the long run, and quite probably the short run, too, didn't alleviate his distress in the slightest.

"Oh, I don't know—maybe there isn't anything *wrong* with it. It's just that—well, don't you ever scold them? Or spank them? How do you discipline them?"

"They don't need it, do they? They're okay. And Leslie takes care of the little ones like a trooper, always helping them—why, she even fixes breakfast for them."

"Doesn't Roberta . . ." I was learning more about his personal life from today than he had ever told me before. It was the first glimpse he had allowed me of what his home life had been.

"No. At least she never used to. Leslie's always done a lot.

And then we've almost always had a part-time housekeeper." That was a true luxury, I imagined, since Roberta worked only sporadically.

"What about Amy? How can you let her behave like that— running around, yelling, talking to strangers? It just isn't right," I ended lamely. It had been so obvious that Amy's problem was much deeper than insubordination.

"Amy's a very special little girl. She's bright, curious, and she likes people. There's nothing wrong with that. And I see them so seldom—always have, because I've had to travel away from home so much. I don't want to always be hollering at them or criticizing them or scolding them. I want them to trust me, and be able to come to me when they need someone—be able to talk to me. I want them to know that I love them."

"I love my father, but he still made it very clear what he expected of me, and God help me if I didn't do it."

"Is that why you're afraid of him?" That he knew this surprised me, because I hadn't talked about it.

"How did you know? I guess I'm afraid of him because he gets so angry inside, then takes it out in silence. I'd rather that he yelled. But who teaches them? Who sets limits and structure? Roberta?"

He shook his head. "They've learned a lot already, Mary. They're not dumb kids, you can see that. What should they know that they don't? And now that Bobbi and I are separated, more than ever they need to be happy when they're with me."

"Isn't it important that they respect you? Leslie called you an idiot today and meant it. And you didn't bat an eye. I wouldn't be able to tolerate that from a child of mine!"

"She didn't really mean it that way. . . ." He shrugged it off so casually, as he did Amy's problems. His perceptions of his children's behavior seemed to differ so drastically from mine. I didn't know then that he really was aware of some of the more troubling aspects of his daughters' personalities but wasn't quite sure what to do about them.

I had fallen in love with a man wise and perspicacious in many ways, sensitive to people's feelings, but a man I thought unwilling—perhaps unable—to see his family situation as it truly was. Much later, in bits and pieces, Stan related that in his work as a management consultant he would devote himself to an assignment until it succeeded, and he had looked upon his marriage, in the best sense, as a project. For years he couldn't bring himself to admit that it was a failure, and that nothing he could bring to the relationship would turn it into a success. His drive for perfection at best, and, at worst, his ability to make the best of a bad situation, led him to continue in and try to sustain a marriage that had barely been a marriage, for more years than most people would have bothered. Once his suspicions were strengthened in the year before the separation that his wife was a lesbian, it became easier for Stan to examine the adverse effects the empty, often angry marriage was having on his children as well as on himself. Staying together "for the sake of the children" simply wasn't the answer.

When Stan and Roberta agreed that their marriage wasn't salvageable, there was little remorse on either side. All she wanted from him was unnecessary reassurance that he would provide for her and the children financially, and stay in close contact with the girls, both things that Bobbi's father had not done when he left her mother when Bobbi was a child. So Stanley already had his lawyer working out a legal separation agreement that would take care of their needs, and assure him continued association with his daughters.

His fantasy (although I didn't know it at the time) was to create a new, fulfilling life for himself, and then to share as much of that life as possible with Leslie, Amy, and Jennifer, as much as they wanted, as much as they needed to become fulfilled themselves. And Stanley was a master at transforming his fantasies into reality.

I had fallen in love with a weaver who had spun for me a tapestry of sunlight and starlight and moonbeams and a curiously hectic tranquillity the likes of which were beyond my wildest imaginings. In the time we'd known each other he'd given me nothing but joy and asked nothing of me in return. Even when he presented to me his most cherished treasures, in need of polishing—a blemish here or there—he didn't ask me to help him. He just trusted that I wouldn't let him down, and as we drove home that rainy night, I knew, no matter how much I might want to, I couldn't.

2

After we celebrated New Year's Eve by Stan's finally moving in with me, he decided with unalterable determination that it was time we spent the weekend together. The five of us. I tried in vain to convince him it was too soon, for me as well as for them.

"We'll have a good time," he said. "It's time they got to know you better. And you'll love them. They're super kids." He seemed to have forgotten he had said all this to me before, and he ignored my plea for delay.

It was as if Bloomingdale's had never happened. We hadn't talked again about the state I felt the kids were in because I knew he would only get defensive if he thought I was going to be critical, or shut me off with a "Wait until you really get to know them." From the brief exposure I had had to them, I'd as soon get to know a pride of panthers or a cage of rattlesnakes.

But as was usual in those early days, I let him prevail, despite the fact that Bobbi still didn't know about me and I didn't think that through the children was the best way for her to find out.

On a sunny winter Friday, the phone rang in my living room as I was hiding the most obvious evidence that my home was now Stanley's as well. It was Stan. "We're in the neighborhood," he said, probably with a straight face. "We thought you might let us drop by for a few minutes. Okay? Amy wants to say hello," he added.

"Hi, I'm Amy. Are you Mary? We met before. Do you really have an airplane? Where do you live? Are we coming to see you? How do you know my daddy?" Stan grabbed the phone and said they'd be right over. I tried to tell him to stall for fifteen minutes. I really wanted him to stall for fifteen years, but he hung up before I had the chance to speak.

I ran upstairs, opened the closet door, and stuffed in whatever remaining traces of our nonconnubial bliss were to be found. A last survey of the open shelves in our minuscule bathroom revealed only one item which I felt might be incriminating—Old Spice aftershave that one of the kids had given Stan for Christmas.

The door knocker rapped, and the sound of children's voices filtered up the stairs. They were all so excited, and I was approaching despair. The idea of being a part-time stepmother hadn't been so frightening or burdensome when I had imagined that Stan's daughters were all that he had said they were. It might even be fun being a stepmother to terrific, smart, super kids, having all that pleasure without the effort of making them that way. But I certainly didn't want to spend the leisure hours I had with my love in the company of three dirty, whining, insecure little brats. Memories of our first meeting at Bloomingdale's still made my stomach churn. I was romantic enough to believe that we were entitled to a delightful courtship, growing and loving and learning together. We were building a "relationship." But Stan, in his gentle, low-key way, had sneaked in three more people who needed a relationship as much as he did. And I wasn't ready for it.

I was suddenly living with a man I had met only ten months before; and for all but one of those months, I had known him only in a professional capacity as my company's management consultant. I didn't understand Stan, didn't really know him— he was totally unlike anybody I had ever met. I needed time, time to adjust to committing myself. Time to get used to living with someone, time to get used to letting someone get close to me. I'd had plenty of boyfriends, a collegiate engagement, and more mature relationships with "men," but these relationships had all had one thing in common: the distance that I cherished and preserved between my inner self and them. Now I found myself thrust into a situation where I at least thought I wanted to be, with someone I thought I wanted to spend the rest of my life with. I wasn't quite sure how it had happened or where we were headed, but up to recently things had been more or less to my liking. Now there was one exception. Rather, three exceptions.

I could count the number of times that Stanley had talked about the kids, before or after that day at Bloomie's, and not need to use all my fingers and toes. He obviously pretended or preferred to believe that the kids were not going to be a problem for either me or him. There was only one time when he'd given any sign of the enormousness of the emotion he felt for them, a week or two before I met them, but I didn't realize it at the time.

We had had a gourmet Christmas excursion, first dinner in a French bistro on Third Avenue, then shopping for a tin fish poacher, a copper omelette pan, and a glass espresso coffee pot. Our first joint purchases made me a little nervous, because somehow this domesticity made our being together more real, more final, and at the same time, more fragile. I hadn't yet agreed to either his proposal or his proposition, but he assumed I would say, eventually, yes to both. It was raining and cold, but we were warm from wine and brandy, weaving down 59th Street, holding hands, pressing our noses against chilly, interesting windows, and pausing in dark doorways for sweet, satisfying embraces.

We passed F. A. O. Schwarz, where Stan and his daughters had had a wild shopping spree the weekend before, he trying to create a very special Christmas they would always remember. The stuffed Stieff animals were piled high, hugging dancing dolls and airplanes. Artfully fake snow dusted the green suede-cloth carpet, and the trains—wood, tin, and plastic, electric, rotary, or pulled by candy-striped cord—were arranged on tracks leading nowhere, filled with things that good little boys and girls had written on their Christmas lists. There was a "bear house," complete with little rooms, and little bears, and little bear furniture, carefully carved from pale wood and displayed in the far corner of the window.

"Is that what you got Amy?" I asked, pointing to the bears, then shifted my eyes toward a string of redheaded rag dolls in chartreuse and hot-pink dresses.

Stan didn't answer, and after a moment I turned to him. He had shoved his hands into the pockets of his camel-hair coat, and scrunched up his shoulders as if that would shield him from the cold or from his sadness. There were frost droplets on his brown tweed cap from the rain. There were also frosty tears sliding down his cheeks, and their salty warmth had fogged his glasses.

I put my arm through his, but he didn't look at me or speak as we turned and walked away. By the time we'd crossed Fifth Avenue, it was as if nothing had happened, and he never told me what he felt or what he thought as we stood looking through the glass at the toys and the warmth in that window of Christmas love. It was years before I fully understood how deeply he cared and how worried he was about his children. The only way he saw to save them was to walk out of their home, to leave them at least for a while, and he was afraid that because they were so young they might not understand he wasn't simply abandoning them.

As my darling Stanley and his three little cherubs waited for me on my front stoop that second day of January of the first year of my new life, every muscle in my body tensed, and a slow dull ache began behind my forehead. I suddenly couldn't imagine that any relationship would have sufficient rewards to compensate for the probable hell that was waiting for me. And if these were the thoughts and feelings I had before the girls and I knew each other, before they knew that I was supposedly going to be their stepmother, what was it going to be like later?

I went down the steep stairs reluctantly, breathing deeply and counting slowly to calm myself. One quick look around the living room—oops—a painting he had brought that they would recognize—quickly under the couch. One more deep breath—open the door. It's too late to turn back now. Do you want to? Yes.

There were hollers and hugs, and a little ball of dynamite attacked me on the porch. That was Amy. Jennifer stood behind her father, and Leslie, holding his hand, stood off to the side.

"Well, hello. It's good to see you all again. How are you?" My voice was warm and my smile welcoming, but my heart was cold and my muscles tight. I looked at Stan over Amy's tangled head, trying to read his eyes, but couldn't. He smiled back with gratitude, seeing only what he wanted to see, and he wanted me to love them all. It was the first moment of a long game of "Let's Pretend . . ."

"Is this your house? Do you live here? Who lives here with you? Can I come in?" Amy pushed past me. "Where's your plane?" She looked around as if there might be an airplane parked somewhere in my eight-by-fifteen-foot living room. She was obviously disappointed.

"You promised we could see Mary's airplane." She had a voice as deep as Tallulah Bankhead's but edged with aggression rather than vibrancy. Without waiting for a response, she began to make herself at home. She removed her faded purple ski jacket, trimmed in fake fur once white, now sooty, torn, dirty, zipper broken, and dropped it on the floor. She was wearing a spotted football T-shirt and very worn blue jeans.

Jennifer had moved into the living room too, quietly, not speaking but watching, looking, and listening. She was close to tears. Leslie gave me a relatively friendly greeting, then unzipped her green down jacket, scanning the room quickly but thoroughly. In a minute her coat had joined Amy's on the floor, and she was on her way to the stairs.

"This is a pretty small house, isn't it? I'm going to look around." She headed upstairs to our bedroom.

"Oh, I'll show you," I said quickly. "Amy, we'll go to the airport to see my plane soon. Jennifer, wouldn't you like to take off your coat?" She shrugged. I felt like screaming. Amy was following, no, leading, Leslie up the stairs. But not before she had managed to pick up and drop a china dish I had not had the foresight to put out of reach. I knew that young children touch and grab, but the more concessions I made to their existence, the more real they would become. Jenny tugged at her daddy. "I have to go to the bathroom."

"I'll take her." I reached for her hand, but she ignored it with aplomb.

The older two had already disappeared up the stairwell. I followed Jennifer, and we came upon her sisters fingering the articles on my marble-topped bureau in the dressing room at the head of the stairs. I rescued a bottle of Chanel No. 5 from one and a bracelet from the other, then planted myself in the doorway to the bedroom so they wouldn't wander in there and open Stan's closet. I directed them to the bathroom.

As soon as Jennifer began to pull down her pants, Amy shrieked, "I have to go, too," and shoved her little sister out of the way. She sat on the john, swinging her legs, gazing up at the shelves (thank God I'd checked them beforehand).

"Who does all that perfume belong to? Is that all your makeup? What do you do? This is a tiny bathroom. How come this bathroom is so tiny? What's this for?" She reached for a squeeze bottle of hand cream, still not showing any signs of performing.

"Amy! AAAAmy! AAAAAmy!" Jennifer's voice rose in a crescendo, and she finally stamped her foot and clenched her fists. Amy looked at her from under bangs sadly in need of cutting, washing, and combing. It was a measured glance, calculating and almost surly.

"Oh, all right!" She got up off the seat, and as she pulled up her jeans, I realized she wasn't wearing any underpants. A moment later, I discovered Jennifer wasn't either.

Stan came up and stood silently by as I disentangled Amy from more of my jewelry, which she had found in a box on the dresser.

"Let's go," I said. I didn't know what to talk to them about, and I hated to have to patrol forbidden territories or keep saying, "Don't touch," "Don't look." Out of the house maybe they'd be better.

While they were putting on their jackets, Amy piped up, "Are we going to sleep here tonight?" She had, as I was to find out, a distinct knack for raising topics that people didn't want or weren't ready to discuss. Stan and I had hotly debated the virtues of their staying (he pro, I con) and had not resolved the issue. My hope that this visit would be short-lived went out the window with that "innocent" little question. Clearly Amy expected to stay out overnight somewhere—and apparently her father hadn't told her where.

"I don't know, sweetheart. We can't really inconvenience Mary like that." He gave her a little hug and waited for me to say, "Oh, why don't you? I have plenty of room if you girls don't mind camping on the floor." That was the scenario as he had proposed it to me the night before. I had told him to take them to a local motel. "I'll never spend a weekend with them in a hotel again. It makes us feel like migrants," he said as he argued his case. "But you'd be close by," I told him. "Besides, it isn't proper for us to be together with the kids. And Bobbi will be furious."

"We won't sleep together. Please, Marila."

"It's too soon." But he hadn't listened to me. So I picked up my cue, like a good girl, although I wasn't at all happy about it. "Unless you had other plans, Stan?" He breathed a sigh of relief and nobody seemed to notice my lack of enthusiasm.

We headed for the airport where I kept my Cherokee 180, without a moment for private conversation, three little heads hanging over the back of the front seat, listening to every word and contributing quite a few of their own. I was glad that I had stopped to take four extra-strength Tylenols before we left, because my headache would have soon reached migraine proportions. The sky had clouded over, and was cold and steely gray by the time we reached the airport.

The girls were obviously impressed. I did a preflight check

with them, feeling nostalgic, wishing I were off flying somewhere instead of being trapped in a . . . downdraft. You aren't being realistic, I thought. You aren't being fair. They were here first. But what if I couldn't like them? Or they me? They were so lost, and needed so much. How could I really help them? And what if, because of them, Stan and I couldn't work things out between us? All those questions—but as my grandfather used to say, "Only time tells the tale."

The tiedowns were secure. Amy kicked the tires to make sure they weren't soft. She was the quietest I'd ever seen her. We climbed up on the wing so they could look at the instrument panel. "Gee!" "Wow!" "Oh boy!" "Can we go in?" Leslie and Amy sat in the front seat, Jenny in the back, and I admonished them to keep their hands off anything and everything. To my amazement, they obeyed docilely.

I jumped down, and Stan caught me, pulling me behind the plane for our first kiss of the day. The silence was broken only by the sounds of the wind whistling and the engines of weekend pilots doing touch-and-go's on runway 27 into a stormy sunset. It was too good to last. Amy opened the door, and we heard her trying to get out.

Leslie informed us that Amy and Jenny were scared and she was hungry and wasn't it time to go? We had been there a total of ten minutes. She took Stan's hand possessively, and they started off toward the car. She must have decided we had put them in the plane to get them out of the way, and she wasn't going to tolerate any hanky-panky. The two little ones stayed close to me, Amy curious and "helping" to lock up, Jennifer confused and a little bit lonesome. When I was finished, I took a tiny hand in each of mine, and without a backward glance we walked peacefully across the concrete to join my lover and his other daughter, who were deep in conversation.

That was the last time I ever went to the airport, and I never flew again. Several months later I sold the plane that had provided escape and flights of fancy, and only occasionally as I view the world from aloft through the windows of a commercial airliner do I feel a twinge of regret that I grounded myself. But I don't need to fly anymore to feel free.

We piled ourselves cheerfully into my little car for the ride home, Stan driving, the "big" girls in the back seat and Jennifer on my lap, nestled against my chest quite contentedly. The fresh air had cleared my head and eased my headache; I was enjoying the excitement of the children, and their lively conversation. Amy's cheeks glowed like roses; she giggled with delight when I told her that. Rose was her middle name, a beautiful one she thought, but I realized she never saw herself as beautiful, or pretty, or in fact, as anything but ugly. "Amy Rose, you look lovely. You have real roses in your cheeks." She didn't believe me, but she liked to hear it just the same, and the glow came as much from the caring words as from the chilly air. For a brief period of time—very brief—it was a sweet interlude.

3

"Who's hungry?" called Stan. "Me! Me! Me! Me! Me! Me!" There were many more responses than people, and hands began to wave and flail about. The level of energy among the girls was on the rise.

"Quiet." The vigor in Stan's voice shut them up, because it was so unexpected. He rarely raised his voice (at them, or anyone else for that matter). "Can we go somewhere around here for a hamburger?" I knew of a Burger King close by, and also a supermarket. I had really not believed I'd have the kids in the house all weekend, and was going to have to shop if we were going to eat.

We opted to go to the Shoprite first, but that was definitely a mistake. This was my first experience of supermarket shopping with three children in tow, and that they were hungry probably compounded my difficulty. The kids wanted anything and everything. They each had a different kind of favorite cereal. Amy wanted strawberry ice cream. Leslie wanted coffee ice cream. Jennifer started to cry because she didn't like ice cream at all; she wanted cupcakes. They all wanted doughnuts, but one wanted plain, one wanted sugar-coated, and one wanted jelly.

Peanut butter was unanimous, but jam was a problem. Then there was candy (I said no), cookies (I capitulated), yogurt (three flavors, of course).

Amy was becoming increasingly difficult. She ran up and down the aisles, shouting, grabbing whatever appealed to her and bringing it to show me. I sent Leslie after her when she was gone too long, or was striking up conversations with unsuspecting and unappreciative shoppers. I was too embarrassed to go after her myself, and at the moment that was more important to me than Leslie's sense of triumph that she could handle Amy and I could not. People looked at us rather strangely; we must have presented a baffling picture to some, and an appalling one to others. There was Stanley, a slightly jowly, bespectacled, balding intellectual, with what little hair he had left radiating two inches up from his head. Dressed in a black cotton turtleneck, brown leather jacket, casual slacks, and expedition hiking boots, he looked like a 1960s Greenwich Village dropout, out of place in a suburban New Jersey supermarket.

Then there was I, twenty-eight and looking twenty if one didn't look too closely, with three wild, disheveled, dirty children in tow. I wanted to wear an advertising sandwich board: I AM NOT RESPONSIBLE FOR THE CONDITION OR BEHAVIOR OF THESE CHILDREN.

I guess lots of kids are noisy. I guess lots of kids run around in stores and are into everything. I guess lots of ten-year-olds declare loudly, "I only eat steak," and three-year-olds cry and stamp their feet when they want to have Apple Jacks instead of Crackle Snaps, and five-year-olds break a 32-ounce jar of pickled beets, or wet their pants in the macaroni aisle. But I'm not quite sure how much of all this needs to be included in a single twenty-minute shopping trip.

To all observers I must have seemed a harried portrait of despair, unable to cope with motherhood and not smart enough to stem the flow of progeny; Stan, a cradle-snatcher, giving me three babes before I was old enough to drive. The kids were marshaling forces against me, Leslie and Jennifer with some degree of subtlety, Amy blatantly for all the world—or at least all the Shoprite— to hear. My headache had come back. But I kept smiling, my expression calm, saying silently to Stanley all the while, "What have you gotten me into?"

We should have gone home to peanut-butter-and-jelly (three

different kinds) sandwiches instead of to Burger King, because they were angry at their life and at their father and their mother, and were unloading on me, an unsuspecting victim, with triple barrels.

But to Burger King we went. There was a long line, and Stan told the kids to find a seat. They took off at a gallop around a corner, nearly knocking onto the floor several Whoppers with cheese, fries, and shakes, not to mention the surprised man who was carrying them. I went after them trying to look nonchalant and in control, amid glaring looks from customers. ("Can't you take better care of your children, lady?")

"They are not my children! I don't have anything to do with them!" I screamed silently, a smile fixed on my face.

"Girls, don't you think you should calm down? Little ladies don't chase in restaurants like that. Now sit down and . . ." My eyes settled on six little hands—six very dark, grubby, dirty little hands. I didn't remember that they had looked like that fifteen minutes ago. Miraculously, our trip to the ladies' room was uneventful. I have since discovered that I was destined to spend a tremendous amount of time in bathrooms, going to bathrooms, talking about going to bathrooms, and wishing one child or another had asked to go to the bathroom.

We all arrived at the table at the same time, they with three clean faces and six clean hands, and Stan with enough food for his army, none of whom was satisfied with what he brought.

First, there wasn't any ketchup. I got ketchup. Then there wasn't *enough* ketchup. I sent Leslie. Jennifer wouldn't eat her hamburger without mustard. Stan got mustard. Then Jennifer wouldn't eat her hamburger at all. She had to go to the bathroom. Leslie took her to the bathroom. Amy didn't want to eat anything but pie. She started a long conversation with a little boy at a table behind her, asking him, as he held a hamburger to his mouth, what he was eating.

"Amy, turn around and eat your dinner." I was very calm. My voice didn't rise a decibel even when once again I had to tell Leslie and Jenny to walk, not run. I was being very adult and deciding I couldn't let the kids embarrass me or get the best of me, and besides, none of these people would ever see me again. I was very much looking forward to going home, popping little people into beds and blankets, and being alone with Stan. I tried to push from my mind the fact that they would be there in the morning when we woke up, and it would start all over again. I was beginning to realize that it was like waking up with a new mole on my shoulder. I could cover it up, but it was always going to be with me.

"Shall we go?" Stanley asked, but he was optimistically premature.

"I have to go to the bathroom," said Amy. The john apparently was becoming some new form of warfare—child against adult. Amy, however, had something far more devious in mind than mild disruption.

"I'll go with you, Amy."

"I know where it is and I can go myself."

There was no one in all of Burger King who didn't hear her. My ESP was working overtime, and I felt it would be a dreadful mistake to let her go.

"I know where it is and I can go by myself," she repeated. Her voice was deep, challenging and loud. *"I don't need help from you."* Jenny and Leslie were looking at me, the one from the corner of her eye, and the other from under thick lashes. They were waiting to see what would happen.

"I think she can handle it," Stanley decided. Well, he was the father and he should know. If only I had known how much he didn't know!

The minutes ticked by in idle childish chatter, fingers picking absentmindedly at leftover fries, before we began to worry about the whereabouts of Amy Rose.

Leslie volunteered to go and find her. And find her she did, firmly locked in the restroom of the "Have it your way" Burger King. My way, frankly, would have been not to be there at all.

"She's locked in."

"We'll get the manager."

"She says she doesn't want to come out."

First Stan went. Then I went. Leslie went again. The manager said it didn't open with a key. We pleaded, cajoled, scolded, threatened, promised, and got nowhere. To me: *"I want my mother."* To Stan and Leslie: "Go away. I'm not done." There were three women waiting to get in; one looked sympathetic, the other two murderous.

Finally, we announced loudly we were leaving, and said we'd leave her behind. Amy called for Stan. He didn't answer. Once she called for me, but I didn't answer either. As she opened the door a crack, to peek out, Stan scooped her up and carried her under his arm outside into the cold winter rain that had started to fall.

He spanked her and scolded her, and from all indications that was a very rare occurrence. Jennifer and Leslie were aghast. Daddy *never* spanked. But Amy didn't cry or show remorse. He loaded her into the car, and we drove home, considerably subdued. The two youngest fell asleep, and Leslie sat gazing out the window at the rain, silently sucking her thumb.

The children had brought a little plastic suitcase for their weekend visit, containing two shirts, a couple of pairs of socks, a bathing suit, three pairs of Leslie's jeans, and a sweatshirt. For all three of them, for three days. In January. I was glad I had remembered to buy underpants in the supermarket, and I tried to find something in my drawers for nightgowns. The best I could do was the tops to my thermal underwear and one nightie that had shrunk but had such fond memories for me that I couldn't bear to throw it away.

The little tub filled with bubbles and warm water for Amy and Jennifer. I scrubbed, they soaked, and I washed Amy's hair. Jennifer screamed and screamed about water and soap in her face—she was afraid to close her eyes, afraid to get her head wet. In fact, I found she rarely got her shoulders wet. We hurried quickly through the ordeal. She was terrified but let me calm her down with words and hugs without much resistance. Both girls needed a shower to rinse off the grime of the bathwater. Jennifer balked at this also, but I managed to get her in and out in haste and swathe her in a bright-orange bath towel twice as big as she was, before she knew what happened. Brave and adventurous Amy, to whom a shower was a novel experience, had to be dragged out forcibly. I was exhausted by this time, and prayed for the night to end.

We had decided that the wisest thing would be for the girls and me to sleep together in the bedroom, with Stan on the living-room couch. So we made a bed on the floor for Amy and Jennifer, several layers of blankets on top of a thick-piled rug. Leslie and I were to share the bed.

Snuggling down under the covers, shining hair on pillows, cheeks glowing, eyes twinkling, their bodies smelling warm and soapy clean, they were different children. They weren't wild, or angry, or pouting, or fresh, or precocious, or obnoxious. They were beautiful and sweet and, above all, happy. It was my first glimpse of Stan's children as I wanted them to be, and it gave me hope for what they could become. Leslie joined us from her at-first-protested bath, as refreshed and calm as her sisters, happy at having splashed herself liberally with my Jean Naté Friction pour le Bain.

Together with Stan, we read aloud *Bunya the Witch,* the five of us in a comfortable heap on the floor, everybody close to somebody. Jennifer fell asleep, her chest rising and falling in a barely perceptible rhythm. Leslie and Amy lay sucking their thumbs, listening to the story, Amy interrupting only infrequently, Leslie engrossed. As Bunya took off on her broomstick to Miami Beach, the ten-o'clock news broke into the Bach concert on the radio.

"Okay, kids, time to go to sleep." Stan disentangled himself from the blankets and from Leslie, who had been using him as a pillow, and stood up. I did, too.

"No, Mary, stay with us a little while, please." Was it a ploy to keep me from her father or was it a genuine request? I gave her the benefit of the doubt, as it seemed like a good opportunity to score some brownie points. Stan turned off the light and started down the stairs.

"Turn off the radio when you come down, Bobbi." There were

audible gasps—from Amy, from Leslie, and from Stan. My knees quickly turned to aspic, and I felt the blood flaming to my skin.

"Daddy!" Amy sounded exasperated. "That's not Bobbi. That's *Mary."*

"Oh, God, I'm sorry," he whispered, and disappeared down the stairs before anybody could say anything else.

Intellectually, it's easy to convince oneself that the habit of seventeen years is very hard to break; that in the dark, in a cozy family setting, it's very easy to forget—or very hard to forget, to erase—those years of memories. But the idea that Stan was unconsciously thinking of Roberta, perhaps even wishing it were Bobbi instead of me, was excruciating. I was still unable to convince myself thoroughly that he really loved me, really cared— that he did indeed want me to answer yes to his three questions: Will you love me? Will you let me live with you? Will you marry me? Shaken by the strains of the entire day, I was suddenly positive that everything was only temporary, and he would go back to his precious Bobbi.

Leslie apologized for her father's mistake.

"You know, it's real easy to get you mixed up. You look just like my mom. She's got hair like you do, and you really look a lot alike." That was not exactly what I needed to make me feel terrific, and I would have bet a million dollars she knew exactly what she was saying.

I broke away quickly and went downstairs, not because I wanted to be with Stan but because I didn't want to be with the girls. Unfortunately, there was no place I could go to be really alone. Stan was sitting at the kitchen table absentmindedly reading *The New Yorker.* We didn't look at each other, and didn't speak. I sat down in the living room, just as absentmindedly thumbing through a *Redbook.* There was a lot in the air between us—thoughts and words, unspoken, almost unarticulated, certainly suppressed through the months we'd been together. The house was so small that even though we were in different rooms we couldn't get away from each other.

"I'm sorry," he said, looking down at me, having walked the

five feet that put him in front of my sagging brown couch. "I don't know what happened; I didn't mean it."

I tried to keep my voice controlled and steady without success. "That's okay," I squeaked. I went right on reading an article on how to tell if you were suited to your mate.

I wouldn't look at him, and couldn't say anything further. It was a tense, silent half-minute.

"Marila . . ."

"Listen." I finally looked at him, but my voice was tight and still high, and I was trying very hard not to cry. "She's your wife. You lived with her for seventeen years. For all I know, you wish you were living with her now. So it's only natural you should call me by her name." I paused to add dramatic effect to my next sarcastic remark.

"Besides, I'm sure that you were reminded of many other evenings when you and Bobbi put the kids to bed. Together." I finished scoring myself on the self-test. I passed with flying colors, and I was disappointed.

"That's so untrue." His calm gentleness, as always, was infuriating and exasperating. "She didn't put the kids to bed or read to them, or stay with them the way you did when Leslie asked you. It was different—it was always different. You have no idea. You just have no idea what my life was like." He sounded tired, beaten. "I don't know why I called you that—but you have to believe me. I'm not at all sorry about us. I'm glad we're together. You're my salvation." He touched my knee, and my blood started churning again, but not entirely from anger. I hated him for thinking that he could pacify me with a few gentle words or a caress, and I hated me for letting him. I wasn't sure I believed anything he said to me, and I hated not having any choice if things were to work out between us. I *had* to believe him. He reached for my hand, and I gave his a half-squeeze, to let him know he wasn't forgiven but I'd try to forget.

"How was the day for you?" We went into the kitchen, because it afforded precious little but still more privacy than the living room. At least there were no cracks in the boards of the ceiling to the bedroom above. "Leslie said something really interesting at the airport. She said, 'You know, Daddy, you should marry somebody like Mary if you're not going to be married to Mommy anymore.' I think she saw me kiss you. She's a pretty smart little girl, you know."

Stan thought all three girls were very smart. He had trouble differentiating between brashness and intelligence, aggravating precocity and freedom of spirit in his darling daughters. At ten, Leslie, besides struggling with approaching puberty, was having trouble in school and had difficulty getting the right change for a candy bar. But since she was able to express her feelings verbally—by demanding what she wanted when she wanted it, and telling you exactly what she thought of you if she didn't get it—Stanley felt she was well on her way to becoming a success in life. The fact that she found it hard to make friends among kids her own age, expected to be treated as an adult, and supervised her younger sisters' activities with shrewish relish gave him no cause for concern.

He was only slightly more realistic about Amy, who even in the best of circumstances was likely to have a tougher time than most in dealing with life. Although her IQ was well within the normal range, she had been evaluated as having "minimal brain dysfunction" and dyslexia. Consequently she had a continual and monumental struggle to meet the norm of kids her age. A few months before, she had begun to spend an hour a week with an educational therapist, and Stan felt that with the individualized attention she was already making progress scholastically. But her demeanor and behavior were another matter.

Amy was destructive physically—breaking things, tearing things—and emotionally, she had an uncanny knack for picking out other people's vulnerabilities and teasing them mercilessly under the guise of innocent remarks or questions. She would hide, or scream, or do almost anything to attract attention, and she had apparently rarely been criticized, given limits, disciplined, or counseled. She was ignored, and excused, and left to her own devices. As far as Stan was concerned, she was "rambunctious."

That was the only problem with his sweet Amy Rose.

Jennifer was perhaps the brightest of the three, although she always seemed sad and somewhat depressed. She was progressing nearly as well as Amy, thanks to Sesame Street and sporadic attendance at a Montessori school, but she rarely spoke, answering queries with shrugs or nods or shakes of her little head. When she didn't get her own way or was very unhappy, she could, and often would, let loose a tantrum—a real foot-stamping, arm-flailing, hair-raising session.

Sometimes she would sit at meals not eating, not talking. She could spend literally hours over two pancakes or half a peanut-butter sandwich, and then, after everyone else had left the table, silent tears would slide down her cheeks. But Jennifer also had a certain special light in her eyes, and a sweet wisdom and gentleness; so the glimpses of personality she treated me to occasionally only made her withdrawal all the more distressing. And she was the only one who didn't suck her thumb.

None of the three had any manners. They talked to grownups with the same respect they accorded to children their own age—none. They interrupted at will, and expected an immediate response to their demands. They took what they felt like taking, from wherever it was, never asking permission or putting things away. They felt they had the right to do anything, go anywhere, say anything, without reproach. They ate as if they had never been taught how to use a knife and fork and spoon, chewed and chattered simultaneously, reached and grabbed at the table, ate whatever they felt like rather than what was on their plate. When finished to their satisfaction, they ambled off without a by-your-leave, to do whatever struck their fancy. They didn't seem to know what napkins were for (or toilet paper, for that matter). Personal hygiene was an alien concept. Baths seemed to be a rare occurrence, and their underwear, on the few occasions that they were wearing any, was usually filthy. They didn't brush their teeth, wash their faces, or comb their hair. I never figured out what happened to the clothes we bought for them.

Much of this was readily apparent to me within twenty-four

hours, but I didn't know how to deal with it because it was so completely foreign to my own upbringing. Fortunately, though with plenty of pain, we were able to educate each other, and as much as I have helped them grow, they have helped me put my until-then-narrow life in perspective.

For fourteen years, at home and in convent schools, my mother (lovingly) and nuns (less so) were always after me. "Stand up straight." "Eat your breakfast." "Eat your crusts." "Leave the grownups alone." "Take a bath" (mother). "Don't touch yourself when you bathe" (nuns). "Don't eat so much." "Eat what's on your plate." "Hurry up." "Slow down." "You're so clumsy." "Do your homework." "Play with your sisters." "Leave your sister alone." "Don't interrupt." "Don't bite your nails." "Pull in your stomach." "Elbows off the table." "Napkin in your lap." When I was growing up, blue jeans were for weekends in the country; otherwise little girls wore skirts and dresses and gloves and hats. I had been taught to say "please" and "thank you" and "pardon me." I read Emily Post and Amy Vanderbilt with a devotion more appropriate to the Bible, and was absolutely convinced that there was a right way and a wrong way to do things. I had a very old-fashioned, straitlaced, narrow-minded, distorted, unreasonable view of acceptable behavior from little children. But it was the only way I knew.

Still, even if I'd been able to be more flexible, Stan wouldn't have wanted to hear that I thought his three precious darlings were three little monsters, or that the idea of their intruding on my life, even on a part-time basis, was enough to make me physically ill. I didn't want to hurt him, didn't want to make him angry, and I couldn't tell him I was angry at him for allowing his children to be what they were. Until this weekend, what we had created between us was the most important thing in my life. I didn't want to risk losing that against the outside chance that his daughters really were "great kids," really were terrific. So I didn't say anything when he asked what I felt, except that any children of his were welcome as children of mine, and I'd try to love them as if they were my own. I remarked that they all looked as if they needed attention and love, and it seemed to satisfy him. Later I would grapple with the fact that if some things about those girls didn't change, Stan and I would probably never make it, but for the time being he was happy, and accepted what I told him as true. If he didn't feel the undercurrents that were operating, I wasn't going to expose them. Not yet.

Fortunately, Stan and I didn't have a chance to develop the conversation. Leslie soon came padding down the stairs. "I can't sleep." Stan and I caught each other's eye, and steeled ourselves for the unexpected. She would probably deluge us with questions, which I in my adult superiority felt were not her place to ask, and which she in her childish innocence felt involved her so deeply that the answers were her right to know. In this particular instance, she was, I am sure, much more right than I.

"Are you going to get married?" She was blunt, and the whole thing, too quickly, was out in the open. Perhaps it would have been better, or at least made things easier, if we had lied about it. But we didn't. For a moment her ten-year-old fancy was titillated at the idea of becoming a flower girl, her long brown hair streaming over her shoulders, and tossing pink petals in our path. That didn't last. The questions poured out.

"How's Mommy going to feel when she finds out?"

"Does that mean you don't love us anymore, Daddy?"

"But now we won't see you anymore. Julie's father got married again, and now he's too busy to see her."

"Are you and Mary going to have any babies?"

"But if I come to visit you on weekends, I'll always have to have a suitcase, and carry my clothes. I can't do that, Daddy, really I can't. Please. I won't really have a home. I'll just be visiting everybody."

Leslie had been struggling to keep her composure, shifting back and forth from hurt-child tears to bravado and even cheerfulness, but it became too much for her to take. She finally broke down into heaving, uncontrollable sobs, and Stan held her skinny body in his arms and rocked her gently, stroking her hair and soothing her soul. He didn't look at me. It was just the two of them, and in spite of myself the exclusion hurt. I didn't relate it at the time to the feelings Leslie was most certainly having at being replaced in her father's life by me.

She finally calmed down, energy spent, though not her feelings. "I just don't want to have a suitcase," she repeated woefully.

That was really important to her: the transience of the situation, the impermanence of her attachment to our world.

"Don't worry, Leslie," I said gently. "You don't have to bring anything the next time you come. I'll go shopping, and you'll have clothes here, so you'll never need a suitcase."

"What about a nightgown? And a toothbrush?"

"Those, too."

"And how about Amy and Jenny?"

"They, too," was my reply.

"But you don't know what size we wear."

"Sure I do. Didn't I help you shop in Bloomingdale's?"

She was satisfied, and we were exhausted. Neither of us had anticipated the trial of defending or explaining our feelings to her.

Leslie felt that this should be a secret between the three of us—she didn't want to tell anyone. But her demands for explanations and reasons forced us to deal with her in ways more adult than her age. I wonder if things would have been easier between Leslie and me if we had been able to ease her into an acceptance of the situation gradually, as we did with the others, rather than confront the facts with her right from the start.

Stanley had to have known, consciously or unconsciously, that sharing our plans with Leslie would have one inevitable consequence. Bobbi would surely find out. He must have realized that Leslie wouldn't be able to "keep our secret."

Later, she and I continued the midnight conversation, snuggled under a warm down comforter, sharing confidences like giggling schoolgirls. We spoke of dreams, boys she knew, men who had loved me, and pink bridesmaids' dresses. She was sweet and vulnerable and frightened of the changes in her life, but that first night, as we fell into sleep in the middle of a sentence, I think she felt a little bit more secure, and not quite so alone. I had done what was needed of me, expected (I thought) of me, and it hadn't been so hard. It had even felt good.

I was far from happy, but my last thoughts that night were that I would become a "Super Mom," the kind of mother the girls had lacked and yearned for. I would fill the void and heal the scars and be their savior. It was an ideal situation for a dreamer like me, who had spent countless hours of idle time creating imaginary situations in which I was all things to all people, and here was a real-life chance. I certainly didn't want to blow it by letting everybody know I was ready to bail out before I even got started.

The next morning dawned gray, a day to sleep late and do nothing. But my life was never to be the same again, no longer uncomplicated. No longer could I stay in bed until I was good and ready to get up. Breakfast platitudes ringing in my ears, I had to rise to the occasion. Faced with instant motherhood, I was determined to serve the kind of weekend breakfast that would do any mother proud.

These kids, who would have been content to eat cold cereal by the handful right from the box, leaving a trail of crumbs behind them and on the floor as they watched Saturday morning cartoons, were surprised and intrigued at the prospect of a family breakfast. They "helped" make French toast and juice, and set the table, wiping the sleep out of the corners of their eyes, a little less discombobulated and a little more at ease by now. More at ease meaning being a bit snider in their comments to their father, a bit more caustic in their remarks to each other, a few kicks here and there under the table. Once again they eschewed my version of table manners, munching their toast with gum-snapping gusto, as much maple syrup on their T-shirts as on their plates, ready for thirds before I'd sat down to firsts. There was one spilled milk (Amy) and one spilled juice (Jennifer), neither of which distressed me too much. After all, Super Mom could cope with little trifles like that. I also had a sudden flash of *déjà vu*, realizing, as I began to eat when everyone else (including

Stanley) was leaving the table, that this was an image from my childhood—except that then I was the middle daughter, and my mother was the cook.

The second priority of the day was to get Amy to her weekly session with Mrs. Unger, the educational therapist who was instrumental in her successful struggle to master letters, words, and numbers. It was a monumental feat just to get everybody dressed and washed, get dishes done, and get out on time, but I did it. Settling into the car, I was suddenly exhausted, feeling after only three hours of sleep as if I had already put in a full day's work.

It took us over an hour to get to Tenafly. Saturday mornings certainly weren't going to be easy, if this was any indication. Dorothy Unger stepped into the waiting room to take Amy into her office. She was a small blond woman, prim, with penetrating eyes and a slightly pursed expression to her lips. I was nervous as Stan introduced me as a "friend," and felt that in one piercing glance she had sized me up, forming an opinion of the weekend stepmother that she would be hard pressed to change. Over the next two years I came to know her quite well, and once my awe had been put in its proper place (she reminded me of nuns I used to have as teachers), I found her a delightful person, with the best interests of her students her foremost concern, punctuality and professionalism running neck and neck for second. More than once she has listened to my tales of woe as an "other mother" with compassion, and often she gave me advice. Dorothy certainly offered me much insight into Amy and her problems, showing me not only how to deal with them myself, but how to help Amy deal with them.

But at that first meeting I felt woefully inadequate, as Amy hid under a chair and refused to come out, and Jennifer, overtired from the excitement of the day before, began to whine. Leslie was half asleep in a chair, at least out of trouble. Mrs. Unger coaxed and cajoled Amy gently, then spoke sharply as she received no response. Amy crawled out reluctantly, and followed her sullenly into the other room to begin her hour-long session.

40

Lunch was another struggle with hot dogs and the bathroom (again!), in a diner this time. To further complicate matters, or perhaps to make them more normal, depending on your point of view, the kids were cranky from being overtired, Stan was cranky from being nervous about how they were reacting to the situation, and I was cranky from both these causes, plus a few more.

I had always wanted to be a mother. I had always wanted sweet little bundles in buntings, who would grow up gracefully and gratefully, albeit with vigor and spunk, into respectful, well-mannered, clean-at-appropriate-times, disciplined, bright, and loving children, of whom I would be very proud. Instead, on this Saturday noon, I found myself once again demonstrating to an unsuspecting public a mother who had failed dismally to instill even one of these virtues in her offspring.

4

It was three days before Amy's sixth birthday, and we stopped on the way home from Mrs. Unger's to get presents and party things, Stan distracting Amy while I shopped. My instincts told me that a six-year-old girl would want dolls or jewelry, but Leslie managed to persuade me that what her sister really wanted, and really *needed*, was a Tonka dump truck; and I let myself be convinced when Stan shrugged and said Leslie would know best. I bought her a ring, though, and Tinker Bell cologne and nail polish for dress-up play (both requests she had made), determined to somehow turn this boy-girl child into a girl.

After we got home, I began to bake Amy's favorite chocolate cake, and our tiny house grew festive with balloons and colored streamers, laughing children, and John Denver, also Amy's favorite. Then the girls wanted to talk to their mother, so Stan dialed the number for them, and handed the phone to Leslie.

"Mom? Hi, Mom. Oh, Mom, we're having a lot of fun, but I sure do miss you." There was a brief pause.

"At Mary's." Another pause. "Oh, she's a friend of Daddy's. We're staying at her house. We took Amy to Mrs. Unger, and we're having a party, and . . ." Leslie chattered her ten-year-old chatter, catching her mother up on the events of the day, thrusting insidious little daggers into Roberta, managing to remind her that she was no longer with Stan.

Amy was yelling over Leslie's voice, clamoring to speak, and making it impossible for anybody to talk or think. Stanley ignored it all, and it was Leslie who finally shrieked, "Oh, all right. You talk, but you're mean. I'm not finished."

She threw the phone at Amy and stomped around, huffing and puffing like the wolf in "The Three Little Pigs," pacing back and forth between the kitchen and living room, a space about eight feet by four. In her own way she was as noisy as Amy Rose had been, but she was also very upset, and beginning to cry. The phone call had proved distressing to her, for she couldn't quite comprehend what had happened in her life, why her parents were getting a divorce. And she couldn't understand how her father could be happy if she was so unhappy.

Amy, meanwhile, was making sure that her mother knew that they had gone to see Mary's airplane, and Mary had gone to Mrs. Unger's with them, and they had slept at Mary's house, and Mary had bought them new underpants, and Mary was making her a birthday cake, and Mary was such a good friend of Daddy's. If Stanley had hoped to keep my existence a secret, he was sadly mistaken.

Jennifer also talked to her mother, more briefly, but with disastrous effects—the tears began while she was on the phone, and after she got off she started her foot-stamping routine, accompanying it with a low, moaning whine.

I heard all this from the kitchen, trying to be nonchalant about the whole mess as I was getting "Chicken Zenorini" into the oven, and the cake out to cool and be frosted. My head was throbbing, and my hands were beginning to shake; the knot in my stomach had grown from the size of a Ping-Pong ball at the beginning of the phone call to the size of a medicine ball by the end. Stanley, the creep, was nowhere to be seen—he had probably gone upstairs to the bathroom, about the only place where one could find even a semblance of quiet.

By the time the call was over, Leslie and Jennifer were competing for the highest-pitched wails, while Amy whooped around, laughing almost hysterically, teasing her sisters about their respective sorrows, certainly not acknowledging her own. There wasn't a door I could close, or a place to go to get away. It was my house, my kitchen, and all these crazy people suddenly appearing from nowhere had totally disrupted my peaceful life.

"Everybody shut up!" The crying and shouting ceased immediately, and three little faces turned toward me in amazement. I couldn't think of anything else to say, being suddenly consumed with guilt for yelling at them when I knew they were genuinely distraught. Besides, I had had to scream so loudly to be heard that my throat hurt.

The toilet flushed upstairs, drowning out "Welcome Home, Country Roads," and Stanley had the nerve to saunter casually down the stairs and say, "Is something the matter down here?" I was torn between murdering him for ducking out and embracing him for making an entrance before his three whirling dervishes recommenced their act.

"We just talked to Mommy," Leslie said, and started to cry again, but with much less flourish than before.

"Why are you getting a divorce, and leaving Mommy and us all alone? Why don't you love us anymore?" Amy asked, sounding tough, righteous, and accusatory. Jennifer stared at her father with unreadable eyes.

"Oh, Amy." He sighed. "We've been through this so many times before, Amy." Stan looked at the three little faces, waiting. He swallowed hard, and said it all over again. "Sometimes mommies and daddies fall out of love, and that's what happened to us. Your mother and I just don't love each other anymore. We tried, because we both love you three girls very much—we tried to live with each other, but sometimes grownups just can't stay married, no matter how much they love their children. And it doesn't mean we don't love you."

"You didn't fight that much." Petulantly.

"Oh yes they did, Leslie," Amy taunted her. "You know they did. They'd go in their room, and close the door, and Mommy would yell at Daddy. And it used to make you cry. I know because I saw you." Amy dared Leslie to deny it, and she could not.

Stan pulled all three close to him, on his lap and in his arms, and repeated again what he had been saying nearly every night for more than a month to them over the telephone. "Your mom and I were just making each other very unhappy, and because we were unhappy, we were making you unhappy, too. This way she can do what she likes to do, and I can do what I like to do, and we can both spend time with you girls and have a good time. Do you understand what I'm saying?"

"You mean like Great Adventure?"

"Great Adventure? What do you mean? We never went to Great Adventure."

"You remember," Amy continued, exasperated. "We were supposed to go to Great Adventure, and Leslie's friend Joan was supposed to come, and then Mommy didn't want to go, and then you went in and closed the door, and she was yelling and crying, and then when you came out you said we'd go some other day, and then you went away and didn't come back until it was dark, and Mommy just cried all day, and we never went to Great Adventure." It was all one sentence, and she was breathless at the end.

"How do you remember that? That was years ago. You're right. We promised we would take you, and we didn't. Your mom didn't want to go, and she didn't want me to go without her. Things like that used to happen a lot."

"And I was embarrassed because Joan was there, and she heard everything, and *her* parents don't fight," Leslie lashed out, thinking about her friend Joan, and her disappointment at the spoiled plans and broken promise.

"But lots of your friends in school have parents who are divorced. And that's why most people get a divorce—because everybody is so unhappy."

"But we *were* happy," Leslie insisted. "We want you and Mommy to be married again."

Stan sighed. "No, you weren't. Did you feel happy when we didn't go to Great Adventure?" He looked from one small face to the other. Leslie looked back, eyes red-rimmed from tears. Amy stared at her feet, twisting them together, sucking her thumb, and trying to shut out what was happening. He sighed again. "Do you understand what I'm saying, Jennifer?"

Her gray eyes met his for the first time, filling with tears, and slowly, sadly, she shook her head from side to side. "No," she whispered, and the tears slid silently down her cheeks.

Stan reached to pull her closer to him, but she tensed and curled into a ball, and wouldn't let him.

The bell on the stove to signal that the chicken was done pinged sharply and broke the spell, although I'm not sure it wasn't welcome. I'd been sitting quietly in the kitchen, watching this scene and feeling like an eavesdropper, totally alien from the little group inside. Forgotten and unwelcome. I turned off the timer.

Stan tried to recoup the situation. "So! Hey! Aren't we supposed to be having a birthday party? Everybody looks so glum! Let's get smiles on, and have a happy birthday party for Amy Rose! Come on, everybody—Mary, where are you? Happy birthday, Amy." He leaned over to give her a hug and a kiss, then did the same for the other two.

"When's dinner?" Stan came into the kitchen, kissed me with his eyes, and reached up on top of the refrigerator for the paper bag full of party hats and favors. "Who wants a hat?"

"Me!" "Me!" "I do!" "I do!" Thirty seconds transformed them from sad little caterpillars to smiling butterflies, and the tears and forlorn moments seemed forgotten.

The party was a joyous, raucous occasion, though overanimated and at times a little forced. Amy and Leslie recounted other birthdays to me in detail, emphasizing the part that Roberta had played and how the celebrations had included the whole family. The birthday girl's brilliant brown eyes shimmered, however, with genuine awe at the seven-candled chocolate cake finally placed in front of her—it was the first cake, she said, anyone had baked especially for her. Her disappointment in the dump truck and her pleasure at the trinkets made me wish I'd followed my instincts and bought her a doll. Next year, I vowed to myself—if I survive.

The rest of the weekend passed in a blur, in a trail of debris through the whole house, pens and paper, party favors, books pulled down from the shelves, crumbs and half-eaten cookies. There were at least three fights, two more tantrums (one major, one minor), one wet bed, one wet pants. It was the longest two and a half days in my life. I was grateful when early dusk began to settle Sunday evening and Stan suggested it was time to take the girls home.

I waved goodbye from the same front porch where I had greeted them with as much relief now as then there had been trepidation. It was over, and I didn't want to think about next weekend. I did the dishes in scalding water because with my hands so hot I couldn't think of anything else.

"Hi, beautiful. How's my girl?" The phone had rung ten times before I answered it. I wasn't in the mood to talk to anybody. It was a voice out of my past, a deep laughing voice, warm and sexy.

"Frank? Is that you? My God, how are you? Where are you?" I sank back on the couch, a little from surprise, a little from relief, glad to be listening to someone from a completely different world than Stan and his kids.

"When are you coming down to the Sunshine State, babe? I just closed today on a house I know you'll love. It's right on the waterway and only a few blocks from the beach. I bought it for us, honey. When are you coming?"

Dear Frank. It had been nearly a year since we'd spoken. Twice that since I'd seen him. He had been moving to Florida then and wanted me to go with him, but I just couldn't do it—I didn't love him enough. I knew this latest phone call came at a terrible time, with my defenses down and my anxiety high. Frank was a safe harbor. He'd always take good care of me—the worst would be we'd start to bore each other.

"Did you really buy a house? How did you find me?"

"Your mother. She said you'd bought a house, too—don't worry, we can sell it."

"Frank . . ."

"And things are going great. You'll love it, babe. And I love you."

"Frank . . ."

"Say you'll come."

"Frank . . . did my mother tell you I was getting married?" There was silence for a moment. "Who is he? What does he do?"

"Nobody that you know. I met him at work. He's a consultant."

"Are you sure of what you're doing? You won't come?" His voice rapped accusingly.

It was my turn to be quiet. The past three days raced across my mind like high-speed film, the fights, the tears, the tension, the relief when they all left. Then I thought about the other times, when we were playing or loving or working, and Stanley made me feel exciting and competent and wise. Frank had always made me feel beautiful, but like a yacht or a Cadillac or a gem, something to show off.

"No, Frank, I can't come." I wasn't sure that what I was doing was right, but I knew that going with Frank would have been wrong. I hung up sadly, because it would have been so easy. Frank made everything easy. But dull. And my life hadn't been dull since I'd known Stan.

I was still sitting by the phone two hours later when Stan came back. In the interim, I had spoken to my mother, calling for solace and getting anything but.

"It was quite a weekend, Mom."

"Mmm hmmm."

". . . They behaved terribly. . . ."

"Well, what do you expect? I'm sure they missed their mother terribly, poor things, and you're not used to dealing with children, you know."

"Maybe it will get better. . . ."

"It's been quite a shock for the children, I'm sure, happening so suddenly."

"It wasn't so sudden, Mother. They'd been talking about divorce for ten years." By this time I knew the call was a mistake. I couldn't hear a single drop of sympathy in her voice, and had hung up more depressed than ever, feeling terribly sorry for myself and wondering if there was any way out.

48

Stan helped me finish the dishes, recounting the relatively un-eventful ride, without too many tears and recriminations, and even some planning.

"I told them I wanted them to spend the whole summer with us. They're even more afraid they are going to lose me now that I have you, and I thought that would reassure them. I knew you wouldn't mind."

"The whole summer?" I was horrified. The last way on earth I wanted to spend my summer was baby-sitting someone else's kids.

"I told them they could decide where we'd go for vacation, too. Leslie wants to go to Hawaii and Amy wants to go to the Grand Canyon."

"Why don't you and I go to Tahiti?" I suggested, casually but seriously.

"We couldn't afford to take the kids. I'm not sure we can swing any kind of a fancy vacation this year." He had missed my too subtle suggestion, and I let it pass. I was afraid of hurting his feelings, afraid one of us might get too angry and we wouldn't be able to work it out. So I changed the subject.

"Did you see Roberta?" I imagined him going in and sitting down for a cup of coffee, chatting about the arrangements for next week, discussing the next steps in the divorce. Very civilized. He was such a civilized person, and took so many things in his stride.

"No, there was just a sitter there. But I do want to talk to her about you before the kids say any more about the weekend than they have. I'll call her later." It was already after eleven. Whenever there was an issue, I was to find, he would "call her later." His impressive organizational skills and ability to act with clarity and decisiveness fell completely apart where Roberta was concerned.

We were lying in bed, talking sense and nonsense, and I was beginning to relax. The reality of the weekend was fading, and in my ostrich fashion I was ignoring the fact that next Friday was only four days away. The phone rang.

"Who the hell is calling at one o'clock in the morning?"

"You answer it," I said. "It's probably Roberta, and I don't want to talk to her."

"No, she wouldn't call; she doesn't know the number or your name. You answer it. It may be another of your old boyfriends." I'd told him about the call from Frank. He hadn't taken it as a threat, or even acted that interested. Perversely, it annoyed me that he didn't seem jealous, or have the slightest concern that I might have been tempted to sunnier climes and less *tzouris*. I let it ring until he picked it up.

"Hello." I could hear a rising crescendo through the wire. Stan tucked the lower end of the phone under his chin and mouthed, "You were right."

"Look, I wanted to tell you myself, but you weren't there." He sounded like someone talking to a slightly retarded child, very patient, very slow.

"It was all very proper. She slept with the kids. . . . Come now, that's silly, of course I want to see them again. . . . No it hasn't. . . . Be reasonable, Roberta, you know I'm not going to do that." His voice still hadn't risen a decibel, nor had it become tense or tight. He was lying back, listening, first cleaning his fingernails with his teeth, then crossing his legs and picking at his toenails, two mindless habits he lapsed into when preoccupied.

"You can tell your lawyer, but we're both adults, and can do what we choose. I haven't said that the kids shouldn't live with you because of what you are doing." It was his first statement that wasn't totally passive, and it unleashed a tirade from her. I couldn't hear what she was saying, but I could imagine.

"Let's talk about it when you're a little calmer. I'll call you later this week. . . . I told you, it hasn't been going on a long time. . . . Yes, we worked together for a while. . . . This isn't getting us anywhere. . . ." He turned to me with a shake of his head.

"She hung up on me."

"How'd she get the number?"

"I don't know. Information, maybe. Leslie must have remembered your last name. She said I can't see the kids again, because they shouldn't be exposed to the flaunting of an unmarried relationship. That's a laugh. It's okay for them to be around her and her lesbian friends." He sounded bitter, and I couldn't think of anything to say. I felt guiltily happy because we would have next weekend to ourselves.

"What are you going to do?"

"Talk to my lawyer, I guess, and see if there's anything I can do. I really would like to have the kids with us permanently once the divorce goes through. I'm worried about their living with Bobbie. They'd do much better with us."

It was the first I'd heard of this plan. "You mean you'd have custody?" Weekends were going to be bad enough. Full time would be a disaster. I lay there thinking about us, and Roberta, and how angry she was and what that might mean. I'd never been able to understand or believe the couples who split and stayed good friends or partners, but a really hostile arrangement, with me in the middle, was downright frightening. I couldn't sleep.

"Stanley."

Nothing.

"Stanley." I sat up on my elbow, and spoke directly in his ear.

"Mmm. What."

"I said, did you cancel all your credit cards?"

"No, why?"

"She'll use them, and you'll have to pay the bills."

"She won't do that. She's not vindictive. Besides, I just won't pay."

"You'll *have* to. And believe me, she will."

"Don't worry about it. Won't happen." He rolled over and began to snore in earnest. I slept fretfully the rest of the night.

5

The first time I met Stan he was working as a management consultant at the pharmaceutical company where I had been employed for several years as a research chemist and then as a chemical production supervisor. The hourly workers had threatened a unionization effort, and Stan's company had been called in to try to improve morale while production was being cut back, overtime was being eliminated, and fifteen percent of the nonexempt work force was being laid off.

The first step was to develop some sort of teamwork among the management instead of the usual political infighting, and to get the managers to understand the role they played in motivating their employees. Neither task is easy. Stan accomplished both these goals to varying degrees during a two-day workshop which included team-building exercises, group process, planning, and objective setting. The workshop I attended with thirty other managers began on St. Patrick's Day.

In the most powerful exercise of the two days each participant shared something about himself that might give others insight into his personality. I had always felt that to hold my thoughts and feelings close to me made me less vulnerable, so to share them publicly was incredibly difficult for me. If I couldn't share myself with family, friends, and lovers, how could I open myself to strangers? But I hadn't reckoned on Stan's powers of persuasion. Everyone else in the room had spoken.

"Mary?" Stan's voice was soft and gentle, coming not from a person in the room, but from a source or force outside us all. He encouraged me the same way he had encouraged all the others before me, and they had all given something of themselves that was secret—and sometimes precious—to them.

"I don't have anything really to say."

"Can you think of anything that was important to you—that changed the way you think about things, perhaps, or what you do? At school, or at home?" I wasn't looking at him, but as I listened to his melodic voice the people in the room began to melt into the murky twilight shadows.

"No. Well . . . nothing specific. But I've always had the sense that no matter what I've done, I've been something of a failure to my father. He never seemed satisfied with me."

"Why not?" Stan's question was supportive, not interruptive.

"Oh, I don't know. It was a feeling I had. Maybe it was because I wasn't married and a mother like my older sister, or married and respectable like my younger one, although my sister Lacey had married as soon as she graduated—'My ten-thousand-dollar gardener,' he used to sigh. 'Why did I bother to send her to college?'—and Liz had married after two years at college. 'Why couldn't she have waited till she finished school?' he'd say. 'That way she'd always have something to fall back on.' And he probably told them that they should have gone to graduate school and made use of their education like me, so in our family you couldn't win either way." I looked out the window, recalling fragments of my youth. "After two years I stopped going to school full-time, the girls' college he had chosen for me. I turned my summer job into a full-time one and enrolled in Fairleigh Dickinson University at night. It took me five years of going to school nearly every evening winter and summer, but I got my bachelor's and master's degrees, using tuition refund programs to pay for all of it."

"What did that mean to you, Mary?" That voice again. I hadn't intended to say any more, but found that I had to.

"When I look at my own life, the things I've done, and haven't done, a lot has been to try to please my father. But some things I did because I knew they wouldn't—you know, I'd say, 'All right, dammit, I'll give you a reason not to be happy with me.' I realized I had to make my own decisions in my own best interests, and not always be stretching to satisfy someone who rarely told me he was pleased with my accomplishments."

I stopped again, finished this time.

"Okay, thank you, Mary. Let's take a break, and we'll begin again in fifteen minutes." I went back to my hotel room, washed my face, and looked at myself in the mirror. The face that looked back was round, with bright brown eyes and clear skin. Many people said that I was pretty; many times I felt pretty. I thought about the successes I'd had in school, the jobs I had held, the money I had in the bank, the people who cared about me.

"You really are okay, you know," I said aloud to that face. "Anything but a failure. You have to live up to your own expectations, not your father's."

When I reentered the room where we were gathering, Stan was standing in the foyer, leaning up against the wall, sipping Coke from a green glass bottle.

"Mary." He called my name as I passed by. "Your sharing," he said, coming over to me. "That must have been difficult for you, and I appreciate that." His voice was gentle, and his brown eyes behind the gold-rimmed glasses were concerned. He made me feel that what I'd said was important, to him and to me.

I got involved full steam in Stan's project, because there were more managers than departments, and I was getting bored with the world of chemical manufacturing. It seemed much more stimulating and fulfilling to change people's behavior and attitudes than to transform one chemical substance into another.

There were lots of meetings taking place and committees being organized, but at first I was never invited. I just went. Meetings on communications, reorganization, systems for performance appraisal, meetings about holding meetings, incentive training—you name it, I was at it. Nobody ever asked me how I got there or what my role was, they just took it for granted somebody knew why. So before long I was getting assignments at meetings, and giving reports, and calling meetings.

I learned a lot about Stan during those months watching him make the same presentation to some fifteen different groups and always making it sound new—different—as if it were the first time. I listened to his same corny jokes and always laughed, and listened to him share the story of his seige with testicular cancer and always cried. He told the story the same way each time, how he had felt a hard lump, and been frightened, postponing the inevitable but finally going to a doctor. Much to his relief, the doctor told him he was fine, nothing to worry about, so he tried to ignore it and hoped it would go away. A year later, with the lump still there, he changed doctors, and ended up on the operating table in less than twenty-four hours.

The operation went well, but the surgeon wanted to do a lymph-node dissection, to remove the lymph glands from his groin and abdomen and make sure the cancer hadn't spread. Stan was given the choice of going home or staying in the hospital for the week before the next operation, and being Stanley, he chose to go home and live what he was afraid might be his last healthy week on this good earth.

"I looked at my kids when I got home," he said slowly, obviously thinking back to those summer days three years before, "and decided that I was going to do a lot of the things I'd been promising them, but never had gotten around to doing. I taught Leslie how to ride her bike, and I taught Amy how to do a backflip, and I read a lot of books that I'd been wanting to read. I tried to identify the most significant events in my life, and all I could come up with was a tennis match I'd won as captain of my college tennis team. And I decided," he went on, "that if I made it, I was going to do a lot of things differently, and stop wasting so much of my life and my time." He would finish his monologue with a wry sad smile. "If it could turn out as well for everyone as it did for me I would highly recommend cancer as a worthwhile experience. It puts life in perspective."

One sweltering day in July our paths crossed by accident in

the middle of a chemical tank farm, and since we hadn't done more than exchange pleasantries over the past six months, he was caught off guard by my impassioned plea.

"Hi, Mary," he had greeted me casually, mopping his sweating brow. "How is everything? Things are moving along well, don't you think?" His collar button was open, and his tie loosely knotted about his neck. He hardly paused, obviously expecting a positive response from me, and preparing to move quickly on to wherever he was headed.

"It's *awful*. Everything is just awful. Things seem to be slipping back terribly. Dan is worse than ever, and Elmer's running everybody ragged. Can't you *do* anything? What are you doing, anyway? Do something!"

He was nodding and smiling inattentively when it dawned on him what I was saying. He stopped dead. "What?"

I repeated what I'd said and then some. "If you don't *do* something, it's all going down the drain," I cried fervently. And that was the moment, he later said, he fell in love with me, and began to dream about me day and night.

The summer turned into Indian summer, and one brilliant day Stan called and asked me to work as one of the internal project coordinators with his consulting group. I accepted, delighted and proud, because to have the "company shrink" tell me I was doing well at something I hadn't been trained for and enjoyed so much was the highlight of the ten years of my working life.

In the months that followed, we worked together several times a week. There was an easy camaraderie among the consultants, and they welcomed me into their little group, made me feel a part of it. I was grateful and pleased, happy and excited. Stan seemed gentle, charming, and brilliant, and I discovered he had a delightful sense of humor; but while I listened to his every word, I could hardly bring myself to talk to him, he awed me so.

One day he phoned to tell me that he had to make a major presentation, and he wanted to check some facts with me. Would I have lunch with him? My heart thumped as I tried to be casual about saying "Sure," excited, I thought, at being singled out by such an interesting and—in the consulting world—powerful man.

My visions of a glass of wine and an expense-account lunch were dashed when he greeted me with "Hi. Let's get something at the deli and eat in the park."

Once there, he quickly chose a ripe Anjou pear. "My father has a supermarket, and I can tell a good pear. Try one." It did look good, as if the juice were ready to burst through the skin. Without waiting for my response he selected another that matched the succulence of the first. He added a yogurt, and I a Diet Pepsi.

"Would you mind paying for these? I don't seem to have any money with me." Shades of the days when I used to carry an extra dime, to call a cab when my date was too unpleasant.

I thought he was joking about the park, since it was mid-November, the kind of dreary damp day that chills deeply. But that's where we went. And then we walked, he in a heavy camel-hair coat, I in a lightweight jacket, he rehearsing his presentation, and I agreeing, disagreeing, or interjecting a comment or suggestion. After a while he sat on the bare ground beneath an old maple tree to eat his pear and yogurt. A brook gurgled nearby. On another kind of day it would have been a romantic setting for a picnic lunch, but for a business meeting it was a cold disaster. I sat cross-legged on a root, trying to keep as much of my bottom off the damp ground as possible, intent on what he was saying. (Later Stan told me that his eyes kept drifting to my crotch, trying to imagine what was under my corduroy jeans. By then he had been having erotic dreams about me for months, and he could barely keep his mind on what he was talking about.)

Back in the car, he said, "You know, I scheduled a kind of postmortem after this afternoon's presentation. Why don't you come? You've been such a help in getting me ready for it, I think you deserve to be one of the first to hear what happened."

Three of us, I and two of his staff, waited in an office for him, and the appointed hour came and went. It was going either very well or very badly. Finally, the door opened. There he was, full cheeks rosy from the cold night air. His glasses had slid slightly down on his nose, and his eyes were as black as midnight and sparkled like the Milky Way. His coat was draped across his shoulders—I'm sure he had worn it like that on the brisk half-mile walk from the executive building, relishing the biting cold, as he had that afternoon. He positively swaggered.

He looked at each of us, and then, grinning broadly, turned two thumbs up. That was the first time I thought he was handsome, and the first time he seemed sexy.

After that, things happened *very* quickly.

The first Monday in December Stan addressed me directly before a day-long workshop. "Mary, I'm going to watch you this afternoon and give you feedback on how you're doing, okay?" I felt he was looking directly into my soul, over the rim of a Styrofoam cup which oozed beads of coffee sweat. "Maybe we could do it over dinner tonight."

Someone in the background clapped hands and called, "Okay, fellas, we're ready to roll! Grab your coffee and sit down."

"Sure." I felt the hot nervous flush creep through me that comes when you think somebody is going to find out you don't really know how to do something that you've been pretending you could do. "That'd be really helpful," I fibbed.

As we went through the workshop that day, I kept thinking about Stan, and the so-casual dinner invitation. It reminded me of so many other invitations I and every other woman had gotten from married men, but I was certain that lasciviousness was the farthest thing from his mind.

He was different from anyone I had known before, and couldn't be neatly labeled or compartmentalized. He dressed like a nebbish most of the time, in baggy trousers and dark cotton turtlenecks (the brown one spotted, the black one ripped along the right shoulder seam). Occasionally, like that day, he would appear in an expensive jacket quickly tossed aside, sleeves rolled up and collar button open, with his tie knotted loosely around his neck. His hands and forearms looked strong and capable, the muscles and veins running in powerful tracks, belying the delicacy with which he would push the sweat across his brow with the middle finger of his left hand (he was always sweating), or adjust his spectacles with the thumb and forefinger of his right hand, the rest of his fingers set as if he were drinking tea from a Limoges cup.

"Mary!" he called to me at lunch break as I was heading down the hall. "Don't forget I'm working with you this afternoon. And we're set for dinner tonight? Hey, Myron, do you have a minute? Excuse me, Mary." He walked off casually with his colleague, leaving me alone with my nerves.

I was educated to be a chemist, played at being an engineer, had taken a fling at law school, and had never had a psychology course in my life. I had always worked with test tubes or kettles or books, never with people, so I guess it was only natural that I should be nervous when it came time for my first evaluation as a trainer, by a pro, in a field so far afield from all my experience.

That afternoon Stan was incapable of sitting back and observing. He often jumped in to ask a question as I struggled on trying to do my best, nervous and anxious that his interruptions were the sign of some deficiencies on my part.

The workshop broke on schedule, and Stan came over to me, not quite so casually.

"Uh, hi. Are, uh, you still . . . I mean, are we still . . . uh . . . that is, is dinner still on? Uh, I'll give you feedback while we eat." I just nodded, clutching my notes to my chest. He seemed relieved. "You did fine, by the way. You're a natural at this stuff."

Who, me? It was hard to believe that he wasn't simply flattering me. "I'm looking forward to what you have to tell me," I lied.

"Great. Let me tie up a few loose ends here, and then we'll leave. I'll be with you in a few moments." Assured once more, he fixed his tie, and was rolling down his shirt sleeves as he walked away, humming to himself. A little bewildered, I took a seat in the lobby and waited.

It was a short wait. Stan was back almost immediately, carrying a well-worn briefcase (with ragged seams) made of a rich brown leather that gleamed with use. He shrugged into a dark-blue raincoat.

Outside, the wind had picked up fiercely as the temperature

dropped, and the clouds were being pushed speedily across the sky by the wind. To the west there was a narrow band of coral; laser beams from the setting sun were cutting through where the clouds touched the horizon. We walked up the hill into the big parking lot, stopping at a brown Lincoln. Stan unlocked the front door on the passenger side, waited till I was settled, then closed and locked the door.

As he slid behind the wheel, he was humming again, softly, and he started the engine.

"Are you cold? The heat will be up in a few minutes."

I nodded.

"Do you like seafood?"

"Yes, very much." I nodded again.

"Good. I know a little place not too far from here where you can get some of the best seafood in town. What do you say we try it?" He had already begun to move the car out onto the street.

"What's the name of it?"

"Sea something." He chatted a little bit, but for the most part there was silence and for me, at least, discomfort. It increased as I realized we were approaching the Lincoln Tunnel and heading into New York City.

"We're going to New York?" The tone of my voice reflected my astonishment. It was still chilly, but I was beginning to sweat. I tried to think who had seen us leave, who knew where I was. The answer—nobody.

"Don't worry." His voice was certainly reassuring, but some-how I didn't feel reassured.

"Where are we going?" I asked again, a little more emphatically when we came out of the tunnel and headed uptown. He looked more the Greenwich Village type.

"To be honest, I'm not exactly sure—it's on 55th or 56th or maybe 54th. We'll find it." That wasn't what I was worried about.

"It's right down this block, I think. It's a little place I've been to quite a few times—one of my favorites—but I haven't been here in a while." We were slowly cruising crosstown on 48th Street, passing the theaters with lobbies faintly lit and shadowed, barren this Monday night when the Big Apple's curtains remain down.

We turned north on Sixth Avenue, then east on 56th and entered Restaurant Row. He pulled the car up to the curb about halfway down the block. "That's where we're going," he said as he held open the door for me. I followed the direction in which he waved his hand, and saw the lighted entrance of the Seafare of the Aegean. It was the only one along the street that I hadn't been to.

And so we came to dine amid the capacious elegance of a "little seafood place," where Stan could give me feedback, ostensibly without distractions. Once ensconced on the red leather banquette, he began immediately to talk about the day's events and I relaxed. From the pocket of his jacket (bought, although two sizes too big, for its colorful Emilio Pucci lining), he whipped out two folded sheets of white narrow-lined pad paper covered with little tiny notes. He had obviously been watching me very closely all day, much more closely than I had been aware.

He unfolded the papers as he ordered a drink, "Jack Daniel's sour on the rocks for me. Do you want anything?"

"Chablis on the rocks, please." I'm usually a vodka drinker, but I had a premonition I should try to keep all my faculties intact.

We scanned the menu, and he ordered for both of us, dishes approved by a waiter hovering over us in his black dinner jacket, hoping to please.

Stan talked enthusiastically about my work over appetizers of stuffed clams, cold lobster, and salad, then we each retreated to our private worlds to savor, for me, stuffed sole, and for him, poached bass. He ate quickly, and leaned back against the banquette, arms stretched casually along the ledge, relaxed by two Jack Daniel's sours and the lion's share of a bottle of Pouilly Fuissé. As he had two weeks before, he had loosened his tie, and was looking quite handsome, flushed this time with alcohol rather than cold. (I found out that he had been on a diet for two months, losing twenty pounds as a prelude to this dinner.

It was probably that that had made him suddenly so much more attractive.)

I was warm and mellow, having enjoyed the wine and the conversation, and not minding that we weren't talking now. Stan ordered two Rémy Martins without consulting me. "You know, Mary, there is something else I've been wanting to discuss with you."

"Mmmmm hmmm."

"I love you. I've been thinking about it for a long time, and you don't have to say anything now, or ever, but it's something I want you to know." As he spoke, looking slightly away from me, his tone remained casual but his left arm slipped off the bench top, around my back, and clutched my left shoulder.

Oh, Jesus. Who needs this?

"I know this may come as a surprise to you."

Of course not. Was anybody surprised when Moses parted the Red Sea?

"You know I'm married and have three children."

Naturally, and you love them very much; you just want me for my body.

Now he turned to face me for the first time, and he shifted his arm back up on the ledge. I couldn't look him in the eye. "I want to ask you something, but it's hard to explain. . . ."

Shit. If you want to screw around, come out and say so.

"One guy once took me out to dinner, told me how much he loved me, his wife and kids, but that he wanted to have a 'physical relationship' with me. Is that what you're interested in?"

He was obviously relieved with my directness, and I think even took it as assent.

"I don't know. I only know I love you. We don't have to talk about it here, or now. I hope we'll have many evenings like this. . . ."

Brother, have you got a case.

I thought I had heard it all: every possible reason why Mary could fulfill some empty part of an empty person, why she should give, and not get in return. I wondered what excuse he would give.

"My wife is in a mental hospital (or suffers from severe depression, or is paranoid). . . ."

"My wife doesn't understand my business, and how important it is to all of us. So she goes her way, and I go mine. If it weren't for the kids . . ."

"God, but you should see the way she drinks. It just makes me sick . . . but someone has to take care of her. . . ."

"We've outgrown each other—we don't think alike anymore. . . ."

"She was pregnant when I married her; it was a mistake from the start. . . ."

"What's her problem?" I was curious how inventive he would be.

"Huh? Whose problem?"

"Your wife's. What's the matter? I mean, how come you don't get along?" It was impossible to keep an edge of sarcasm out of my voice.

"It isn't exactly that we don't get along. It's just that, uh, ah, we have very different interests." His expression belied the innocuousness of the statement. "But I love you."

"And I'm suddenly one of your interests? I don't want to have an affair with you, Stanley. I don't even know you."

"I don't think I'm interested in an affair either," he said slowly. "I don't know what I want."

"Let's not talk about it anymore, okay?" I stood up. "Let's just go. I'll meet you at the door."

I went to the ladies' room and had a warring conversation with myself in the mirror. Trying to figure out if he was serious or only thought he was, and what I was going to do.

He's crazy.

Why me?

Why not?—it happens to everybody, surely.

But he seems different—he's always so honest; he doesn't seem like the kind who screws around.

They all will if they're given half the chance.

He didn't say he wanted to.

He didn't knock his wife.

He tried to impress me by bringing me to a fancy restaurant.

63

So what if he wants to impress you?

Shit.

I felt I knew him well enough to know that he was too sincere and ingenuous to be giving me a real line. I fervently wished he hadn't brought up having an affair. Come to think of it, he hadn't. I had. He had just said he loved me. I went out in a state of confusion, to meet that sweet gentle man, and wondered if any other adventures were in store for me that night.

He was waiting by the cash register, popping pastel-colored peppermints into his mouth, trench coat draped casually over his shoulders. He looked like a cross between Woody Allen and Humphrey Bogart. Once he saw me, it was all Bogart.

We were quiet in the car. The music was on again, and it once again made conversation an option rather than a necessity. We made our way out of the city, down Lexington to 53rd Street, across to Fifth Avenue, and then down and crosstown to the tunnel on 39th. The store windows were beginning to show signs of Christmas: animated mechanical elves, wreaths, lights, silvered trees, and golden doves. The big spruce at Rockefeller Center rose behind the promenade, glowing in the December night.

"Would you mind if we rode a bit?" he asked me. "I don't feel quite like going back."

I agreed, hesitating only slightly. Stanley reached over and took my hand, gently squeezing my fingers. My hand lay limp in his, not returning the pressure, tingling from the effort to keep it a fraction of an inch from his. After a minute, he put both hands back on the wheel.

Once out of the city, he began a steady stream of conversation, a monologue about his past and present and dreams of the future. He told tales of his first job out of college as a typist, which he owed to his father's fruitman, and a hilarious account of his second job, as assistant contributing editor of an encyclopedia. (There was no contributing editor.) It was here he compiled his first book, an anthology of radical sixties articles which he sold to the founder of Ballantine Books in a Cuban restaurant in Greenwich Village. Then to an attempt at having his own business,

64

its near bankruptcy, the novel he had written, the great American novel he planned to write.

The wheels hummed on the concrete as the miles sped by. We were soon fifty miles from the city, and he apparently knew where he was heading. He had lapsed into silence, and I slid down farther into the seat so I could rest my head. The green glowing dial on the dashboard clock had both hands moving swiftly toward the Cinderella hour, and a long day at work, alcohol, and the stress of this unexpected situation were beginning to tell.

"Barry Fields, the guy I work for, lives near here. And there's a beautiful park somewhere close by, too. I remember I took my oldest daughter for a walk there one time."

The red light which indicated only reserve fuel flickered, and then glared its warning steadily.

It took many miles to find gasoline, many miles away from the park that Stan wanted to show me, which was far from everywhere and next to nothing. That would have influenced most people to change their plans, but not Stanley. He had created a script for that night and was determined to follow it through, a script based on dinner in the city, a ride in the country, and a walk in the park, and by God that was what we were going to do.

We reached Jockey Hollow at nearly two o'clock, and crept along the roadway. Two deer stood petrified in the headlights' glare, their eyes reflectors, and jumped backward as we came abreast of them. Stan pulled up next to a post-and-rail fence, at the base of a tilted meadow which stretched a quarter of a mile up the hillside. It was dusted with frost, and glimmered against the blackness of the forest which surrounded it on three sides. He turned off the lights but left the engine running, his hands resting lightly on the base of the steering wheel. I glanced at him from my corner of the car, and he was gazing at the sloping earth in front of us, somewhere in the world of his mind. My eyes followed the direction of his, and I became entranced by the patterns of the almost leafless trees against the night sky, and the pools and rivers of shadows that were scattered over the meadow. I wondered what he was thinking about as he sat so still and looked so intense.

"Would you like to go for a walk?" He was still looking through the windshield, and his voice was very low.

Since the restaurant, his conversation had been casual, and although he had shared a lot about himself, he had never again mentioned how he felt about me, or even that he cared. He had made no other attempt to touch me after I had not responded to the warmth of his hand, what seemed like years ago although it was only hours.

One reason I didn't call a halt to the evening was that I was too intrigued with discovering who he really was—what lay behind the gentleness and caring and perception. I was curious: about what he thought, what he believed in. The tale he had been telling about his life was full of surprises, facts and feelings I could never have imagined. So by the time he asked me to go for a walk, I was more curious than ever.

"Do you want to go for a walk?" he repeated and turned to me expectantly. I just nodded, and we stepped out into the frosty air.

It was night quiet, winter still, and the sound of the air as it whispered through the branches became part of the background silence. We began to walk along the base of the meadow, not touching, not talking, heading toward the Wyck House used by George Washington when he camped in the park with his regiment on his way to Valley Forge. Stan unhooked the wooden latch on the gate in the garden fence, and began softly to give me a history lesson. I didn't hear his words, only the hypnotic music in his tone, and I drank in the fragrance of a garden full of drying herbs and late-fall flowers. As we paused by a bank of rose bushes, Stanley reached down to pluck a still-live rose and handed it to me.

(Now he's going to try to kiss me.) He looked into my eyes for a flicker, and then continued walking, hands back in the depths of his coat.

We left the garden through the same gate and walked along a fence silvered with age. We approached a grove of trees, and he turned and leaned his crossed arms on the top rail. "See the horses?" he whispered.

There were two of them, large and white. One was lying on the ground in the shadow of a cherry tree, the other standing in the clear, seeming to glow in the dark. He looked up from the grass he was chewing, and gazed still as a statue in our direction. An eternity of maybe twenty seconds passed, and then as the specter of one horse moved closer to us, the other unfolded himself to an upright position. They meandered over to where we were standing, so close that we could see the smoky breath shooting from their nostrils, flared and crusted with frost.

"Aren't they beautiful? They make me want to write poetry."

"They look like ghosts," I answered. "Maybe they're haunting the pasture, and they really belonged to George Washington."

Stan turned his head, slowly, so as not to disturb the mammoth creatures hardly an arm's length from us, and looked, first, I imagined, at my mouth, and then into my eyes.

(Now he's going to try to kiss me.)

"I don't believe in ghosts," he said gently, and turned back to the horses. "This is all there is."

We continued walking, up the side of the meadow, up through the sloping forest. Once there was a noise, a snort, and pounding hoofs, coming from behind and to our right, from the direction we had left the horses. When we stopped to listen, only silence met our ears. Twice more as we climbed to the top of the tilted meadow we paused to try to place the sounds keeping pace with our position, always at a measured distance from us. There was no headless horseman in this sleepy Jockey Hollow, only a riderless horse, posting his territory and protecting it from trespassers such as us.

Finally the crest of the hill, with the open expanse of winter grass below us. Still we hardly spoke ("Are you cold?" "No," I lied), there being nothing for us to say, and no need to say anything. There was a final snort as the hoofbeats passed behind

67

our backs, through the forest and away. Stan and I looked at each other nervously and embarrassed, both a little frightened.

"Sounds like it's gone. Do you think it was one of the horses?" I was relieved, because I didn't think Stan would have been able to fend off an animal attack.

"I thought maybe it was a moose. It sounded awfully big, and I don't think horses make noises like that."

"A moose? Here?" Again, I imagined he was looking at my lips. I wondered what it would be like—if his kisses would be wet or dry, or if he would use his tongue.

We started to walk down the hill, footsteps crunching on the frost and leaves, each of us wrapped in separate thoughts. It was at the halfway point, Stan walking a few steps ahead of me, that he turned and waited for me. I stopped several feet away and caught my breath, enjoying the burning cold in my lungs as I inhaled deeply, wiggling my toes and fingers to produce a little warmth.

"Would you mind very much if I kissed you tentatively?" I almost didn't hear him.

I was twenty-eight years old. I had been kissed passionately and dispassionately, by friends and by lovers, with restraint and with abandon. I had been kissed by single men and married men and men in the limbo in between. I had been kissed by surprise, and with foreknowledge and thought, and I had, on a few rare occasions in high school, been asked for permission. But no one had ever asked if he could kiss me tentatively before.

So I said, "I guess so," and waited to see what would happen.

Stanley took a step forward, his hands still in his pockets, and then leaned over toward me, bending into the space that separated us. His lips rested lightly on mine for a fraction of a second, hardly long enough for me to know that they were there, but I imagined them to be soft and warm and gentle and slightly parted. It was over before I realized it had begun, and I wasn't sure if I had imagined it or if it had been real, that slight, electric tingle that you feel through an improperly grounded wire.

Then Stan took my hand in his, and we walked in silence

back to the car, with my heart pounding much more than I would have predicted.

The rest of the night flew by, with conversation, and laughter, and kisses that were no longer tentative. He never tried to do more than kiss me. He never suggested making love. And when we realized that it was long past time to part, I knew him differently, more deeply, having caught snatches of the thinker, the dreamer, the poet and the clown.

That first evening had stretched into the night, and ended at dawn, as we rode into the sun rising in the crystal-clear sky behind the New York City skyline. Rays of golden light poked their fingers through the narrow streets. If you believe in omens (I do, Stanley doesn't), you would have seen in the energy of that silhouette and the intensity of the morning all that was to follow in our lives.

We drove in silence, holding hands, and this time they were clasped firmly. The night had been mystic and romantic, and extraordinarily sweet. We parted gently, without passion, and at least on my part, no expectation of other dinners, nights, or dawnings. I left him that morning with a treasure, and that was enough.

But it wasn't enough for him. Two days went by, in which I tried to recapture some of that night, but the memories became as spectral as the visions of the horses. The Wednesday after Thanksgiving was a blustering, stormy, wet, dreary day, and I had just about succeeded in relegating my adventure with Stanley to its proper place.

The phone rang in my friend Cowen's office, and he answered it by giving his name in his usual marble-mouthed fashion. "Haalo," he added. "Sure. She's here. Yeah. Okay." He stood up and held out the phone. "It's our crazy shrink. He wants to talk to you. Want me to leave?"

"Of course not." But I must have blushed, or perhaps he heard my heart begin to thump, because he left the room, closing the door behind him.

"Hi," was all he said. I took a deep breath.

"Hi," and waited.

"How are you?" It was inane.

"Okay. You?" That was equally inane.

"Okay." About twenty seconds of silence.

"Mary, I haven't been able to stop thinking about Monday night." I waited some more. "Was it real? Did it really happen? It seems like a dream."

"Yes. It doesn't seem real to me, either."

"Those horses—I keep seeing those horses. . . ." His voice trailed off lamely, and I just sat there, hunched over, gripping the phone with my left hand, and wrapping the cord around my right. I didn't know what to say, so I said nothing.

"Mary, I meant what I said, in the restaurant, but I know you need time, and we need time to get to know each other better."

(Jesus Christ, this is like something from a movie.)

"I have to go to Florida tomorrow on business, and I thought you might like to come along. You could swim and spend the days on the beach while I worked, and then we could be together the rest of the time."

I still didn't say anything, just twisted my feet around the legs of the chair. I was beginning to look like a contortionist for the Ringling Brothers.

"Mary . . ."

Nothing.

"If you're worried about . . . well, let me just say that there are no strings attached. Honest. You don't even have to talk to me if you don't want to. Just give us a chance to get to know each other, away from here, away from everything. At the very least you'll have a rest. What do you say?"

I didn't know what to say, so I said, "I don't know what to say."

"Don't say anything, then—at least don't say no. Think about it, and I'll call you tonight, and you can let me know for sure. Monday night was such a beautiful night for me, and I think for you, too. Remember, no strings. You can do what you want— walk the beach—sail—I promise I won't bother you."

"Okay, I'll think about it." No strings attached. That's a new line.

He was off the phone before I knew it, and those five minutes became as dreamlike as the other night in Jockey Hollow. And I wasn't sure what I was going to do.

He called me from an airport between planes, assuming that I'd be home for his call and that I would go with him.

"The plane leaves at ten tomorrow night, and I have reservations for us."

"I'm not sure I'm going."

"I promise nothing will happen. Trust me. I just think it's important that we get to know each other. Meet me in the parking lot at seven, and we'll leave from there." His voice was pleading, and he was gone.

He was back at the plant the next day, and we worked together, another workshop, but I couldn't keep my mind on where I was. I was still trying to decide if I would go to Florida with him. He didn't talk to me all day, didn't give me a chance to tell him no.

I met him in the parking lot, and he never followed up on the business he said he had. I walked the beach, and swam, and sailed, and soaked up the sun, with Stanley by my side. We picnicked in a bird sanctuary among the flamingos, terns, egrets, and pelicans, and we picnicked on the beach among people and sand crabs. He kept his promise; there were no strings attached. Only once, on a sandy jetty, he kissed me with more passion than I had ever known before, but it was brief, and he didn't kiss me like that again. And he told me he and Bobbi were getting a divorce.

That was how it all began: a month-long courtship beginning at the Seafare and ending when Stanley camped on my doorstep just taking it for granted that I would want him there as much as he wanted me.

It was a courtship filled with poetry, Stan engraving images for us to recall. The first poem was inscribed in one of the few remaining copies of the novel he had written:

71

Mary—

Two star lit white reincarnations
Dreamt where Washington slept . . .

My first poem in fourteen years.
                    Stan

There were the lines from the day we sucked dripping persimmons in Central Park:

Such ripeness
I hesitate to pick up,
not to break the skin
and let spill down the sweet juice
before my mouth's taste of the
pitless orange fruit can even begin.
So I go slow—
only pillow you in the hollow of my palm,
court you with braked haste . . .
All my fantasies of you
remind me doubly of persimmons:
your circling lips over and below,
the fruit dripping onto your lap
in Moist Central Park
reilluminates images of you
like in movies
interlocking with me in slow motion . . .
Oh, Mary, you whelm me with shadows,
touching, and kisses from your
exquisitely tasteful form—
Let me be your fruitman
and crush a persimmon about your
breasts, lips and thighs . . .
Then I lick you
and I warm.

All that, with no strings attached.

6

It was not my custom to bring my gentlemen friends home to meet my parents. When they did meet, it was more by accident than design, because from the time my first love picked me up wearing his prized basketball varsity jacket, they disapproved of every one of them for one reason or another—they were too old or too married or too hippie or too poor or too ethnic or too something, and everybody had to be taking advantage of me. My very straight parents had a suspicion, I think, that I drifted from affair to affair, besmirching my virginal character (and consequently their reputation) with no intention of settling down and becoming an honest woman.

So it seemed pointless to go on having them meet the instigators of my supposed imprudences. Their fantasies of my decadent life were far enough from the truth, but since we'd never discussed my sexual activities or lack thereof, or sex in general for that matter, I couldn't deny what they never outrightly accused me of. Besides, it wasn't any of their business.

Stan had more of his belongings in my house than anywhere else, although he didn't officially "move in" until after that fateful day in Bloomingdale's. My parents had been barely aware that he even existed. When I first met him and began to get involved in the project he was working on, I would talk to them about what we were doing and some of the other things he had done for other clients, but my father's reaction had always been skeptical. "My business," he said, "has been successful without consultants."

He would add, "What about your education? You went to college and graduate school, and studied chemistry, and now what are you doing? You're wasting all that time and money on what sounds like bullshit to me." The son of an Italian immigrant, my father had gone to Lowell Tech to study textile engineering, then had joined his father's well-established embroidery business and married my mother. When I started college as a science major he had given me his cherished *Handbook of Chemistry and Physics,* and his slide rule.

So I stopped talking about Stan at all. Now, however, Stan was optimistically planning on getting married by the end of January.

By mid-December, both Stan and Roberta had retained counsel and begun to work out the details of support, alimony, and distribution of property. All he wanted was for it to be over with as quickly as possible, and his attorney assured him that could be easily accomplished in six to eight weeks.

He paid every December bill without question, and arranged to begin paying a fixed sum in January (a sum subject to change when the separation agreement was signed) as well as a mortgage on some land, a bank loan, insurance, and other sundries. All of which, he felt, should have satisfied Roberta, who, being deeply involved in the pursuit of equal rights, was about to embark on "getting in touch with herself" and securing her independence. She was, Stan said, as relieved as he that the marriage was over.

So while the papers were not yet signed, there seemed to be agreement in principle in most areas, and Robert Begert, Stan's Philadelphia attorney, was certain that the remaining points of discussion could easily be resolved. It was his optimism and apparent lack of knowledge that New Jersey required eighteen months of separation before divorce that fed Stan's delusions about an easy divorce and an early remarriage.

In light of the fact that it was now late December, we decided that it was time we told our respective families we were about to get married. In our anxiety to get it over with as quickly as possible, we scheduled a doubleheader—first a trip to Long Island for a drink with Stan's father, followed by a late dinner at my parents' home.

The drink with Harry wasn't too bad. Stanley monopolized the conversation, forestalling his father's criticisms and overdramatized reactions, telling his father exactly what he was going to do, and just a little bit about why.

"What will become of the little ones? Be good to them, Mary, because this will be very difficult for them. Are you sure you're doing the right thing, my son?" He shook his head in sadness. We sat with him in the dark Formica restaurant, his feelings a little bit hurt because we wouldn't eat more than a salad with him ("What, you won't let me break bread with my new *tachta?* Stanley, I'm an old man. Humor me a little, and let me buy you something to eat"). I was glad when it was time to leave.

The week before I had called my mother.

"I have someone I'd like you to meet, Mom. Could we come by on Tuesday?"

"Why, of course. What's his name?" She had been speechless for a moment, but recovered quite nicely. My mother was smart enough to know that something was up.

"Stanley Silverzweig. He's the consultant whom I've been working with the past few months."

"Oh, I see. He's Jewish?" My parents liked to consider themselves ecumenical and were proud of the fact that my older sister had married a Jewish doctor, but another Jew in the family might be too much. "Why don't you plan on coming to dinner?" Then she changed the subject, not asking me another thing about him, and I was too nervous to share my excitement and trepidation without at least a little encouragement.

They were, I am sure, quite unprepared for someone like my gentle Stanley, with his casual dress, curly hair, and thoughtful manner. We were a little bit late, fortunately, so were able to dispense with the predinner chitchat and proceed right to the main event.

"I hope you're not kosher," my mother said with a nervous smile as she placed a beautifully arranged platter of meat on the table. "This ham looked so good in the market!"

Stanley waved his hand as if to say, "Don't worry" and proved his own ecumenism by more than doing justice to the bounteous meal his future mother-in-law had prepared so carefully. My father talked incessantly. From the time we sat down at the table, he went on and on and on and on. Stan is good at getting people to talk and putting them at their ease by getting them involved in conversations about things that interest them, but this was one time he didn't need to try. My father, Joseph, launched into a three-hour monologue about his business, his vacations in Mexico, right-wing politics, plans for retirement to a farm in Vermont—everything that he could think of that might not touch on us.

Each time he paused for breath, Stan would open his mouth to speak, trying to turn the talk to our plans, but as soon as Papa saw him start to say something, he would jump in with a new topic.

As my mother and I cleared the food and the coffee cups, she whispered in the kitchen, "He seems very nice," and gave me a knowing, motherly squeeze. My father brought out his collection of brandies and old-fashioned moonshine, along with an assortment of cordial glasses for a tasting party. It was something he did for company he liked very much or didn't like at all. I wasn't sure which was the case now. Stan politely sipped from this glass or that, catching my eye occasionally with a twinkle and a suppressed smile, knowing full well what Joseph was up to.

"How about letting me show you the slides of our last trip to Guatemala? It was a fascinating trip, and I'm sure you'd really enjoy them. I'll go set up the projector." He half rose from his seat, but this time Stan stopped him.

"Joe, sit down, please. I'd love to see your slides someday, but right now there is something else that I think we should all talk about. I love your daughter, and I want to marry her. I'm going to marry her. My divorce will be final very soon, and then we'll be married." It was done. He looked from Joe to Mary, my mother. I just looked at my lap. There was total silence for the first time that evening.

Then came the questions, about Roberta, about the kids, about our plans, and Stan answered them all as best he could. I sat by in silence watching him handle my family much the way he handles clients, running a workshop on them, getting them involved, trying to get them committed to the changes that were about to happen in their lives.

The remainder of the evening passed quickly, and we finally departed, my mother hugging Stan and inviting him to their Christmas Eve party, hugging me and saying, "I hope you know what you're getting into. I hope you'll be happy." There was worry in her eyes behind the smile.

"Thanks, Ma. I'll be okay." By this time I felt I was mature enough to distinguish between a married man who had no honorable intentions (I'd known a few of those), a married man with honorable dreams, but no intention of carrying them out (I'd known a few of those too), and one who meant what he said, was what he said he was, and would do what he said he would do. By this time I knew that Stanley was in fact about the only man I'd ever known, married or single, who fell into that last category.

My father shook Stan's hand overvigorously, and didn't say anything to me when I kissed him goodbye, just patted me on the back.

And then it was Christmas Eve and I sat alone in my bedroom, wrapping the Christmas presents Stan had bought at Schwarz for three little girls that I had never met, waiting for him to call from the children's house and let me know what time he'd be picking me up. This was the first time in ten years I was bringing a man to my parents' traditional Christmas Eve party. It was a command performance, and a test. The hands crawled around the clock as I waited for the phone to ring, and I dressed the boxes and books and toys in shiny Santa Claus paper and red satin ribbons.

When the phone shrilled I jumped up and answered breathlessly, "Hi."

"Oh, are you still there? I thought you would have left long ago." My stomach sank. It was my mother. She sounded hopeful, I imagined, that my plans had fallen through.

"Stan will be calling any minute to let me know when he'll get here. I'm wrapping his presents for the girls." I tried to sound nonchalant, and probably didn't.

"Oh, well, try not to get here too late." She asked me the question I was refusing to ask myself. "Are you sure he's coming?" She was wearing her high distracted voice, the one she used when she thought that you were in trouble and didn't want her to know, but she was clever enough to know—and clever enough not to be in trouble herself.

The phone rang again immediately, and this time it *was* Stanley. He was calling about ten minutes after he was supposed to have arrived.

"Hi." He sounded apologetic before he began. I started to have hot flashes as I imagined what was coming.

"Hi. What's up? I . . . uh . . . I thought you'd be here by now." I tried to conceal my panic.

"Well, it's been kind of hectic, and hard to get away. The kids, you know . . . they thought I was going to spend more time with them tonight." He paused, sounding as if there was more to come but he didn't know how to say it. So I said it for him.

"You won't be able to come then, right?" My voice was very controlled and flat. I couldn't bring myself to fake cheerfulness, since I was half an hour away from suicide. Why couldn't the little brats go to bed early on Christmas Eve, to wait for Santa Claus? It was after seven. Besides, they were Jewish, so it shouldn't matter anyway.

But I didn't say any of that. There was a significant, pregnant pause.

"No, no, I'll be there. I said I would come. Just remind me how to get to your folks, and I'll go there directly as soon as I can."

"What time?" His voice sounded tired and I guessed he had had a tough visit, but I pushed him anyway. Nothing had ever been so important to me as his coming through for me tonight, proof to my skeptical parents that I could indeed make a wise choice, that I was right and they were wrong.

"I don't know, Marila." He sighed, using the Yiddish form of my name as an endearment. "After the kids go to bed."

"Yes, but what time?" I was relentless, and angry at myself for being that way, but angrier at him for the situation he was putting me in with my family.

"You know how excited kids get. . . . As soon as I can. Please understand."

I was being singularly ununderstanding. "If you aren't going to be there by ten at the latest, then don't come at all."

"What do you mean? I said I'd be there. But the kids—"

"But me, Stanley, what about me? You told my parents just two days ago that you were going to marry me in less than six weeks. And now I'm supposed to tell them you can't keep the commitment you made tonight. Fine. I'll tell them that your other family came first, you decided you'd rather spend tonight with them." My chest was heaving as if I'd just run a four-minute mile.

"Marila, that's not fair—you know it's not true. I promised you I'd come, and I will. I'll just be late, that's all. Please . . . I'll get there as soon as I can. I love you."

I let him hang up without the ritual return of "I love you too." I put all the Christmas packages in the car and left, dressed in a blue Moroccan dress with white silk braid trim I had bought that afternoon to wear for what I still hoped would be a very special Christmas.

My mother was solicitous. "Oh, I'm *sure* he'll come."

My father said in a gruff voice, "That's what happens when you have children—there are responsibilities and obligations. It's always the kids who suffer when adults get selfish. These things just never work." My sister Lacey was, thankfully, silent.

The doorbell rang at precisely five minutes to ten. My relatives exchanged meaningful glances, and assumed I would answer the door. They were making private wagers as to whether or not the caller was my guest or theirs.

Unshaven and very unkempt, it was Stanley, and I felt a deep wave of relief and gratitude. He kissed me quickly and said, "I have to wash and shave. Is it okay?"

"Sure." I led him up to the green-tiled bathroom at the top of the stairs, gave him clean towels, and headed back down, feeling like joy to the world.

"Stan's just freshening up," I informed everybody casually, and I can only wonder if they had any idea of the panic I had felt not too long before.

When he came into the room, Stanley was wearing his traditional, uncolorful turtleneck, but fortunately it was one that was untorn. Around his neck was a string of wooden beads, bright orange and bright blue, little wooden barrels and blocks, about one inch long and half an inch in diameter, strung on white kitchen twine.

"My daughter made them for me . . . Amy . . . she's almost six. Yes, it is difficult for them. I have three. . . . Yes, it's hard on her, too. But this is something we both wanted for a long time—it's really better for both of us. . . . Seventeen years. . . . Yes, I see them as often as I can. . . ."

Daddy, will you please shut up and leave him alone!

We exchanged Christmas presents. He gave me a crystal bowl, a pewter tea service, candlesticks, a back-packer stove, a down vest, and a down sleeping bag. I had wanted an engagement ring.

I gave him a cashmere turtleneck and a necklace. It was the year silver and gold chains came into vogue for men, but I still couldn't let myself believe it would all work out, so I settled for silver. He said he liked it, but for two days he wore his wooden beads instead.

7

The next weeks after that mad midnight call from Roberta were a delight for me, being in love, playing house, planning for the future that not so long ago had been bleak and empty. (It wasn't as easy for Stan, who was trying to work out the trials and difficulties of this new way of life, because Bobbi would no longer let him see the girls. She felt that his living with me was setting a bad moral example for their daughters, a sentiment she communicated through her lawyer.)

I'd lived alone for six years, and had been given the dubious honor of "old maid" of our branch of the family. When I bought my house in Mount Tabor, my grandmother said—in her inimitable fashion—"I guess that settles it. You'll never get married now." I had fairly well resigned myself to that as well, never having met anyone who didn't wear on me after a while, or bore me. My mother had always said I was too fussy, but I just preferred to be by myself than to be with people whose company I didn't enjoy. There was many a Saturday night during my college years when my roommate and I had more fun watching the girls go out with various specimens of so-called manhood, most of whom we wouldn't have been caught dead with, than going out ourselves.

So it was a treat for me to have found someone who was continually entertaining me without even trying, regaling me with tales of his Jewish mother, his childhood, and his youth. He told me about his sweethearts and his college chums, his travels and his work. He gave me a copy of the anthology he had published, and when he wasn't around, I ripped out the dedication that said "To Bobbi." We went to movies and to a basketball game, and we looked at real estate ads for houses. He began to introduce me to some of his friends from his other life, and then was hurt, and I embarrassed, when these encounters turned out awkwardly. I cooked, which I love to do, for two for a change, and he promised to cook for me. "A crab omelette," he said, but the Alaska king crab meat he had so carefully selected stayed in the freezer for weeks until he finally confessed that he had cooked so much for Bobbi and the kids that he couldn't bring himself to do it. He asked about me, and my life and my thoughts and my feelings, and he listened and seemed to truly care about me. That was a new experience for me, and a constant joy.

But there were also his nearly daily phone calls with the kids, staying in touch, trying to explain, trying to sort out their feelings, trying to help them understand, particularly now when Bobbi wouldn't let him see them. The same questions and answers over and over again. Why? Will you come home again? Was it my fault? And there were conversations with *her*, where he was just as patient as with the kids, infuriatingly so. He never raised his voice, never expressed his own frustrations by tone or inflection. It took me a long time to understand that the unpleasantness of dealing with Roberta was a small price to pay for freedom.

She continued to keep him from seeing the kids, and when once he went anyway, she didn't answer the door. His lawyer said to let it be for a while, that short of an all-out custody battle, which he didn't recommend, there was nothing that could be done. "You can't win. Unless you can prove maternal neglect, or the children strongly voice a preference, the courts will rule in favor of a homosexual household with the mother over a heterosexual one with the father, especially if you aren't married. Until you're divorced and remarried, she's in the driver's seat." A very different tune indeed from the "everything is just about worked out" he had been assuring Stan of up to now.

The bills began to trickle in from the charge cards that Stan hadn't cancelled—Saks, Lord and Taylor, Bamberger's. The lawyer said he had to pay them because they were in his name. Ditto with the telephone, fuel-oil, local supermarket, and gas-station bills that Bobbi forwarded to him. It seemed endless.

He had signed the credit application for a car loan on Bobbi's new station wagon several months before, so the bank was sending him repossession notices, plus overdue notes, etc. His lawyer said he had to pay until the formal settlement was worked out. Ditto with the mortgages on the two houses they owned.

His father called, apparently having had second thoughts after accepting me into his family too hastily, and told him he should stop his foolishness and go home. My folks seemed to imply, "I told you so" between every sentence when I spoke to them.

Nearly a month had gone by without Stan's seeing the girls, although one of our major topics of conversation that month without his daughters was what he thought they needed and what he thought would be good for them. That wasn't difficult. Harder to figure out was how we could give it to them. Stan was increasingly exploring in his own mind the idea of gaining custody. He ignored the fact that the lawyer told him it would be impossible, as he always ignored what he didn't like to hear. "I'll never forgive myself if something happens to them," he said.

I was really in a bind, full of conflict and guilts. The last thing I wanted was to raise somebody else's failures—if anything, I wanted to raise my own, and now I wasn't altogether sure I even wanted to do that. But if I told him that I didn't want his kids permanently—didn't want to be their baby-sitter, or their pseudo mother—what would that do to us? And they were so pathetic; it would be so easy to help them if they would let me.

I knew that he really loved them, and I could understand his concern for their environment, his worry about their emotional problems. My gut response was "Why the hell didn't you do something about it sooner?" He has two alternatives, I said to myself. He doesn't pursue custody, because he knows I don't want it. But if the kids end up in trouble he'll be bound to feel that it's my fault—he wanted to save them but I wouldn't let him. Or he pursues it anyway, knowing I'm resentful and unhappy, and everybody ends up miserable. Except maybe Roberta, who could enjoy her children with minimal responsibility, while I took them to the dentist and the doctor and washed their clothes, and saw to it that they took baths and did their homework.

And if Stan had his way, I imagined the reality would be a dreadfully, expensive court suit, a nightmare that would drag on interminably and be debilitating, embarrassing and destructive for all concerned, including the children. Begert had told Stan that although he would like to be involved in the case, odds on success were less than slim. It was his preliminary opinion that Stan should get his divorce and remarry before he seriously contemplated initiating a custody suit.

"He should know what the chances of winning are. But if you really feel you have to do it, you have to do it." I tried to appear as if I were maintaining a moderate, middle-of-the-road position.

"And you'll back me? Mary, it will be tough."

We had no idea then just how tough it would be.

We talked about it, examining it from every angle, and it has been one of the longest conversations we have ever had, literally stretching out over years. The final decision to pursue legal custody was made by the children themselves rather than by us, although we told them often that they would be welcomed with delight if they chose to live with us, and we'd do everything we could to make it happen if and when they made that decision. But the idea had been implanted early in Roberta's head that she was somewhat vulnerable in a suit, and that pressure turned out to be to the kids' advantage. In her efforts to prove to the world that she was a "fit mother" she increased at least a little the attention that she gave the girls. They needed so much that every little bit helped.

It had been an idyllic interlude for me before Bobbi capitulated and let the girls come again to visit. She must have felt her freedom limited by having the kids all the time. She had lost her best baby-sitter after the separation, as Stan used to take over while she went to her feminist meetings, to women's consciousness-raising sessions, or to their cabin in the woods. Selfishly, I hated to give the idyll up. "It's only for two days," I kept saying silently, and convinced myself I'd survive, and even enjoy it, at no cost other than constant indigestion and migraine headaches.

We'd prepared for the girls' future visits by setting up "the garden room" with cots and chests and toys. It was on the lowest floor in the house, below street level, saved from being a basement by double French doors opening out onto a garden and yard. One wall was fieldstone, the others rough-hewn wood, and while not completely finished it was a charming room. We had brightened it up with posters and paint, filled the dresser drawers with playclothes and underwear. I'd spent many pleasant hours getting things in readiness; it was something like having a baby: getting the nursery completed, and then waiting for the blessed event. In this case, three of them.

Stan and I had decided several weeks before, and after much discussion, that it would be wise for me to quit my job. My continued functioning as internal coordinator of the project Stan was managing could be considered conflict of interests by some, and the project had been too difficult and too successful to jeopardize it at the eleventh hour. Besides, I had been working for ten years in chemical laboratories and plants. Now that I had another option for survival, the nagging fears about what all the little molecules I had been breathing were doing to my insides were able to come to the fore.

So I was going to work for Barry Fields doing training, as well as writing and developing training materials, trading in a steady paycheck for the world of free-lance work. I was nervous about plunging into a new career at the same time I was becoming a consort and a part-time surrogate mother, but the idea of a flexible work schedule and working with Stan was tantalizing. More tantalizing, in balance, than the trepidation I felt making such an irrevocable commitment. I prayed Stan was as good and honest and caring and genuine as he appeared to be.

The Friday night we finally picked Leslie, Amy, and Jennifer up for their second visit was cold and rainy and ugly. It had been my last day at work. I was weary from the round of farewells and fare-thee-wells, and a series of exit interviews with assorted executives who were trying to find out why I was leaving. One VP spent fifteen minutes staring at my tummy with his X-ray vision, wondering if the excuse of "personal reasons" meant I was "in the family way."

Arrangements to get the girls that night had been rather complicated, as Roberta was refusing to talk to Stanley and Leslie acted as go-between. We were, she said, to pick her up first at dancing class, and then pick up the other two at home.

Stan and I walked hand in hand across the parking lot to the brick, ivy-covered building, and down the stairs to the one-two (clap), one-two (clap), one-two (clap) rhythm of a slightly out-of-tune piano and the teacher's "Higher, girls, higher" to the same beat. Behind me, as I stepped into the classroom, I heard him mutter, "Oh, shit," and quickly turned to see what had happened.

"Roberta's here."

"Okay, girls," (clap, clap), "that's it for today." Leslie turned from the barre, looking sharply from us in the doorway to a woman on the other side of the room.

I wanted to die.

She didn't look in the least the way I had imagined from Stan's sketchy comments. ("She spends lots of time in bed." "She never wanted to do much." "She used to like me to bring her coffee but would never get it for me.") I put these comments together with the images from the pictures in my father-in-law-to-be's scrapbook—the pictures he took such pains to show me. ("This is Stan and Bobbi before they were married." "This is Bobbi when she was expecting Leslie." "This was a wonderful family picnic we had.")

Roberta began to move toward us, arms swinging determinedly from her sides, a maroon down-jacketed ball with faded jeans and stringy hair, a sweatshirt showing beneath the jacket. She looked old and tense and tired, nothing at all like my fantasies. I remembered the sound of her screaming through the phone at Stanley's patience, and the tremendous need I had sensed in the girls in only the few days I'd known them, and I understood my love and his daughters a little bit better.

By the time she had reached us my palms and armpits were soaking, and if I had had anything to eat, I'd probably have thrown up on the spot. She approached with determination, and a fraction of a second before she paused in front of us, Stanley turned around and walked away, to talk to Leslie and her dancing teacher.

I wanted to kill him.

We were face to face, but she was looking over my left shoulder, and I was looking over hers, then down at our shoes, then over the other shoulder. Inevitably, though, our eyes met. I was speechless, but felt I had to speak. I wondered if she noticed the sweatlets on my upper lip. I noticed hers. "You have wonderful children," I lied.

"You don't have to tell me what I already know."

She turned her back to me then, for the first time but not for the last, and with as much purpose as she had walked toward us, she walked away. And so did I, outside where it was cool and damp, and it didn't matter if I cried or if my mascara ran. I cursed for the millionth time in a five-minute eternity when I discovered the car was locked, and chose to wait in the freezing rain, getting chilled and sodden, rather than go back inside. I knew with a dread certainty that Roberta and I were enemies, and any latent hopes I had had that we might be able to work things out rationally were totally irrational.

"Leslie's coming with me," Roberta called to Stan, she and Leslie chattering gaily as they came out of the school after him, holding hands. (It was the antithesis of the scene to be enacted five years in the future, standing in the judge's chambers, Leslie already ours, Amy and Jennifer clinging to my skirt as they waited for their fate to be decided.) Bobbi and Leslie started to skip through the rain and the puddles to a brand-new station wagon. Stan was silent, simply unlocking the door of the three-year-old Volkswagen Beetle he had gotten in trade for his Lincoln Continental and some much-needed cash.

"We have to pick up the girls at the house," was all he said, but he reached over to take my hand. I put it in my pocket instead, steaming as much as the windows, and sat silently.

"I'm sorry about this, Mary," he said two stoplights later, and reached again for my hand, again without success. "It was Leslie. She arranged it. She told me to pick her up and she told Roberta to pick her up. Neither one of us knew what she was doing. Bobbi was as surprised as we were. I'm really sorry." Stanley sounded truly contrite.

"I know you didn't do it—don't worry about it. It doesn't really matter. We had to meet sooner or later." I really wanted to scream at him, "How could you do that to me? How could you put me in that position? How could you let that little girl manipulate us like that?" But I didn't say any of that, and since it turned out to be the mildest of my confrontations with Bobbi, it was just as well.

The ride to our house, after picking up Leslie and Amy and Jennifer, was subdued. Leslie did appear somewhat embarrassed and crestfallen, although she didn't admit to having done anything Machiavellian. She also seemed a little disappointed. I don't know what she thought might happen at the dancing class—fist fights, or a screaming match. More probably she hoped that by a head-on comparison Stanley would see the error of his ways, and repent and return. Amy thought the whole thing great fun when she heard about it and discussed it ghoulishly and at length. Stanley didn't stop her.

The weekend passed relatively peacefully. It was a little like Christmas with the new room and new clothes and new toys. Enough time had passed for them to get at least a little used to the idea of two families. Tantrums, fights, tears, and fits of hysteria were kept to a minimum, and on a scale of 1 to 10, my headache never exceeded a 7.

8

Once we started to see Leslie, Amy, and Jennifer on a regular basis, things began to settle into a routine. Each Friday Stan drove three hours back and forth on the Jersey Turnpike to pick them up, all four tired and cranky by the time they got home. I'd give the girls baths and wash their hair—it always looked as if they hadn't done either since we'd seen them last. Saturday morning we'd all get up at the crack of dawn for a "family breakfast" (wasn't I terrific!) and haul them the hour plus to Mrs. Unger for Amy's lesson, and the hour plus back. The day was ready to begin at one in the afternoon, with all five of us worn down by the strain of spending so much time confined in a car, and the tension of a weekend half gone before it started. Then there were dishes to wash, dinner to fix, laundry to do. Once in a while there was a movie, perhaps sleigh riding when it snowed.

And, of course, there was the inevitable weekend cry. One or the other of the three kids would start it with "Daddy, why are you getting a divorce?" which would progress to "When are you going to come home and live with Mommy?" to "Don't you love us anymore?" That was the signal for tears. Always theirs and sometimes his. They would gather on the couch, huddled together, the four of them, and he would patiently explain once again. I would tiptoe around, trying to melt into the walls, feeling like an intruder in my own house. One Sunday, after a particularly bad session and a particularly bad weekend, I fell apart. I went upstairs and began to cry for the first time since I'd known Stan, and since the girls had been coming to visit. My frustrations at the problems Stan and I faced just learning to live together, as well as the ones caused by the tremendous feelings of guilt Stan had over the kids, plus the strain of their presence, plus dealing with a very angry not-yet-ex-wife, were more than I could bear. So I cried and cried, and I cried alone because Stanley was downstairs comforting the girls, and that made me cry all the more.

After their session had concluded, and it began to get dark, and they began to get hungry, Amy came to seek me out. "When are we going to eat? Hey, have you been crying? What have you got to cry about?" There was amazement in her voice, and I couldn't have begun to explain. She told Stanley, "Hey, Daddy, Mary's crying." But by then it was over, and I was spent. He thought it was for them, and how could I tell him that it was for me? That I'd given up my freedom for a part-time family that didn't want me, for Bobbi's spiteful torments, for more of my parents' disapproval, and for what seemed like not much in return. I didn't—couldn't—tell him any of this because I didn't think that he could do anything to change things, or even that he'd understand. So there was a little more resentment, and I'd sigh a little deeper after each of their crying jags.

"Doesn't anybody care about me?" I wanted to scream. *"Am I a goddam lousy piece of furniture that doesn't have any feelings? Maybe I feel as lousy as all of you about things."* But I didn't. I never said anything, and he always took my silence for the acceptance and approval that he expected.

A serious problem for me was that I really didn't have anybody to talk to. My friends were single, like me, or childless, and none were involved in second marriages. Lacey, my older sister, passed off most of my questions with "That's what all kids do when they are ten or six or four," as if it were all perfectly understandable, and any dimwit should see. My sister is thin and cool, and it was hard to keep asking her advice when I got that kind of response. She thought she was helpful, and to a degree in fact was, but it was far short of the encouragement and support I needed. I had hoped that my sudden acquiring of a family might bring us closer. Instead, I had these nightmarish imaginings of her and my mother discussing my situation—my inadequacies, follies, and failures. And this assumption was fed by my getting the same reaction from both of them about certain issues.

Like the lesbianism. To me, that was one of many valid reasons for Stan to decide marriage to Roberta couldn't work, and was part of my answer to their questions. Their usual response in those early days was twofold: "Why did he stay married so long?" and "She can't be much of a lesbian if she had three children. Where did they come from?" At least Lacey was merely skeptical. My mother's disbelieving tone infuriated me (as did her ability to take the same fact and argue it the other way—"How can he let those little girls live with a lesbian?").

I spent a lot of time stewing about the problems that arise when a single woman lives with a not quite unmarried man and his children, in a society where open relationships are often frowned upon. I could even remember not too long before looking with disapproval on a similar situation, thinking it disgraceful and immoral. So it had taken many months of soul-searching to arrive at a feeling of relative equanimity, to decide that Stan's leaving Bobbi created no fresh victims. What it provided was a way for Stan to have a normal love life, and at least occasionally for the girls to have a normal environment.

My mother and I had one particularly memorable conversation that succeeded in reinforcing the negative feelings and guilt about our situation I had been beginning to temper. It took place after my parents had met the girls for the first time, and I had blown up at Stan (he barely acknowledging my distress) over Roberta's bills that were still rolling in and his checks rolling out in silent acquiescence. The kids had spent two days trying my patience beyond belief, Stan encouraging them by not discouraging them.

I was nearly in tears as I related the latest sordid details, including the report from Stan's lawyer that Roberta was going to make the divorce as long and drawn-out as possible.

"You knew what you were getting into. And you certainly

didn't want any advice from us about getting involved with a married man. You've always done what you wanted, and now you're taking the consequences. You can always change your mind, you know. He certainly seems to be taking his sweet time about getting the divorce. Are you sure he really wants to? And of course she's angry. Wouldn't you be if your husband was shacking up with somebody else?"

I had never considered what Stan and I were doing to be "shacking up." That was what college kids did, or irresponsible people having a fling. I believed we had a clear and lasting commitment to each other, and that made what we were doing at least marginally acceptable. My mother, in a few well-chosen sentences, made the whole thing seem dirty.

My father knew that I knew he thought I was immoral without articulating it, so he tried a different approach.

"Don't you two think that you should take a closer look at what you are doing?" He had begun calmly enough, assured of a captive audience since Stan and I were in his car driving to Stamford, Connecticut.

"Huh?" We looked at each other. We thought it was perfectly clear that we knew exactly what we were doing.

"Do you really want to take the responsibility for ruining those children's lives?" He was a little more agitated now. "Stan, you decided to get married, and you decided to bring those children into the world. You have an obligation to provide them with a good home."

"Joe," Stanley said in his calm consulting voice, "the marriage was bad from the start, and I don't think children should be raised in an environment where the parents don't get along. It's better for them to see both their parents happy separately than unhappy together. Besides, eventually I'm going for custody of the kids. I think they would do much better with us."

"With you, maybe. But what about Suzanne?" He always used my middle name. "She doesn't know the first thing about kids, and certainly isn't capable of taking care of them full-time. She won't even be able to manage them on weekends and vacations.

Besides, how will she be able to work? She should work, and not waste all that education. You're being totally irresponsible and selfish, both of you!" He had turned nearly purple with rage, and I was trying very hard not to cry. Sitting between them on the front seat, I felt like an inanimate object being discussed.

"She'll be able to handle it okay, Joe. I have tremendous confidence in her, and the girls like her already." He didn't react to my father's harsh words and tone in kind, and I wanted him to be more vigorous in coming to my defense.

"They're very difficult children, you know that, and she just can't cope with them. You should stay with them and Roberta and try and help them, rather than run off." By now he was positively apoplectic, and I was afraid he'd have a heart attack on the spot.

"They're my kids, Joe, and I know them and what they need better than anyone," said Stanley, almost patronizing in his quiet assurance. "I'm not exactly running off. I see them almost as much as ever, and they get more from me when we're together now."

"Well, if I were you two, I'd think things over carefully, and stop before it's too late." The conversation ended on that bitter note, and we drove the rest of the way in silence.

My biggest disappointment was that my father didn't seem able to support me in doing something that basically displeased him, even though I was an adult and this was the most important decision of my life. And my mother, who had been invariably by my side when I needed her, this time I felt wasn't there either.

It shouldn't have surprised me that they were so disapproving, because I was doing what I had disapproved of in others until I found myself in the same situation. But they couldn't seem to understand that what they saw as their failure with me was really of my own choosing, and didn't reflect on them or the values they had taught me. And their disapproval was still as painful at twenty-eight as it had been at eighteen or eight.

Fortunately, they never took out those reactions on Leslie, Amy, and Jennifer. They have always been kind and loving toward their three new "grandchildren," making them feel welcome, giving them the sense that there is someone else who cares about them. For that, we've always been grateful.

Unfortunately, my parents' initial experience with the girls had been disastrous and probably prompted my father's tirade. They had been totally unmanageable, Jenny throwing a prize tantrum, Amy teasing Leslie till war was declared, and Amy wetting her pants for a finale. After that, it felt as if my parents rarely passed up an opportunity to compare my "daughters," to their detriment, to my sister Lacey's kids, who were smarter, prettier, handsomer, more talented, and better behaved. They seemed to relish discussing at great length how the trauma of the divorce was something that children shouldn't have to go through, and deploring the selfishness of adults like us who would inflict that on helpless youngsters. And after they accepted the reality of the divorce, their favorite topic, one they could discourse on for hours, was our lack of concern for the children's well-being because we let them go on living in a lesbian environment, and didn't immediately institute a full-scale custody suit. We never quite convinced them that the legal system didn't necessarily agree with their point of view.

It was true that Lacey's children were attractive and bright and had their heads pretty well together. It was true that Leslie, Amy, and Jennifer had a haunted look in their eyes, Amy was barely controllable, Leslie sounded more like a fishwife than a little girl, and Jennifer, except in a tantrum, was as quiet as a churchmouse. It wasn't true, at least in our case, that the children would suffer in the long run as a result of the divorce. The tensions they had faced were worse than simply having two families, at least one of which was normal and happy. But the girls weren't the real issue.

The criticism was of us: I was faced with a task beyond me, I was unprepared and unqualified to solve any of the girls' problems, and our selfishness was the cause of many of them. Still, however distraught my parents made me feel, their criticism only increased my determination to become a fairy godmother instead of the wicked stepmother, to wave my wand and transform all my Cinderellas into princesses. But I didn't want them to be dressed in fragile glass slippers, and go up in a puff of stardust at midnight. I wanted them to grow up to be strong and competent, so that years from now Stan and I would be able to look at them with pride instead of having to say, "My God, how much have we hurt these kids by making our life what we wanted?" And, of course, I wanted to prove my parents were wrong. I wanted to have them say someday, "She's done wonders with those children. I don't know what they would have done without her."

Every weekend I threw myself into the monumental task of teaching, cajoling, comforting, and loving the three fauves. By then, I had had enough glimpses of what they could be to feel hopeful—at least sometimes—that it was only a matter of patience, time, and elbow grease before they would live up to my tremendously high expectations.

I hugged them and held them and wiped away their tears. I scolded, corrected, praised, and occasionally spanked. I clothed them, groomed them, trimmed their hair, and tied it in ribbons. I'd get up early to cook breakfast—or spend hours cooking dinner so each meal would seem like a special occasion. We baked bread and cakes and cookies together. We went shopping, and read to each other, did homework and played.

Leslie and I talked endlessly about school and friends and growing up. Amy was tough to get close to, and the toughest to deal with. I drew on my patience and tried not to get angry with her, because she was used to having people be angry with her and tell her she was ugly or clumsy or mean. I didn't have the foggiest notion what to do with four-year-old Jennifer, who barely spoke, and, once her tantrums ceased, clung to me like Velcro. Yet without intending to, without even realizing it, during those early months of metamorphosis I began to care more and more about each of Stanley's daughters, because of who they were and could be in their own right, not because they belonged to him.

After three months of weekends all this feverish activity had us doing quite well. Although each weekend saw at least one outburst as regular as clockwork, they were becoming shorter and less intense, and in between the girls were turning to me more and more for comfort and attention. Their manners had improved to the point where I was quite proud of them (usually), and I'd found the secret to keeping them looking tidy. They had their Mount Tabor clothes and their "home" clothes, and instead of sending them off spiffily dressed, as I did in the beginning, I just put them back in whatever they had come in, because otherwise their clothes disappeared.

I chose the christening party of Lacey's new baby to display my efforts, and force my family to eat crow with their cake. My trio almost blew it.

We had shopped for party dresses and patent-leather Mary Janes, and the three angels were scrubbed and shining, ready to go on exhibit. We were only slightly late, and I was putting the finishing touches onto their hair with a curling iron. Leslie was delighted at looking so pretty, Amy was excited at going to a party, and Jennifer was very quiet. Amy started to tease her by pulling on the ribbons in her hair.

"Stop it, Amy!" she shrieked, with cause.

"Now, Amy," I intervened calmly. "Leave Jenny alone. We'll be ready to leave in a few minutes."

"Aaamy! Cut it out!" Jennifer started to cry, and slapped out at Amy with vengeance and enough accuracy to make Amy start to cry as well.

I decided to try persuasion rather than lose my temper, although, as usual, by Saturday afternoon I was at my wits' end and had a roaring headache. Besides, I didn't want to be late. This christening party was to be their "unveiling," so to speak, the first time we'd gone as a family to one of my family gatherings. It was important to me, because although I usually hated these get-togethers, I was sick of hearing about the poor dear children whose home had been broken, and wasn't it dreadful, etc., etc., etc. I intended to use the christening to prove to my father and mother and sisters and relatives that Stan and I and "our daughters" were making it okay, and I wasn't about to let these silly little twerps screw it up at the eleventh hour.

"Come on, girls. Let's not fight now. You all look so pretty, and we're ready to go to the party," I pleaded.

"I don't want to go to any party," Amy roared.

"I want to go home," wailed Jennifer.

"Oooh!" and Leslie joined in. The three of them stood there, looking as lovely as you could imagine, and as miserable. So was I.

"Staaaanley!"

I hollered down the stairs, trying to be heard over the din of one of the basketball playoff games. He couldn't have cared less about the party, and was quite put out, in his quiet sort of way, that we would be leaving at the halftime of a very good game. He ignored my calls for help and their concert of near hysterics as long as he could. Finally he came upstairs.

"Why, don't you girls look beautiful!" he crooned at the three upturned, tear-streaked faces, puffy eyes still spilling over. I had gathered them to me but could give them little comfort, and they quickly swarmed around their father, the cause of both their torment and salvation, as he came into the room.

"Daddy, we don't want to go anywhere. Can't we stay here?"

"Daddy, I want Mommy. I want to go home. Why are you getting a divorce?" And we were off again.

Everybody sat down on the bed, and for the millionth time Stan tried to explain that just because he loved me instead of Roberta didn't mean that he loved them any less.

"And now you even have two families that love you—that's why we're going to the party today." The kids had calmed down, the tears had stopped, and they were only sniffling. Jennifer had cuddled against me, Leslie against Stanley, and Amy was sitting off just a bit, wiping her nose on the sleeve of her brand-new dress.

"Okay, everybody, let's go!" I jumped up and took Amy off to get a Kleenex, then dispensed them to everybody else. Within five minutes they were angelic again, and once more dissolved in hysterics, this time giggles, as we made great ceremony of powdering shiny noses and red eyelids so that the tears would be our secret.

We drove to the christening party only about an hour late, all in good spirits, and we four ladies listened to the Irish and English folk songs that we loved to hear their father sing.

We made our grand entrance, last of the forty or so arrivals, and began the tedious round of introductions, to aunts and uncles and cousins and half cousins, and people whom I had never met as well. My little princesses, thank God, did me proud. Leslie and Amy felt at home relatively quickly—a brief introduction to Lacey's kids (close in age to them) was immediately successful, and the four took off to parts unknown. I said a silent prayer that Amy would not wreak too much destruction, since one of her new "cousins," Raish, a seven-year-old boy, was as rambunctious as she could be.

Jennifer didn't fare so well, however, and clung to me desperately, scared at the confusion, the strangers, and the attention. I walked over to talk to someone, and a moment later she was clutching at my dress. I turned around and nearly tripped over her. She wouldn't talk to anyone and began to look frightened, and I dreaded that she was going to produce one of her tantrums. Once I took her upstairs to the playroom to be with the other kids, but ten minutes later, I felt a little tug, and there she was again. It was one of the first times that she had come to me of her own accord, that she chose me over her sisters or her father.

We were, of course, a major topic of the conversation that day.

"When are you getting married?"

"Is his divorce final yet? No? Oh, I see, but he *is* getting one, isn't he?"

"Those poor children. They look so forlorn. It's terrible to break up a happy home, isn't it? Oh, dear, of course I don't mean to imply . . ."

"How old is he, anyway? Had he been married a long time?"

"How does his wife feel about all this? It must be quite a blow to her. Did she have any idea . . ."

"And he's living in *your* house? And you quit your *job?* And you aren't sure *when* you are getting married? Dear, are you *sure* you know what you're doing?"

I pulled Jennifer close to me, warm and tangible, and I realized that all these catty, callous, and cruel questions were coming from gossip-relishers feeding on my very real problems, prompted, I suspected, by the lurid stories they had heard from my mother and sister before we arrived.

There was an older female relative who so innocently asked, "What does he do for a living? From what your father described, it doesn't sound very honest to me." My father had probably used the description he still uses (but now with fondness)—"I don't know what he does—he's some kind of a bullshit artist." I tried to explain, but soon found she wasn't really interested at all.

I was glad we'd gotten there late, so we would be subjected to their cold-eyed scrutiny and unsolicited advice for a shorter period of time. My head was pounding, and my cheeks ached from smiling so much, but somehow every time I tried to explain anything or answer a question, it came out sounding so defensive that it was better left unsaid.

They'll find out for themselves, I thought, finally responding only with monosyllables or "It's really a very complicated situation."

Meanwhile, Stan was faring little better. He had somehow gotten cornered by my younger sister, Liz, and was being given the third degree. She wanted all the details, all the particulars. What was he planning to do? When was he getting his divorce? When were we getting married? Did he know I was vulnerable and easily influenced and he shouldn't take advantage of me? Did he know other men had promised to marry me, and it had never worked out? During the patronizing whipsaw from Liz,

Stan assured her, just as patronizingly, that at our ages we were mature enough to know what we were doing, and gently disengaged himself.

My parents were cordial, but never once mentioned to us the obvious changes in the girls.

The party broke up early, to our delight. For once my three little women had behaved totally above reproach, and, except for Jennifer, seemed to have had quite a good time. Stan and I had our most pleasurable moments of the day when, after the kids had gone to sleep, we mimicked as best we could the idiotic and mean-spirited conversations we had heard, the implications that our moral fiber was far inferior to that of the other guests. And we reveled in the positive impression that the girls must have made.

9

So things weren't all bad, despite the tears, the tantrums, and the teasing. The girls began to adjust to two houses, enjoying two sets of toys and two sets of clothes. Leslie enjoyed playing one parent against the other, and as long as I didn't ask her to do anything remotely resembling a chore, stayed in fairly good spirits (apart from, of course, the family weeps). The rest of the time she played with her sisters, mostly with Jennifer: dolls, or house, occasionally school. She was always the disciplining teacher. The two little ones looked up to her with a mixture of admiration and resentment, because the games were always played by her rules or they weren't played at all.

Amy spent a lot of time watching TV, sucking her thumb, and, out of the corner of her eye, watching her sisters play without her. When she did join in, there were invariably fights, which seemed to me, as I eavesdropped, to be largely engineered by Leslie. She would create a situation which had to result in dissension, then step in and resolve it, assuming the role of mediator and surrogate mother. It was a very unattractive role, this little ten-year-old martinet shrieking and bossing, then cajoling and comforting Jennifer, who would be in tears, and brushing Amy off with "You're always causing trouble—why don't you leave us alone?"

At first it seemed slightly bizarre, Leslie's and Jennifer's relationship, but the more I thought about it the less strange it felt to me that the girls would look to each other for companionship, particularly in a situation in which their whole life had been turned upside down, and what was once so familiar was now so discombobulated.

Knowing what I knew of Amy, I realized it wasn't so odd that she disrupted peaceful play. She was usually hyper in her activity, with a frantic, unsettled look in her eyes. She didn't listen when someone spoke to her, and she constantly interrupted. When she played outside she was the wildest and the loudest of the neighborhood children and always came home the dirtiest, with Leslie not far behind tattling about Amy's fights.

That was one side of Amy. The other was the sweet warm little girl who always asked if she could help me, and didn't often have to be reminded to do her chores, always the first to say "Good morning" or "Hello." In many ways she seemed very bright. But she felt she was different, and it bothered her. She said to me one time when she was about seven and a half, "There are so many things I want to say, and I can't, and when I try to write it doesn't work. It's so *frustrating*. I wish I was like other kids."

Stan had always treated Amy with the same permissiveness that he used with the other two, hoping that all three interpreted it as love, the way he had as a boy with his own parents; and though he might have blocked his awareness of Amy's difficulties previously, he was now beginning to recognize that she needed much more attention and direction than he had given her before.

The previous year he had had Leslie and Amy evaluated by a psychologist, and had been appalled at the description of his middle-class daughters as resembling "ghetto kids," emotionally and maternally deprived. That was when Amy was discovered to have a learning disability, and it was at the psychologist's suggestion that she was taken to Mrs. Unger. As time went on and Stan began to accept her day-in-day-out behavior as troubling rather than "cute" or "rambunctious," he realized that she responded well to structure and limits as long as they were provided with consistency and love.

But Amy's mother didn't seem able to face Amy's problems. One of her ways to deal with the hyperactivity and lack of self-control, according to Stanley, was to have the children play in a room carpeted on the walls as well as on the floor. Then she couldn't hear when Amy went into one of her rampages, Jennifer had one of her tantrums, or the three of them had one of their battles royal.

Had Amy been my natural child, if I had had to deal with her from birth, caring for her would have been difficult for me, too, although I probably would have handled her differently right from the start. But I chose to devote a great deal of time and energy to Amy after she entered my life, simply because I couldn't bear the thought of what her life would be like when she grew up if she didn't change. It was as much for my salvation as hers that I put so much energy into turning Amy Rose from an ugly duckling into a swan, transforming her from cocoon to butterfly.

Amy's expression was often sad in repose, and she gazed with such longing at her sisters when they played without her. But she was so easy to scold, so often at fault, that in the beginning I was very quick to jump in to stop the arguments. "Amy, leave them alone. They were playing very nicely until you started to tease them. If you are going to disrupt, you'll have to play by yourself." Sometimes she would cry a tear or two, but mostly she would just go off and suck her thumb and wet her pants. Occasionally I'd spank her, a well-placed, well-deserved whack across her bottom, but mostly I simply scolded her. For just about everything that went wrong, Amy Rose bore the brunt. Yet after a bath in the evening, she'd be so sweet and mellow, and she never seemed to bear a grudge against me no matter how rough the day had been; I'd fall in love with her all over again, and we would both vow to be different the next day.

One of the things that changed my relationship with Amy, and affected the process of change in her behavior, was our shared talent for burping at will. In her estimation that made us kindred spirits.

It began at a Sunday breakfast, all of them around the table, while I was cooking pancakes with my back turned. I was half listening to the undercurrent of conversation, which was just short of a quarrel, over who was going to get the syrup first. Then there was a belch to beat the band, a shriek from Leslie, and a horrified "Oh, Amy" as the orange juice spilled over the table and began to dribble in Jenny's lap. I did my usual "Can't you all be more careful!" in a voice about six pitches higher than was necessary, and was down on the floor wiping up the juice when Amy belched again.

"Cut that out, Amy," I snapped.

"I can't help it." She didn't look at me when I climbed up off the floor, and I'd no sooner turned my back than she did it again.

"*Amy*. You are doing that on purpose. Stop it right now. It sounds terrible, it's unladylike, and there is absolutely nothing cute about it. Cut it out."

"But I can't help it." She was whining a little, but staring me right in the eye.

Stan peered around the Sunday *Times.* "I don't think she can help it, Mary. She probably drank her milk too fast. Right, Amy?"

"Yeah, Dad." You tell 'er, she implied. Sock it to her!

I ignored Stanley, and gave Amy as direct a look as she had given me. There we were, eyeball to eyeball, the challenge of the week, over a stupid burp. I opened my mouth as if to speak, swallowed a large mouthful of air, and let out a belch of my own. Amy's mouth dropped open. So did everybody else's.

One more, just so they would all know that it wasn't a fluke.

"See, Amy, I can do it too. That's how I know you were doing it on purpose. It sounds different from a real one, and I can tell the difference. You can't fool me, so don't even bother trying. You were doing it on purpose, right?" She nodded, in solemn amazement. I had suddenly jumped several rungs in her esteem, and thenceforth had powers attributed to me that unfortunately I did not possess.

My next breakthrough with Amy was the realization that she was unwittingly the scapegoat for a lot of the sibling rivalry and quite possibly even for some of the incidents that one or the other of her sisters should be taking the rap for. Amy acted like the kind of kid who was always doing something wrong, so it was easy for Leslie or Jenny, when they did something they shouldn't that I wasn't witness to, to look sadly in Amy's direction and let me draw my own conclusions.

Jennifer was always very meek and mild except for her tantrums, but I quickly came to dread the part they played in the frustrating routine of weekend-mothering. I felt helpless with her because she found it so difficult to communicate her feelings or her preferences. Her answer to anything, more often than not, was a hunched, scrunched shrug. My mother, of course, was quite eager to tell me that it was natural. What could I expect from a nearly-four-year-old who had had her home ripped apart and thrown into a turmoil, and was being transplanted on the weekends away from the mother who loved her so much, and the only home that she had known? Lay it on, Mother, you're right and I feel guilty, but how do you stop the tantrums? That she didn't know.

For some two months I suffered through at least one of these episodes each weekend. The other kids would watch surreptitiously to see how upset I got, and seemed to have secret smiles in their eyes. Anywhere from five to twenty minutes into the performance, with Jenny screaming hysterically, "I want my mother," I trying to comfort and calm her, and she pushing me away with increasing vigor, Leslie would gently but forcefully interject her body between me and Jennifer. "I'm here, Jen, I'll take care of you," she'd say, and Jennifer would capitulate and begin to calm down.

Finally, I decided that come hell or high water, the tantrums had to stop. Leslie was insinuating more and more that this timid small child was too much for me to handle, and Amy was constantly plotting diabolically how she could best set Jennifer off.

One cold Saturday night in late winter, Jennifer, tired after a busy day of playing in the snow, was actually falling asleep at the dinner table. I put her to bed in our room, and she began to whimper, "I don't want to go to bed!" With an admonition to go to sleep, and an attempt at a kiss that was fought off, I left her and went downstairs to join the others.

The crying continued, and increased in volume. Stan called up to tell her to be quiet, and that only intensified the tears. She came to the top of the stairs, and we put her back in bed. I was getting angrier and angrier at Jennifer for being disruptive, at Stan for getting me into this to begin with, and at myself most of all for not being able to cope with a toddler.

"Okay, that's it," I said half aloud, to no one in particular, and everybody in general.

"Do you want me to go to her?" said Leslie sweetly.

"I'll take care of it," I muttered. It was a declaration of war by a twenty-eight-year-old adult on a not-yet-four-year-old child, and it was anything but a sure bet who was going to win. Most of the smart money probably would have gone on Jenny.

She calmed for a second at the sound of footsteps on the stairs, but one look at me, and she began to scream, "I want my mommy, I want my sister! Go away! I want my mommy!" She screamed and kicked and clawed. She lay on her back, knees drawn up, tiny feet hammering the bed, tiny arms sometimes reaching frantically toward the darkness, sometimes shielding her face, sometimes just pushing the air between us as if that would make me go away. She began to bang her head against the wall; I picked her up and put her in the middle of the bed, so she wouldn't hurt herself. I knew there was no reasoning with her; I wasn't even sure she could hear me. So I tried to soothe her, from a distance, when she paused for breath—"You'll see Mommy soon," "Leslie's downstairs, I'm here."

Then she climbed down from the bed, picked up a chair, and began to pound it on the floor. Her strength in her anger and frustration was incredible, and I fought to get her to the safety of the soft bed. Her cries were at fever pitch for more than fifteen minutes, the most frantic, tortured sounds I've ever heard. My heart went out to her, because I was sure that this was her expression of feelings about the disruptions and sorrows that had occurred in her little life since she was born.

Once Stan came up. "Can I help?"

"No, thanks."

Once Leslie silently appeared out of nowhere and I sent her downstairs, annoyed at her for thinking I needed to be rescued, and renewing my determination to come to peace with Jennifer. It must have been terrifying downstairs: the cries, the moving furniture, the pounding head and feet and chair legs, as if what was needed was some kind of exorcist.

After Jennifer glimpsed Leslie, she began to scream continually, "I want my sister! I want my sister!" until her voice grew hoarse and her body weary, and she drew herself into a corner on the bed, as far away from me as she could get, still sobbing, but more quietly now. I reached out to touch her leg and was rewarded with a kick and a shriek. She had rested enough in that minute or two to have the energy to start all over again.

I was beginning to get scared, because I had no idea how long something like this could go on, and I was afraid Jennifer would hurt herself physically, or damage her vocal cords. The second episode was much briefer than the first, lasting only five minutes or so. This time when her lungs gave out, I gave her a glass of water. At first she pushed it away, spilling it over me and the bed, but I talked to her in what I hoped was a calming voice, saying how much her throat must hurt and that the water would make it feel better. After a while she took it and sipped it, looking at me over the rim of the glass.

She pulled again into a tight little ball, far from me, and I began edging nearer, talking about how much I loved her and how badly I felt when she was so unhappy. The bed was in an alcove, surrounded by windows that looked out onto our little narrow street, illuminated by one weak lamp. There was enough snow on the ground to shimmer, and our town, quaint and charming in the light of dusk, looked like a fairy-tale village from where we sat. One window was open slightly, and the chilled fresh air was soothing; Jennifer inched closer and closer to the window, her back to me, just looking out at the night. I didn't try to touch her; I stopped speaking to her. I moved quietly beside her, and sat looking out of the window too. She was silent now, breathing regularly, but her body was still tense. I didn't want to say or do anything that might set her off again.

We sat like that, almost touching, and the air began to mellow, and Jennifer pressed her forehead and nose against the window pane. "What was that?" I exclaimed.

"What?" she turned to me, and then back to the window. "I didn't see anything."

"A hobbit. I was sure I saw a hobbit. He ran along there by the fence—see, there he goes again!"

"No, you're teasing," Jenny said, almost giggling, and smiled and looked out to where I was pointing. I put my arm around her, tentatively, and to my delight, and near-surprise, she snuggled into my lap, and we spent a very pleasant time looking for hobbits and imagining their footprints in the snow.

10

Monday through Friday, Stan and I would rise early, with the dawn filtering into the cozy alcove where we slept. We rarely needed an alarm, because the light and the warmth of our close bodies was enough to make us stir. One of the earliest feelings that I can recall about our being together was the tremendous sense of peace and completeness that I had, waking up to find someone who loved me next to me—day after day after day. The endlessness of it was sweet and precious, and still is.

Stan would go off to work, sometimes to New York, sometimes to Connecticut, sometimes to Boston. Unlike the longer business trips he used to take, these were day trips, and he'd always come home at night. We would go downstairs together, and, if we had enough time, have coffee together and, rarely, breakfast. He would delay leaving as long as he could, lingering over a second cup and idle lovers' chatter, until he would be at least five minutes late to wherever he was going. Then he would kiss me gently on the lips. "Goodbye, my darling. You really are my darling." I'd watch him through the lace curtains, driving down the hill, and we would wave one last time. It was terribly romantic.

My days would be spent with a mixture of housewifely chores, laundry, and shopping, and I caught up on some reading. I was also working more than half-time doing free-lance writing for Stan's consulting company. At least twice a week we had people in for dinner, almost always old friends of his and hers, people he had been close to in his other life. I would slave in the kitchen for hours cooking elaborate meals, including breads and cakes from scratch. He had said Roberta's usual idea of a meal for company was to send out for Chinese food—or have him cook it. I was determined to prove what a better second choice he had made. One day when a couple was coming whom I particularly wanted to impress I painted the entire kitchen, and laid a brick-pattern stick-on linoleum floor—besides concocting the veal scallopini and zabaglione. Stan walked in the kitchen that night absolutely flabbergasted, because the transformation was remarkable. That feat probably contributed to his expectations of me that I could do anything at all.

Some of these attempts at entertainment were more successful than others, and it was usually inversely proportional to how close the women were to Bobbi and how much of the evening they spent talking about how she was starving herself, weeping oceans, and falling totally apart at the seams. A topic carefully avoided by all of us, however, was Bobbi's lesbian relationship with her friend Joellyn, which she was no longer taking any pains to hide.

Most of the men sympathized with Stanley, and even admitted that they weren't at all surprised. The women, naturally, tended to side with Roberta, as did my mother. Mama couldn't understand why I didn't have more empathy toward this woman whose home and life I had "destroyed." I thought it rather obvious that no matter how beautiful, brilliant, chic, and desirable I was, my charms couldn't possibly be sufficient to ruin a marriage that was thriving—or even holding its own. Stan had made up his mind to get a divorce before he knew me—had talked first about it with Roberta more than ten years earlier—so, though the reality must always be a shock, how much of a surprise could it have been? And while I was quite easily persuaded by my family, Roberta's friends, and, in a very subtle way, by the three little cherubs that I should be feeling guilty, I continually struggled with myself because I didn't really believe that I was. After all, Stan was happier with me, Roberta was happier with Joellyn, and the kids—even before we began to grow genuinely fond of each other—couldn't be any worse off than they had been.

Occasionally, the visitors we'd have in would be connected with work, some of them people I had known from my old job, and these evenings were easier for me to take. Instead of being criticized for being so happy, we'd be congratulated, and I'd feel that I'd accomplished something instead of ruining something (or someone).

Stan usually didn't get home from work till seven, and then he would call the girls to talk about The Divorce. The same conversation every night. It was shorter if there were guests, and occasionally, when he was feeling especially sad or guilty, he would skip it; but generally the daily call was part of the ritual. By the time we'd eaten, and discussed our day's activities, it would be time to go to bed. Once in a while he would have an evening staff meeting, once in a while we would go to a movie, but we were usually too tired. Stan has always kept a hectic— in fact, frenetic—pace, and he tries to carry those who are close to him along. If you can keep up with him, fine. If you can't, he leaves you in the dust.

So I worked to stay even, and he's taught me to accomplish ten times as much in a given period of time as I ever thought I could. Because he was so smart, and professionally so competent, I thought that he was very wise in the ways of the world, very capable of doing just about anything that had to be done. I sorely misjudged him. In our first six months together, I discovered that he was much too trusting, a good judge of people objectively and professionally, but not always when it affected him personally. Not only couldn't he get done what needed to be done in his personal life; he usually had difficulty even acknowledging the need.

I reacted to this, once I began to figure it out, in three stages. The first was to nag him into facing and doing things, figuring that someone as smart as he just needed to be reminded, or pushed in the right direction. Then when I realized he simply was going to ignore what I thought were necessary urgencies, I took care of them myself. I did get things accomplished more or less, but

I also built up an incredible reservoir of resentment toward everybody concerned, especially Stan. When he noticed that things were happening despite him, he thought I was wonderful, and begin to take it for granted that I loved to keep myself busy with his problems. Finally, I would explode in absolute rage, tell Stanley I wasn't going to have anything to do with anything or anybody remotely related to him, and he'd have to clean up his own messes. When he still didn't act, I'd do whatever anyway, but scream and rant and rave all the while.

What I found most harrowing, and where I found Stan most inadequate, was in the mechanics of his getting his divorce. Although he lived in New Jersey, he had chosen a Philadelphia law firm that had done some other work for him. He didn't know the partner who handled matrimonial disputes, but this was preferable, he thought, to picking someone from the Yellow Pages. So he had hired Mr. Begert, jovial and relaxed, who had so blithely assured Stan when he first separated from Bobbi that everything would be worked out in no time, that he would soon be on his honeymoon. But we were still no closer to the wedding day, and the only concrete advice Mr. Begert had given was to pay all the bills Roberta was piling up.

Stan waved my increasing concern at his having hired an out-of-state lawyer aside, with an "It's okay, he knows what he's doing. I'll handle it, don't worry." I believed him. But when more than a month after Stan had engaged him I finally met the barrister Begert and experienced at firsthand the unique way he was representing Stanley's interest, my opinion of my beloved's wisdom plummeted.

Begert had been in touch with Roberta's attorney in December, telling him that Stan wanted a quick settlement and was willing to pay for it—generous alimony and child support, car, large property settlement, all the existing bills, insurance, camps, private schools, doctors, dentists, lessons, swim club, cleaning lady, babysitter, and a shrink for Roberta. Stan had made it very clear from the start that he wanted to take care of Roberta and the girls, but even he thought that this was going a little too far. Begert looked rather pleased with himself for accomplishing all this without having to consult with Stan. The next piece of good news he had was that her lawyer had said that there was no way a quick divorce was possible—that New Jersey had an eighteen-month separation requirement—although he thanked Begert profusely for Stan's generosity, and said his client was prepared to let the process drag on as long as was humanly and legally possible. Which Mr. Begert had acknowledged, telling us, laughingly, "But you two certainly don't look like you are suffering, ha, ha, so I guess it doesn't really matter."

This legal advice resulted in a bill for twenty-five hundred dollars which Stan was asked to take care of right away.

In our spare time we were house hunting for a place big enough for the two of us, his three children when they were with us, an undetermined number of the children of our own we wanted if it proved that we could have them, and any number of assorted guests who hadn't visited us yet but who Stan was sure would not be able to resist our hospitality.

One morning he took me in the frosty mist of a winter sunrise to see The House. It was a federal mansion on about ten acres of ground, with a swimming pool and a tributary of the Passaic River flowing right through the middle of the property. It had enough bedrooms for a family of twelve, a formal parlor as well as a dining room and living room, five bathrooms, a kitchen that needed remodeling, a fantastic brick-floored basement family room, with the floor and beams worn polished and smooth from two hundred years of wear. There was a root cellar and a wine cellar, and the fireplace in the playroom, one of seven in the house, had a bread-baking oven built right into it. It was only moderately in need of paint, would have needed a staff of at least three to keep it going, and was about twice as much as we could afford.

"I showed it to Roberta once, a few years ago. She loved it too, but it would have been too much for her—she didn't want that big a house. But I know you can handle it." We were walking around the grounds, peering in the windows. He wanted to arrange for the real estate agent to show it to us.

"You looked at it with *her?* I want my own house, Stanley, not one you were going to buy for her." I started to sweat and feel guilty about the house I ultimately deprived her of—if it weren't for me, she might be buying a house like this with him.

"Don't be silly. We weren't *serious* about it. Just look at it with me. We don't have to buy it. It'll just give us an idea of what we like. But you'll see, it's got plenty of room for lots of kids— inside and out." He was certainly right about that!

We discussed the house for days, how we could finance it, where we'd get the money for a down payment, what it would mean to us to live there. We had no money to speak of in the bank, but that didn't faze Stanley. Nobody in his right mind would have given us a mortgage then, but that didn't faze him either. Those were just minor annoying details, and shouldn't be allowed to interfere with our getting what we wanted. So I ignored them too.

The real estate agent, Peg Duke, was waiting for us as we pulled into the driveway, from where you could look through the hundred-year-old spruce trees at the stony remains of a mill that had ground flour and wheat during the American Revolution, perhaps even for old George himself. We wandered through the halls and passageways connecting the rooms, up the front stairs and down the back, imagining in the lengthening shadows what it must have looked like in its past grandeur, and what it might look like in the future if it were ours.

As we checked ceilings for leaks, and lifted carpet to make sure the floors really were pine boards eight inches wide and pegged, Peg told us a little of what she thought it would take to fix it up. Paint and plastering she thought could easily be done for eight thousand or so. The outside could wait another year, and then probably wouldn't cost more than five. The furnace looked okay—the heating bill for the previous winter (and this when oil was forty-three cents a gallon) had not been over three thousand. Taxes were in the neighborhood of four thousand a year, but of course it was a very good town with very good schools, and we could rest assured that the girls would get a good education. (Stanley had told her that they would definitely be with us in the fall.) Domestic help would be easy to get, and yes, the kitchen did need remodeling, but look at the lovely view from the kitchen window, and we could probably include an extra twenty or so thousand in the mortgage to cover most of the necessary renovations.

Quick mental gymnastics told me that, not counting the mortgage, it would take at least eight hundred a month just to keep the place going. Right now we were paying $169.99 a month to my father for my house (Papa could indeed be a darling—he had loaned me a large portion of the purchase price at low interest) and were having trouble making ends meet, given Stan's generosity to Roberta. So I listened to the agent's patter as a kind of idle exercise, and regarded the house as something that might be right for somebody but certainly not for me. It was too big, too empty, too formal, and I just couldn't imagine filling it up. The two of us could go for days without ever finding each other, and it didn't look too likely that his kids would join us soon, either.

Finally Stan had seen enough, and thanked Peg profusely. "We'll get back to you after a couple of days once we've worked out the finances. Okay? I think we'd like to make an offer on it." I was stunned speechless. "By the way," he added, "how about things like termites, and the boiler, and that sort of thing? Is there any way we can check those things out?"

"Oh, yes," said Peg in her throaty voice, the kind of deep, vibrant tones that Amy would probably grow up to have. "We'll arrange to have our consulting engineer, Mr. Partekamp, survey the house for you, and he'll give you some estimate of what the costs of fixing things might be. If we sign a contract, that will be the next step." I had heard Stan say that we would be making an offer, and he hadn't even asked me if I liked what I'd just seen. Not to mention that there was no way on God's earth that we could afford it. But once in the car he began chattering away about this feature and that of the white elephant we had just seen; in fact, he was already beginning to furnish the damn place.

"I'm so glad you like it as much as I do. Now all we have to do is figure out a way to get together the down payment, and we're all set. We'll be able to move in by the summer, and the girls will have a chance to get adjusted before they start school."

I couldn't handle all the crazy things he was throwing at me in so short a space of time.

"What about what Begert said about not being able to get custody until we get married?"

"Oh, he probably doesn't know what he's talking about. I'm going to get a New Jersey lawyer anyway, because it doesn't sound to me as if he knows what he is doing." I felt relief, then dread when he added, "I just wish I knew a lawyer I could count on. Isn't the house a beauty? We'll really be happy there."

"Where are you planning to get the money for the house? And do you have any idea how much it's going to cost us to own it?"

"Huh? Cost? Why, no, not really. Probably close to a thousand a month. Why?"

"Just because we're having a hard time now. And you're right, but you're not including the mortgage, which will be a thousand a month by itself. And where are we going to get the ten percent for the contract, never mind the twenty-five percent for the down payment we'll need to get the mortgage?" I was dumbfounded at his seeming lack of comprehension about the step he was suggesting we take. I hoped he was kidding.

He whistled. "That's a lot of money—more than I thought. But I'll just work harder, that's all." He was already working sixty hours a week, and driving another six hours back and forth for the kids, plus the Saturday trips to Mrs. Unger. There wasn't much time left over if he wasn't going to kill himself. "And we can borrow the money for the down payment. I'll make some calls tomorrow."

He still hadn't asked me if I liked it.

The folly of the house lasted about three weeks. He convinced me with his sweet-talking ways that it was okay to go ahead and buy it, that we actually could afford it. Which, I guess, made me as crazy as he, because we spent hours poring over bills, budgets, and bank accounts, until we had to acknowledge there was no way that any of it added up. We were thirty thousand short of the immediate cash outlay we required, since we had no money at all in the bank. I would have to work full-time again and he about fifty percent more in order to only be a little behind the bills each month.

But on he went. In a couple of years, he reasoned, we'd be making more, so we'd catch up. In his own inimitable persuasive way, he and his nonsense began to make sense—and that was how we came to find ourselves one brilliant Sunday morning sitting in the living room of Stan's boss's *House Beautiful* home, situated high on a wooded mountaintop near our own memorable Jockey Hollow Park.

"Barry, I need some capital."

We both hated to ask Barry Fields for help. Despite the fact that Stan and his boss worked together as management consultants in human relations, Stan preferred to go his own way and do his own thing; as long as the clients were satisfied and the billing came in on time, Barry tended to leave him alone. Once, Stan told me, he and Barry went nearly three months without seeing or speaking to each other. He often mused wistfully about starting his own business someday, but he knew that even with his boundless energy and his ability to harness wild schemes, this was a time to establish more security for everyone, not less.

"Barry and I could be a good team, Marila, if we could get along better. He's a theoretician, and uses all that behavioral-psychology jargon that turns clients on. I'm a practitioner, and get the job done—that turns the client on, too. And people are getting smarter about consultants, demanding accountability. Barry and I could be really successful if we worked together instead of against each other. Maybe our need for this house will be a means for us to work things out."

So by the time we got to Barry's, somehow the house had become a symbol of a good new life for all of us. "This divorce bit is really expensive, and my cash is tied up. Until things are settled, I don't have the money to get things together. I'm going to institute a custody fight, and I want to be sure to have a place to live that the courts will approve of. . . ."

To our surprise and Stan's delight, Barry came through with a loan of enough money so that Stan was convinced we'd be able to borrow the rest. And once again I got tired and quit before I could convince Stan that this wasn't a wise thing for us to do. Without even beginning to use my imagination, I had the money Barry had just lent us spent at least a million ways, and none of them was a down payment on a monstrosity of a house that, despite my having said so, Stan couldn't believe I didn't like as much as he.

We got a check from Barry one day, and the next we gave Peg Duke the ten percent required to come to contract. She then arranged for Mr. Partekamp (for a fee) to tell us how much it would cost to bring the thing back to "mint condition."

Thank God for Mr. Partekamp. Two weeks later, while Stanley was trying to figure out where he could borrow the rest of the money we needed for closing on the house, that month's alimony and child support, and a needed Caribbean vacation, not to mention painting, furniture, and general repairs, we received in the mail a twenty-page manuscript documenting the health and well-being of every nail and board from the basement to the roof, and the tiles in the swimming pool.

Fortunately, Mr. Partekamp refused to vouch for the shingles (replacement cost, thirty-five hundred dollars minimum), for the furnace (replacement cost, eighteen hundred), or for the retaining wall which kept the land the house was on from falling into that gently flowing river you could see from the kitchen window (shoring-up costs—twenty thousand). Termites seemed to pose no threats—they had been moved out by the army of carpenter ants. But he recommended rebuilding the chimney that three of the fireplaces were joined to and installation of a sump pump because the house was located in a marginal flood basin area. In fact, in 1902 the waters had risen high enough to cause minor damage. His minimum estimate of what we would want to invest over the course of two years in order to make the house structurally sound was in the neighborhood of thirty-three thousand dollars. He thought that would cover the retaining wall but he wasn't sure, and it certainly would not cover any cosmetic alterations, which he knew, of course, we would want to do immediately, like plastering the cracks in the living-room and dining-room walls.

I read that letter with an increasing feeling of euphoria stealing over me, and as I read it aloud to Stan, tried to keep the glee out of my voice.

"Jesus, that's a lot of work, and a lot of money," he said with awe when I had finished. "I don't know where we can get that kind of cash, and I don't think we can get a big enough mortgage to cover it, do you?" He sounded so dejected, and I felt so good.

"It sure does change things, doesn't it? Do you know anybody else you could borrow from?" I knew there was no one, so it was a safe question. Yes, it sure had changed things—and for the better!

We called Peg, and told her that the results of Mr. Partekamp's survey really made the deal unworkable. It all might end up in the river anyway. She was, needless to say, disappointed, and tried to convince us that most of what Mr. Partekamp suggested wasn't absolutely necessary.

"You could cut costs by doing some of the work yourselves, perhaps," she said, not realizing that Stanley could barely hang a picture, let alone do a remodeling project.

Armed with Mr. Partekamp's appraisal, it was a relatively easy task for me to convince Stan that it wasn't only the money but the hassle of handling that big a house and getting it into shape that was more than we needed at the time. He finally, reluctantly, agreed, and we got our check back. Instead of paying back Barry, we paid bills.

There has always been a "project" in our lives: buying houses, property, or boats; building houses or additions; starting businesses; writing books; the pros and cons of child custody. Some of it we do and some of it we don't do, but we always spend endless amounts of energy and time investigating, then debating whether or not we should proceed.

I've discovered it's a process, that discussions aren't decisions, and where some of the wild, bold ideas used to make me upset, now I let them go full circle, with Stan doing the majority of the thinking and talking, and me reacting. But in our early days, a lot of the activity was, I think, sheer distraction, so we wouldn't have to get to know each other too well, and, God forbid, find out we'd made a mistake.

11

Another consuming discussion, and one that would have a significant impact on our lives, followed shortly after the white elephant—starting a family of our own. As usual for us, it was not uncomplicated. We weren't sure anymore exactly when we would be able to get married, but we were both getting older, and were afraid to wait too long. We also wanted a chance to grow together and know each other better before we added another dimension to our already extended family. Then there was the question of how it would affect our relationship with the girls. Finally, and most difficult to resolve, was that getting pregnant the usual way might in fact be impossible for us.

I had known before we planned marriage that Stan had had testicular cancer, and I knew the implications—because of the lymph-node dissection, certain nerves had been cut, and he had retrograde ejaculation, that is, backward into his bladder, so it was one in a million that we'd ever have children without major medical intervention or a miracle. I was afraid of the one, and Stanley didn't believe in the other.

"Are we going to talk to Dr. Roberts about having a baby?" We were crossing the George Washington Bridge, on our way to Columbia Presbyterian Hospital. It was time for Stan's semiannual cancer clearance exam; it had been four years since the operations, with no recurrence.

"Yes, I want to, don't you?" He reached across the front seat and took my hand, then brought it to his lips. "I'm sorry, Marila. Maybe we can do something, though. I heard that women can get pregnant if their husbands pee in their vagina. Would you like that?" He recoiled as I punched his right rib.

"Yuk."

"Then there's always medical students. At least we'd know the kid would be bright."

"Ah, but what if I didn't like him? Or what if he wasn't any good in bed?" This time he punched me.

"Dummy. You won't get to do it with the student. The doctor does it with a syringe." I was looking out my window, down at the Hudson, the blue choppy waters, freckled with sailboats and Circle Line cruisers, reflecting the sky.

"Well, I've known a few doctors who were pretty good!" Our banter masked our true feelings, which were mixed. Natural childlessness would have its advantages—we certainly would have a lot of freedom, at least during the week. On the other hand, our weekends were always shot with his kids—so we might as well have some of our own. And I'd always wanted children.

I thought back to a winter night early in our courtship. It was raining, and cold, and I was underdressed as usual. No cabs were to be found in the city, what with the weather and the hour, so we made our way from doorway to doorway, trying to run faster than the rain was falling hard. We paused to catch our breath in the iron-curtained doorway of a men's clothing store on Madison Avenue.

"You know I can't have any more children." It was a statement, not a question, and totally unconnected to whatever silly conversation we were having.

"Because of the cancer. . . . I have to tell you that, because I know you want children of your own—of our own."

I had known it, hadn't believed it, didn't want to talk about it. But it was a fact I had to face.

"I know." My face was buried against his chest.

"How does that make you feel?" He stroked my hair and held me close.

I thought of wanting to have four or five or six children ever since I was a little girl. I thought of my sister's kids, and the baby she had just had. I thought of Stanley dying, and leaving me without a child of my own.

When he lifted my chin, so he could look in my eyes, I hoped he thought the tears on my face were rain.

"Terrible," I said. "It makes me feel terrible."

"Does it matter?" he whispered, his eyes and his face pleading not to let it matter. "Will you still marry me?"

"Yes, it matters. But yes, I'll still marry you."

So now there we sat, Stan, me, and his doctor. For a threesome celebrating a victory over a too often unbeatable foe, we were very downcast and somber.

"The alternatives are not very good," intoned Dr. Roberts, in a monotone voice as friendly, I am sure, as he is capable of. "There is an operation being performed with modest success, but it's major surgery, and not a guarantee of fertilization. It involves total restructuring of the internal duct system." He sounded so clinical, like someone giving a paper at a medical convention.

"On the other hand, there is a new technique, in which the urine of the donor, in this case the husband, you, Mr. Silverzweig . . ." It was Stan's story. I thought he had been kidding.

". . . is then centrifuged and concentrated in order to extract any live sperm. This has on occasion proved successful.

"The third, and preferable, alternative, if your religion doesn't forbid it, is artificial insemination, by a donor. The donors are chosen carefully, and are compatible with the parental characteristics," he concluded warmly. "If you decide to pursue this further, here's one of the best men in the country in the fertility field." He wrote a name down on a slip of yellow paper and handed it to Stan, who folded it carefully into quarters and slipped it in his wallet. "Any questions? If I can help you in any way, please don't hesitate to call."

Handshake. Handshake. Thank you. Thank you. And that was that. At least we didn't have to worry about birth control.

12

Stan and I were in accord that making a baby of our own was too big a problem to deal with at the time, particularly since the outcome was dubious. I didn't want to devote a lot of what little energy reserve I had to a project that seemed doomed to failure from the start. So instead I dedicated myself with renewed vigor to being the best stepmother in the world.

And as we all adjusted to each other, the relief that I used to feel when they left on Sunday night began to be replaced by frustration at the way the weekend was chopped up by the long drive to Roberta's and back. It would have been *so* nice to have had that extra evening to ourselves, once they had gone to bed.

One day, Stan had the bright idea of taking them back not on Sunday night but Monday morning, and dropping them off in time for school. So Sunday night he called Roberta to tell her he couldn't make it, and either she could pick them up, or he would take them down in the morning. We weren't surprised that she didn't want to pick them up, but we were surprised she didn't protest. This was the beginning of our discovery that she seemed to prefer to let us have them as long as possible on weekends and vacations. Even though that spring there was no written agreement with regard to visitation, the children spent nearly every weekend with us, and half their spring vacation. Sometimes I was certain that Bobbi only wanted them for women's-rights rallies, or occasions like Father's Day or a holiday when she felt it would be psychologically hard on us not to have them. Still, despite her hostile attitude toward us, I often had a great deal of sympathy for her, because it must be devastating to watch your children grow close to someone else and begin to thrive and benefit from that relationship, even though they still love you, and even though—no matter what—you'll always be their mother.

The first Sunday they stayed over, we all went to bed early and planned to get up early. Stan and the girls had to leave before six o'clock in order to be on time for school. My job was to fix a hot breakfast and get them all on their way. We had very good intentions, but it didn't quite work out.

First, we overslept by half an hour. Then Jennifer didn't want to eat. Amy couldn't find her shoes, and Leslie was sick to her stomach. They piled sleepily into the car nearly an hour late, which meant that Leslie had missed her school bus, and since both Amy and Jenny started school at the same time, in different towns, one of them was also going to be late. But Stan drove off valiantly into the rising sun, and I went back to bed not particularly caring how he handled it. I thought there must be a better solution to the way we had organized things, but I was too tired to think of it right then.

There was, of course, and it took us a couple of weekends to work it out, but in the end it seemed to be satisfactory to everyone. Except me.

We moved the alarm clock to the other side of the room, so we had to get up to turn it off. Then we would put on John Denver, and turn the volume up very loud, so loud that I think everybody in Mount Tabor woke up to "Country Roads" on Monday mornings. Everybody except Amy Rose. It usually required at least three trips to the girls' room, several shrieks at the top of my voice to get her half dressed, and a few more to get her dressed the rest of the way. And I soon discovered that she had to eat first and get dressed later in order to stay neat.

Jennifer never wanted to eat much, and before too many weekends had passed, they all began to complain of sick stomachs as we gathered round the table. I decided it had to be that they were nauseous because they were tired and it was too early to get them up, or it was a way to get out of drinking milk, or it was because they were sad at leaving. But they were quite adamant that they would rather stay over, even with all the problems and the rude, early awakening. Even Amy, who always got yelled at on Monday mornings.

After the first time, Stan didn't try to make Leslie's school bus, but instead would drop her off directly at the private school she was going to. Then he would drop Amy off at her school, and Jennifer at the house so Roberta could take her to Montessori. The only remaining difficulty was that Stanley lost nearly a morning of work each week, and since as a consultant he was paid by the day, it began to add up. But the obvious solution didn't dawn on us until one Monday when Stanley had to be in Boston at the same time he was to drop Amy off at her kindergarten class.

We knew on Friday that he had to go, so I had expected that when he picked them up he would make arrangements to return them, this once, on Sunday. But he didn't. All weekend I expected him to call Roberta and say he'd be down Sunday night. But he didn't. Not, that is, until nearly eight o'clock on Sunday night, at which time he was surprised to get no answer, a reaction that was beyond me, because if she didn't expect them until Monday morning, there was no earthly reason why she should have stayed home that night.

He finally decided that he would call his client first thing in the morning, and cancel out until noon, by which time he'd probably be able to get there. But we knew Barry would be furious, because this was an important client and he was already expressing displeasure at the fact that Stan wasn't working a full day on Monday anymore.

Suddenly it hit him—like a bolt of lightning. *I* could drive them. He could catch his early plane as planned, and I could bring them all to school. Sheer brilliance, he thought—how could we have been so dumb not to see it before? I tried to tell him that I couldn't—wouldn't—take them, that I didn't want to see Bobbi and didn't want to make the trip, but it seemed a rather selfish response. If it meant so much to him and the girls to stay, wasn't that the least I could do?

That morning we got up half an hour earlier, because Stan had a six-thirty plane, but it took everybody half an hour longer to get dressed. The weather was miserable, an icy fog, and it was so dark it might have been midnight. By the time we were ready to go, it was forty-five minutes to plane time. We were forty minutes from the airport, and the roads were slick. It didn't look good.

"Why don't we not even try to get the plane?" I suggested. "Why don't you take the kids back as usual, and catch a later one? I'll call and say you'll be up later." I really dreaded driving the kids to their home.

"No, I can't do that. Let's try to make it, and if I miss it, I'll just try to catch the next one. It'll be a lot easier for me this way. Please, Marila?" When he called me Marila, how could I deny him?

We took off for Newark Airport, driving more quickly than was safe on the icy highway, where he made his plane. Not by much, but he made it, and the four women in his life bade him goodbye tearfully, and began what was to be a new way of life, with me as head of the Transportation Department.

That Monday it worked out fine. Leslie and Amy got to their respective schools on time, and Jennifer scooted into the house without so much as a glance over her shoulder. I'm not even sure that Roberta knew that I was the courier that day. It had worked so well, gone so smoothly, that a couple of weeks later, we decided to try it again—and sure enough, it was okay. No problems. My worst fears of head-to-head combat with Roberta did not come to pass, and the drives became less of a chore, and almost fun.

Now Stanley would make the breakfast, and see us off, waving from the porch as we drove off, then get off on time himself and keep his clients and his boss happy. I'd give him a call about eleven-thirty when I'd get home, clean up the debris of the morning, and work until it was time to get ready for the inevitable company.

The girls enjoyed the trip with me, too, I think. We had a chance to be alone and got to know each other a little better, and that was good for us. There were, at first, some dreadful fights, Amy teasing, car "games" that got out of hand, so there was a lot of yelling that took place on those trips, too. And then there were the times, an average of once every second trip, where I would pull over to the side of the road and shout, *"If you girls don't cut it out right this minute, I am going to spank you so hard you won't believe it!"*

That would be greeted by dead silence, and usually nobody got spanked, though now and then one or two bottoms would receive one firm smack, not enough to really hurt, but enough to show that I meant business. Gradually the rides became more peaceful. We even began to talk together about why they acted out so in the car.

The major problems seemed to be they were tired from getting up so early, they really didn't like school, and they wished that they could stay with us forever. We imagined that they told Roberta they never wanted to leave her either, trying to make both sides feel good. Once we were able to talk about it, and they began to realize I wouldn't let the ride be a two-hour, three-ring circus, they settled down, and were pretty easy.

I discovered early that they were looking for limits, first to be set for them, and secondly to be enforced. When Stan and I would compare notes about our respective trips with them, he seemed to have more trouble and be more frustrated than I. We finally boiled it down to the fact that the girls were wary of me—they weren't used to adults' getting angry at them for their behavior, and then going on normally when things were quiet once again. It didn't take long for them to understand what I expected of them in the car, what I threatened I would do if they didn't live up to my expectations, and that I would always follow through on my threats. Stan, on the other hand, would let things get too far out of control before he would even acknowl-edge that there was a problem, and then weakly confront his darlings with the consequences if they didn't stop. But he almost never followed through, so the girls knew they could pretty much do what they wanted.

"You know, the kids are always better-behaved when you're around. Why is that? I can't get them to stop the fighting in the car, or Amy to stop acting out. They never listen to me the way they do to you." He was genuinely puzzled.

"I beat the shit out of them if they don't do what I want," I said as calmly as if he had asked me what time it was.

"What? Beat them? They never told me that. They always tell me they like it when you take them to school."

I laughed. "Well, I don't really beat them, but I tell them that I will if they don't cut it out—and they're afraid I will, so they do. And I have given enough well-placed whacks that they believe me."

He said shortly thereafter that his rides with the kids were improving, and I thought with satisfaction that he must be using my techniques on them. What it was, he sheepishly told me, was that he began to threaten that he would tell me if they didn't behave better. And that often enough was able to do the trick!

My driving them back seemed to make life easier, and we began to think how nice it would be if we could have Friday nights together as a family too, instead of getting the girls home too late to do anything but go to bed. Of course, the only possible way that could happen was if I picked them up after school on Friday. That way we could all have dinner together on Friday night, nobody would be too tired and cranky on Saturday when we went to Mrs. Unger, and it would really feel as if we had a long time together each weekend. The girls loved the idea, Stan thought it was one of his strokes of genius, and I thought it stank.

When he wanted me to do something that I didn't especially want to do, particularly where the girls were concerned, he would play on my conscience, making *me* feel guilty about all the things that he had done that *he* should feel guilty about.

"After all, they really miss us, and they are getting to love you, and they really like to be with us. And it hasn't been so bad lately, has it? I mean, things seem to be settling down, and it would just mean so much more to them if we had that extra day. And to me." Here came the clincher. "I could never forgive myself if they grew up troubled, Marila, and I could have done more to prevent it."

At first, I told him it was okay with me as long as he went to get them. I refused to ferry both ways. That didn't work at all, because at least every other time he would have an appointment, and not only would they arrive late, tired, and cranky as usual, but disappointed to boot.

"They felt so bad, Marila, that I didn't get there when I said I would. They really like getting here early on Friday, you know. It's too bad that they can't always count on me, Marila. I hope it doesn't hurt them too much."

So Marila gave in. Now I would leave Mount Tabor at one o'clock on Friday afternoon, pick up Jenny and Amy at two-thirty, then get Leslie at three. We'd get back to Mount Tabor just in time for me to fix dinner. My week without the cherubs suddenly seemed shorter than my weekends with them—and there wasn't enough time with Stan. But he was happy, and the kids seemed to be getting happier all the time. I met with both Amy's and Leslie's teachers (Stanley's business appointments kept getting in the way, and finally he said to me, "Marila, could you . . . ?" and I didn't want to, but I didn't say so, and I did what I knew he wanted). They assured me that the girls did not seem any the worse for the "ordeal" of divorce. And exhausted as I was, it wasn't over yet.

Stanley had published two books during his career as a consultant. In the middle of our weekly commutes, custody debating, buying and not buying houses, he decided to begin his third. Like everything else he puts his mind to, he began to work with fervor. Early in the morning, late into the night, he would pound away at the keys of his portable Olivetti, the typewriter on which he had produced his novel and political anthology.

Sure enough, there came a Saturday morning when he arose earlier than all the rest of us and immersed himself in page eighty-four, first draft. As the sun came up, we all got up, too, and began to get ready for the trek to Mrs. Unger. It was part of the weekend ritual that we all go together, because it gave us more time together as a family. This morning, Stan decided there was no real rationale for that, and since he was writing so well, perhaps I could take Amy.

"Marila, I'm really into the book this morning. Would you mind terribly if I didn't go with you? I'm really moving, and I think I've made a breakthrough. It would be terrific if I could just keep on writing." And he smiled his most charming smile, and I knew how much he wanted to write that book.

"Okay. But I'll leave the other kids here."

"Ummmm. Do you think that you could take all three? I'll be able to concentrate better. Please, Marila?" And I took all three.

The next Saturday morning, he was still writing, and I left him alone again. Later that day I got my revenge.

It was spring by then, and sunny, and I opened all the windows and the doors to blow away the staleness of winter.

Stan was busy typing at the kitchen table, eating carrot and celery sticks that he had asked me to prepare for him. He liked to nibble while he wrote, and the rabbit food was insurance against gaining back too many of the twenty pounds he'd lost to capture me. The girls and I were sitting on the front porch, putting our hair in pigtails, Amy quite excited because it was the first time her hair had been long enough to do so.

"Daddy's hair is so long, I bet we could do it to him!" she said with a delightfully devilish look over her shoulder to where her father was hunched over his typewriter. "Let's try it!"

They all turned to me expectantly, as if they thought I would be sure to veto the idea. Instead, I said, "Let's!" and we attacked him. Sure enough, Amy was right, and by the time we were through, he had six little bunches all over his balding head, and he more than a little resembled Topsy.

Consensus was that he needed a haircut, and that a bushy afro really didn't do him justice. We gathered our tools, a pair of sewing scissors and a razor, and my fan club stood around in silence and awe as I began.

It took me about twenty minutes, and for the first fifteen he was still so engrossed in his writing that he didn't realize the extent of what was happening. It wasn't until he felt the shaving cream on his scalp and glanced down at the mound of graying curls on the floor that he began to get nervous.

"Let me see what you're doing. *Stop. Don't shave my head.* I don't want to look like Yul Brynner."

"Why not? He's very sexy."

"Oh, Daddy, you look so funny. You look so handsome!" Amy clapped excitedly.

When I was finally done, we let him look in the mirror to see what a miracle had been wrought. He seemed younger, thinner, and smarter—much more a wise man of the world. I hoped he wouldn't turn out to be a Samson, who got his strength from those bushy locks. Fortunately, it seemed to work quite the opposite. Eventually.

13

After our abortive escapade with the white elephant, we decided that we should get away for a while. First one thing and then another got in the way, not the least of which was that the girls were getting used to our weekends, and were now enjoying themselves. But with the last vestige of winter hanging in the wind, the time had come to indulge ourselves for a week, and fly to a sunny island.

"I have this friend who works for the UN, stationed in Haiti now. He'd love to see us. I'll see if he can recommend a place to stay." Within a few days, Stan had spoken to Peter Warren, talked to a travel agent, and made arrangements for two weeks hence. I had been so sick I didn't think I would make it. What had started as a cold had progressed into what I hoped was pneumonia, hoped because I was thinking how delightful it would be to be hospitalized for a month, and not have to drive anywhere.

This also turned out to be the first of my traveling illnesses, a phenomenon I have attributed to my Catholic, guilt-inspiring background. Until we actually got married, every time we took a vacation, I would develop a monstrous cold or flu, or sniffle, or have diarrhea or some other nonconfining malady for the duration. I'm sure it was because the nuns and my parents had so convinced me that living in sin was a damnable offense that when I'd do it in a particularly enjoyable fashion, I would punish myself.

The week before we left was unusually hectic, even for us.

Stan was away on business for the first time since we had been together, and I was trying to finish a writing assignment from Barry. Stan called from South Jersey twelve hours before the plane was due to depart, more than slightly drunk.

"You have to come and get me," he slurred.

"You were supposed to get a ride. I'm not done with the training manual," I sneezed, then blew my nose very loudly into the phone. "And I have a miserable cold. I can't drive and we're not packed."

"Marila, please come. I need you. I can't get home any other way. Please, Marila. I celebrated a little too much, it went so well. I'll help you finish when we get home."

I coughed some more, and he pleaded some more. He won.

I went (two hours) and got him (two hours back). He was sober by then, and my fever was up to 102, so he finished the manual while I packed our things, and then I passed out. He never got to bed at all. We almost missed the plane because an incredible fog swallowed the dawn, and without a sunrise he lost track of the time.

Just after takeoff, we broke through the clouds into a brilliant blue sky, and blinding sun. I drank orange juice, took a Contac, and quickly fell asleep in the feeble warmth of the sun through the window. Stan had a double screwdriver, and fell asleep feeling me up underneath the blanket. It was the first time we had ever been truly footloose and alone together, away from our past lives and the business of trying to make a present life, away from parents, bosses, children, and an almost ex-wife. We didn't have anything to say to each other, and I sensed we were both very nervous.

Peter met us at the airport, and gave us a guided tour of downtown Port-au-Prince from his jeep, on the way to our hotel.

"You won't find any Americans here," he said as we pulled up to the entrance, and were greeted by a slender coffee-colored gentleman. "That's Julio. He'll take very good care of you."

And he did. Within an hour he had shown us to our room, ensconced us on lounge chairs by the pool, and presented us with tall frosty rum punches. The water glistened in the tropic sun, and the heat penetrated to all the sore places in my sick body—it was even beginning to hurt me to breathe, and I was looking forward to spending the rest of the day doing nothing in the sunshine and going early to bed.

The courtyard where we sat was an oasis in a poor city, the pool surrounded by mango and banana trees, bougainvillea and other flowering vines winding over the garden walls. There was a chicken or two crossing the brick paths, and a dog lay lazily in the shade, his rib bones rippling visibly against his sweaty black coat as he panted quietly. A Hershey-skinned lady barefoot in a pink dress sauntered across the yard into what might have been the kitchen, a yard-wide basket full of fruit and breads balanced easily on her flowered turbaned head.

I should have counted on Stan's ingenuity to keep us from having to be alone together.

"Peter is going to join us later for a swim, and then we'll have dinner with him and his daughter. I thought that would be fun."

I didn't. The last thing I wanted was to have dinner with strangers. I said so, as I sipped a smashing rum punch.

"Stanley," I whined, "I don't feel well, and I'm tired, and I don't know these people. Can't we just be alone tonight?" The second last thing I felt like was sex, but I rubbed his leg suggestively, deciding it would be a small price to pay for my freedom that evening.

"They're not strangers. Peter is a friend of mine. And we've already made the arrangements, so there isn't anything I can do about it now anyway. We'll have plenty of time alone together." He took my hand and rubbed the inside of my wrist, but I didn't respond.

The sun began to drop, a golden mass behind the banana and mango trees that secluded our hotel, Le Chatelet, from the rest of Port-au-Prince. Most of the patio around the pool was shady, so Stan moved two heavy wrought-iron chairs into the last sunny corner. We sat back, eyes closed, and felt rather than heard someone standing by us. It was Peter. He pulled up a chair for himself.

"My daughter Alex used to live here when we first came to

Haiti. As you can see"—he waved vaguely at the foreign clientele—"it's not a stopover for the usual American tourist." He talked easily to both of us, as if he had seen Stan a week ago and known me for years as well.

As the sun dropped even farther, and the air cooled, Peter and Stan swam companionably, doing laps, and I felt rather left out.

When they got out of the pool they sat with towels draped around their shoulders, sipping their drinks, and comparing notes from the last eight years, Stan's corporate world versus Peter's stint with the United Nations. The talk turned to Haiti as the stars began to appear in the blackening blue of the sky, and a sliver of moon could be seen suspended over a huge banana tree. There was an easy sense of intimacy, as they made plans to play tennis the next day at Ibo Beach, and perhaps go sailing the day after that. That would take care of the first third of our vacation, I thought crossly.

Peter's daughter was a sophisticated and delightful hostess. Dinner was served by a native cook—skinny chickens, succulent rice, fried bananas, frozen bread, and rancid butter. Dessert was Alex's own creation, a concoction of bananas and rum, a true masterpiece, but I felt too lousy and tired to do it justice. I excused myself to try to revive a little bit, an eyelash away from tears, feeling frustrated that this vacation I had so been looking forward to was turning out to be just one more big distraction in our lives. I imagined Stan was carefully engineering things so we wouldn't ever be alone, because by the time I got back, more company had arrived and more plans had been made, this time to go for nightcaps and more conversation. Terrific.

My parents used to not quite fight all the time, and my mother would often rummage around slamming drawers, clanking dishes, being overly polite.

"What's the matter?" my father would ask innocently.

"If you don't know, I'm certainly not going to tell you," she would snap.

That was how I felt that night, upset enough to want Stan

to know it, but not wanting to tell him why I was so frustrated, and getting madder by the minute.

The next morning I spelled it out for him, as we lay in the early-morning sun by the pool, watching the world wake up around us. I was buried, sniffling, under a blanket, and he was rubbing suntan oil over his arms and chest. The young women in their colorful costumes were making preparations to lay the breakfast tables, and a skinny young boy was climbing up a tree to get bananas.

"I was tired, and didn't feel well, and I didn't come all this way to meet some more of your friends. Don't you want to spend some time with me?" I probably sounded about six years old, but I couldn't yet believe that we would have a lifetime together.

"I'm sorry. I didn't realize that you weren't having as good a time as I was. I thought it was a fascinating and quick way to learn about the people and the way they live. Marila, if we were here on our own, you know that it would take us a week to learn what we learned last night, and now we'll have a chance to see and do things that we wouldn't have known anything about. Don't you see? Of course I want to be with you. But we're only here a week, and we'll be together a long time." He was actually using my rationale that time was short to prove his point. I hated him momentarily, because he was probably right.

And in fact, he wasn't probably right, he was completely right, and the rest of the week proved it. We went sailing, and played tennis, and were taken to the kinds of restaurants a tourist never knows exist. We spent a couple of languid afternoons around the pool, with Peter and Alex telling us marvelous tales. Alex tried to describe the trip she had taken not too long before to Jacmel, a deserted coffee port, a ride through rivers and jungles and mountain passes.

"If you had more time you might want to go there," she said, not realizing that once she had stirred Stanley's imagination, he would find time. So Peter and Stan spent the afternoon trying to rent a four-wheel-drive jeep, before Alex and Peter departed, a welcome departure from my point of view, giving us our first evening alone since we had arrived three days before.

A beautiful evening it was. My cold was on the wane, and our skin had a good warm glow to the touch as well as sight. We walked through the streets, winding our way past the tiny open stalls, vendors selling strange-looking things to eat, and trying politely to fend off the beggars.

Our walk took us up the hill to the famous Hotel Olafson, where we drank good wine, ate good food, and danced and danced, for the very first time. We wandered about the gardens of the gingerbread mansion, expecting intrigue at every turn, but finding only couples embracing in the shadows of the mango trees. So we did, too, and the best thing about the night was that it didn't end, it just turned into another day that we were together, and I was a little surer that we always would be.

The next morning, Alex brought a bon voyage gift for us—a detailed road map of the whole country. We spread it out over the table, and she showed us the dotted line which represented Baby Doc's new road, being built for his new Maserati, and the nearly imaginary line that would be our route if the new road was closed. She bid us goodbye, leaving us to linger over a last cup of coffee, and perhaps another swim before we left.

We did swim, then had a midmorning rum punch and yet another swim. The jeep was ready and waiting, polished by four little boys for a quarter until it shone, but it was late afternoon before we finally got started.

Alex's directions had been good, so we made our way out of the city easily, and into the poverty of the outlying districts. Beyond the villages were the sugar-cane fields, and miles and miles of railroad track to carry the cane into port. The roadside stands here were thatched instead of wooden, and the roadway vendors sat on the ground instead of on crates. We found the beginning of the new road, certainly built for the Maserati, the white dividing lines on the newly paved lanes painted with careful precision so that our mustard-colored jeep would not pass a farmer on his burro in a dangerous place.

We wound our way up the mountainside, the climb gradual at first, stopping frequently to absorb the scenery. The sun was often hidden by the serious thunderheads that were building up, and they cast weird shadows on the hills. At what seemed to be a crest was a small cluster of shacks. One, larger than most, was close to the road, and a hand-lettered sign nailed to one of the porch posts read ANNELLE'S. There was a bench on the porch, and a table, and two very black, very grizzly men sat looking at us. We kept on going.

Not more than fifteen minutes farther on we came to a dead halt. The bulldozers were bulldozing, and the backhoes were backhoeing, and along the side of the road stood a group of engineers with their sights and flags, pointing and talking. Stan stopped the jeep.

"Is road oh-pen at five?" Enunciating each syllable as a separate word, he held up his hand with his fingers separated, so the engineer he was talking to could see what he meant.

"This road won't open until eight tonight, folks," he said, grinning, surprising us with a slight Midwestern drawl. "We're trying to make up for some lost time, so we're working from sunrise to sunset till we catch up." He told us that if we wanted to get a bite to eat while we waited we could turn around and go back to Annelle's, the only restaurant between Port-au-Prince and Jacmel. We didn't, it seemed, have much choice.

It might have been the only one, but even if there had been others, it would have had to be the best. For about a dollar apiece, we had succulent meat (I hope it wasn't dog), firm potatoes, a delightful rice-and-bean concoction, and sweets for dessert. We washed it all down with Coca-Cola, remembering Alex's other admonition: "Don't drink any water." Annelle, a small round woman with soft brown eyes and a gentle smile, took care of us herself. American tourists were a great novelty, and we became the object of attention, with the locals coming to stand around and watch us eat and drink.

While we were eating, the rains came, and we were glad to be sitting on her dry porch as the heavy drops spattered the dust all around. Because nobody could leave until the deluge stopped, she plied us with seconds, and even with thirds, always with a smile that showed her gleaming white, if somewhat crooked, teeth.

When the rain finally stopped we still had nearly two hours to wait before the road opened up and we could continue to Jacmel. Hand in hand we began to walk down the highway and across to the very edge of what turned out to be a lush green slope. The sun was low in the sky behind us, breaking through the angry clouds that were pouring their wet hearts out somewhere else, and fingers of purple and rose and golden sunlight were pointing across the deep valley to the damp mountain on the other side. It was purple mountains' majesty, and you could actually see the stillness and the clarity. The air had cooled and the dust had settled, and we could see a man and a boy climbing up a winding path from below, followed by a burro laden with a basket.

"God has really done remarkable things, don't you think?" I broke the silence with a whisper.

"What do you mean, god? There isn't any such thing. You don't really believe in god, do you?" He said God with a small "g."

"Of course I do. Where do you think this all came from? I believe in evolution and all that, but I have to believe that it didn't just come from nowhere."

"It's just nature, Marila; god had nothing to do with it."

He still hadn't gotten over the day before when, on a sightseeing walk around Port-au-Prince, we had gone into a cathedral. There was a mass in progress, and my natural instinct was to kneel and steal time for a prayer or two. Stan turned and couldn't find me. Out of his line of vision, he never thought to look down, and when I got up a few seconds later he was a little stunned. "You don't still believe in all that, do you?" Only slightly embarrassed, I just nodded and hoped the subject wouldn't come up again. It had, sooner than I expected.

"You can't believe in god, Marila. I'm surprised at you." Stan's teasing was gentle, but teasing nonetheless. "And he's up there now," he continued, "with a long beard, and a flowing mane of hair watching over us as if we were a lot of little tin people that he plays with."

I looked at the shafts of light fanned over the valley, the original of all the holy cards the nuns had given me in school, or the set for *The Ten Commandments* with only the actors missing. The man trudging up the hill was closer now, and both he and the boy were barefoot, their meager clothes still wet from the storm. The shadows were lengthening, and moving across the country-side, the tips of the mountains shimmering in the last sun. I wanted to cry, it was so beautiful.

"Of course not." I felt defensive. "But it had to start somewhere, with something, and God is just the force that made it all begin and keeps it going."

"You mean nature. Nature's a force, and keeps it going."

"You call it nature, I call it God."

"Well," he said, kissing each of my ten fingers, "that's not as bad as I thought. I'll be able to convert you to atheism yet, I think."

The rest of the ride to Jacmel was unadventurous, if you don't count the hairpin turns down the other side of the mountain on a barely bulldozed rough roadbed. We found a room in a strange haunted hotel that stirred our imaginations, run by a spinster and her mother fresh from the pages of a gothic novel. We bought a machete and mangos in the market place, roamed the deserted streets with boarded buildings at every turn, and found a shriveled little man who spoke no English but offered himself and two horses for an afternoon in the hills. We rode for miles as he walked ahead, leading where there were no paths, and we didn't look down as we wound around the narrow stony ledges on the edge of the cliff. We tied our horses at the home of what may have been a friend of his, or a band of hill robbers, and walked the rest of the way to his destination, which he still hadn't shared with us. He had a long rope coiled over his shoulder, and we were going, we assumed, climbing, or to a hanging.

Pushing through the trees, more jungle than forest, he pointed out different fruits and plants to us, naming things in patois, occasionally cutting something for us to taste. He pointed to a group of bare-breasted women washing their clothes and their long black hair in a rushing stream. The sound of the water got louder, and we came upon some rapids, the water spilling out of a peaceful lagoon. Our guide went for a swim, taking off only his shoes, and we did the same. We thought that this must be what he had taken us so far to see, but he indicated with his index finger "one," and with his other hand "three."

The path continued around the pool, and followed the stream again at the mouth of it, winding upward only a short distance this time, and he indicated "two." Once again, we all went for a swim, then set off wherever the stream and he would take us, the path much steeper, the growth much thicker, and soon he stopped ahead of us and began to make ready the rope.

We caught up with him, breathless, at the third and last lagoon. It was surrounded by cliffs, sheer slate and granite, the water blue in the sun and greener in the shade, water rushing downward through a channel, roaring over rocks that were smooth with years of water coursing ever downward. The lagoon was fed by a waterfall some eighty feet high, cascading gloriously onto a ledge, and bouncing in a froth into the pool below. There was a small island of rock in the middle, a monument to my God and Stanley's nature.

The guide tied the rope securely to a tree, and we swung down like Tarzan and Jane to the edge of the water. Once down, he repeated the ritual of removing his shoes and dove into the water. He swam a few strokes, then rolled over on his back and motioned us to follow him. So we did.

He climbed up on the monument and waited for us there. Once we joined him he gave us a toothless grin and pointed toward the waterfall, making a diving motion. Stan and I looked at each other, and shook our heads no simultaneously. He laughed and jumped in again, quickly paddling to where the water was pounding down the wall. He disappeared under a mound of foam, and we held our breaths, knowing he was all right, but nervous just the same. To our surprise, he appeared not bobbing in the water but standing on the ledge, thinly veiled by the falling water. He waved and laughed, and dove under the waterfall in our direction, then surfaced and swam back to us.

"What the hell," I said, and took off. Stan watched me do it, encouraged by the gleeful, applauding Haitian, then followed suit. Once he had seen that we could successfully manage the acrobatics (which were not as difficult as scary), he indicated in his animated sign language that we could stay and frolic, and he would wait for us back by the rope. At least we hoped that was what he meant. It briefly crossed our minds that he might pull up the rope and leave us behind, but he seemed too friendly a soul to do that.

He had left us to make the most extraordinary discovery for ourselves. Just a few feet away from the waterfall was a damp cave, about twenty feet square, and from inside we could look through the falling curtain which was now catching bits and pieces of the sun as it passed over the quarry. We had no choice but to make memorable love in that sparkling secret alcove.

From then on our vacation was continuous adventure. Although we left Jacmel at three in the morning to avoid the construction, Baby Doc's road had such a high priority that the caterpillar trucks were out ahead of us shoving gravel and boulders, so we could not pass. The only way back to Port-au-Prince was the old road, barely more than a dirt rut, which snaked its way through jungles and rivers. The first crossing was the hardest, because the river was too wide to see where the road came out on the other side. Although people had told us it was possible to make the crossings in a jeep provided the water wasn't too deep, we had no idea whether the heavy rains of the day before had made the crossings too dangerous to attempt. Alex's last words of caution had been "You'll be okay on the old road as long as it doesn't rain." We just gritted our teeth and plunged ahead. I prayed silently.

Stan was letting me drive, his job scouting for the road on

the other side of the river. He was convinced I was a brave adventurous spirit, but I found it a struggle to live up to his swashbuckling image of me. We had crossed more than halfway, about forty feet, before we saw where the hardly more than a path emerged from the bank of the running stream. The bright beams from the headlights picked up the rutted muddy roadway directly in front of us, and we shouted with glee, having gotten in no deeper than our hubcaps, and with renewed optimism that we could traverse the course we literally plunged ahead. The only detour occurred when we couldn't find the road on the other side of one crossing, and followed the riverbed for over a mile until we found ourselves dead-ended in a canyon. We retraced our ripples and tried again.

Breakfast at dawn was flat bread and bananas bought from a roadside market, the Haitian equivalent of a tiny country store, and we drove into the courtyard of the hotel in time to have a second breakfast of mangos and pancakes prepared with care by Julio. We swam, changed clothes, and repacked the jeep for a wild and bouncy ride to Cap Haitien, at the other end of the island. It was there, all by ourselves, in a cool, ancient church at the foot of the hill leading to the Citadel, that we first promised to love, honor, and I to obey, with swallows swooping in and out through the glassless windows beneath the dome as our only witnesses.

14

We returned different people than we had left, feeling much closer to each other. Stan came back with the start of a marvelous beard that made him look rabbinical, and I came back feeling a great deal more confident that despite the rapidity with which we had merged our lives we hadn't made a mistake. Besides that, I had a much better understanding of the kind of life we were going to lead—fast and furious, grabbing the adventures of life, pausing only briefly to savor the sweetnesses before moving on.

Two weeks after we got home I began to write my first book, an adventure mystery, stimulated by our Haitian escapades. I would see Stan off to work in the morning, then type with great fervor on his Olivetti until it was time for him to come home. The first few days he noticed nothing amiss, and didn't seem to mind an omelette or a pizza for dinner. Then he began to notice no clean clothes in the drawer, two days of dirty dishes in the sink; everything was falling apart. I hadn't told him what I was up to because I wanted to write it, not just talk about writing it, and the best way to accomplish that seemed not to mention it at all.

Bobbi had been bugging him for months to "return" the typewriter, one of the first presents she had ever given him. In my righteous anger, I had been able to convince him that since she'd let him take the damn thing when he moved out, she didn't have much grounds for coming around six months later and asking for it back. Not to mention the fact that it was his.

One Monday morning, one of the rare occasions when he took the girls back, I went to work on *The Old Road to Jacmel*. The title suddenly changed to *The Mystery of the Missing Typewriter*. I hunted high and low, turned the house upside down, and could not find it anywhere. The truth was nagging at the back of my mind, since I couldn't conceive of anyone's breaking in just to steal a seventeen-year-old typewriter.

"Hi. How's your morning been? I got the kids back all right, and made my first appointment on time." It was his usual morning phone call, and he sounded his usual self.

"Stanley, I can't find the typewriter, and I need it." I had finally told him what I was doing, and he had spent some time on Saturday reading my manuscript and given me encouragement. "I hope my typewriter brings you luck," he had said.

There was absolute silence on the other end of the phone.

"Stanley?" It was an unspoken question, and I knew what the answer was.

"I gave it back to Roberta. I took it down this morning." I could barely hear what he was saying.

"You what?" The typewriter issue was the fodder for our first real fight, yelling and stomping on both sides. He was eager to pacify Bobbi if he could, any way he could, and I felt he was too eager to give everything away. And it seemed as if the more he acquiesced to her demands, the more she made. To me the typewriter was symbolic of the place to draw the line, something that would prove to me, and to her, that he wasn't always going to give in, that my feelings were as important to him as hers were. To him, returning it meant one more giant step away from his debilitating ties to Roberta, but even though he told me this I didn't hear him.

"I'm sorry. But I thought I'd better give it to her. The lawyers are meeting next week, and I wanted to get her on my side. Anyway, she gave it to me, and it's a symbol I'd like to get rid of. Giving it back is a real message that it's over between us."

146

I felt that was pure rationalization.

"How could you do that? You *knew* how important it was to me. How could you possibly do that to me? And what about your book? How are you planning on finishing your book?"

"I'll do it longhand, this draft. I think I write better longhand anyway. I'm sorry, Marila, but I really thought this was best for Roberta—for everybody. I think it will satisfy her enough to leave me alone."

"You're always so goddam concerned about her and what she wants, and what she feels. What about me? Don't I count? I don't write in longhand, Stanley. I *type*. Think about doing something for me, Stanley, for a change, would you mind?" I slammed the phone down as hard as I could, and wished that he were in front of me so I could punch him.

He brought me home yellow roses, and I threw them in the trash.

"I'm sorry, Marila. I didn't know it was so important to you," he cajoled. "And I wanted to surprise you with a new electric typewriter." I ignored that piece of news.

"Didn't know? What do you mean you didn't know? We talked about it and talked about it, and you knew perfectly well how I felt about it, and then you went ahead and did it anyway. I think you are perfectly abominable. Now go away and leave me alone." He had found me in the bedroom, dinner unprepared, and for the first time in all the time we'd been together, I didn't meet him at the door. He tried once more.

"I just thought it would be best, Marila. After all, the lawyer—"

I didn't let him finish. "Lawyer be damned. You wouldn't have to worry so much about what was best if you would hire somebody who wasn't a jackass like yourself." I was furious, and we were both shocked, but I didn't want to stop.

"You've been doing all kinds of things for her for the past six months that you thought 'would help,' " I sneered, "and where the hell are you now? Not a single step closer to your divorce, that's for sure, and a whole lot poorer." By now we had just about cleaned out our savings.

I was also getting angrier and angrier about another area where I felt Stan was sorely lacking in giving me support, moral or otherwise.

One weekend at supper, the girls were fooling in the shorthand that children have, half-jokes that would send them into gales of laughter. They made it clear they were making fun of Joellyn.

Leslie went "This!" and picked her nose; Jenny roared "This!" and picked her teeth. Amy shouted, "But the best is when she picks her ass!" shifting her body from side to side, and shifting her emphasis on every word. It was wicked, but she was hilarious, and I hoped she didn't talk about me that way.

Up to that point, all we knew about Joellyn was that she was divorced from an attorney, and when she wasn't staying at Bobbi's, lived with her son and daughter in her house in Camden. The bits we heard from the girls added up to a picture of a tough, thoroughly angry person who seemed bent on revenge against men for all the wrongs that had ever been done or imagined against her. And right from the beginning all three girls expressed a dislike for Joellyn; the dislike grew with time, as did their fear of her violent and bruising temper. Joellyn's Irish Catholic upbringing might have been similar to my Catholic Italian one, but somewhere we'd taken different roads, and that made all the difference in the way the children felt about us.

All of a sudden they sobered up, and Amy said, "How come you two never say anything nasty about Mommy and Joellyn?"

"Because the way we feel about them has nothing to do with you, and it isn't right to talk about other people or to criticize them," I answered.

"They talk about you all the time, and to their friends. They say bad things about you. Especially about you, Mommy." Like Jenny, Amy had taken to often calling me Mommy spontaneously, and I hadn't tried to discourage it. It made me feel very good, actually, that they cared enough about me to think of me that way several days a week.

"What do you mean? What do they say?" Stan was curious.

"You won't let us say those words." This from Jennifer, who—

a few months before—had come as close as the sink and the soap in my hand to having her mouth washed out for calling Amy a "little fucker."

Later, after the little ones had gone to bed, Leslie embarrassedly filled us in on the litany.

"They call her doo-doo face, and they say . . . should I say it, Daddy?" She went on when Stan nodded. "They . . . they say . . . she's a motherfucker, and she sucks cock." With that she burst into tears.

The image of several mature women, as the children described them, sitting around a kitchen table, drinking coffee, and calling me a name like "doo-doo face" should have brought tears of laughter to my eyes, instead of tears of anger. The other names— well, I just felt ashamed that they needed to talk like that in front of young children.

As usual Stan shrugged the incident off, certain that there was nothing he could do to stop her. But I was insistent that he talk to Roberta about it, tell her that it upset the kids, and that they shouldn't talk about me—us—in front of them that way.

"If I make an issue of it, they'll just do it more," he said. So it continued, until a year later when the judge, at Stan's specific request, amended the final divorce decree to read that neither parent should denigrate the other to the children. But it's totally unenforceable, of course, and like life, the abuse at us still goes on.

The typewriter episode in conjunction with "doo-doo face" was more than my unfounded jealousy could stand. Stan, swinging between ignoring Bobbi and trying to appease her anger, couldn't understand why I was so upset, why I wanted him to stand up for me, as well as for himself. It was so clear to him that I was his love and his darling that he was totally confounded by my need to be reassured that my feelings came before Roberta's.

Because it liberated him further, he was probably right to give the typewriter back (although I think he should have broken it first!). If he hadn't, I might just as easily have accused him of wanting to keep it around *because* she'd given it to him, a link with the past. But after the "Typewriter Affair," Stan began at least to hear, if not heed, my need to once and for all and always be given priority over Bobbi.

Anything I could do to differentiate myself from Roberta in Stan's mind, I did, or at least tried to do. Bobbi and I were about the same height and we both had long dark hair, but although the resemblances ended there, I still wished we were much more strikingly different, one of us blond, one of us tall. And our faint likeness became an obsession the afternoon I picked up the girls and a neighborhood child called "Hi, Bobbi," as I was walking up the front walk. I was dumbfounded and destroyed.

I spent the next few weeks plotting how to change my appearance. I knew I'd have to do something with my hair, which was halfway down my back and my pride and joy. It had had no more than a trim for over twelve years. This was the year ringlets were in, and while I knew it wouldn't be easy to get my straight hair to look naturally curly and cute, I decided to take the plunge. I went to bed the night before, dreaming about how I would look with an afro, and it was a nightmare. I couldn't go through with it. Instead, I had about six inches cut off, and stopped on the way home for a bottle of Clairol blond dye.

I put it on my almost black hair, and waited twice the required length of time. It really didn't make any difference, so I went back to the pharmacy, bought ultra ash blond, and dyed my hair for the second time that day.

Stan didn't notice anything at all, but Amy did.

"Mom, you got your hair cut. I like it. Can you still wear pigtails?" She was relieved when I told her I could. "My other mom got her hair cut too, only she got it cut real short in little curls all over her head. She doesn't look like you anymore." Amy didn't understand why that made me cry.

15

If you could discount the tears, the fights, the tantrums, the sulks, the harassment, and the fact that Stan was no closer to his divorce, it was a beautiful spring. I was working more, writing training materials for Stan's firm, and still finding time to look at an occasional house with Peg Duke. We made plans to plant a garden and put in a bank of forsythia bushes, and began to plan for our vacation to the Grand Canyon. Amy hadn't let us forget an impetuous promise made months ago during a family crying jag, and we had decided that nothing short of nuclear war or a natural disaster could keep us from going. It was a test to them, to prove that they could count on our word.

That spring we often packed picnic lunches and went for long hikes and practice camping trips on weekends. Stan was working on his book, and looking very literary. I was feeling very motherly, enjoying playing at having children, and buying them clothes and toys, and reading stories, and doing all the wonderful things that wonderful mothers do for wonderful children. And they did seem wonderful to me a lot of the time. They'd bring me flowers for my buttonhole, or a pretty rock, or come to me for their skinned shins or bruised feelings. I was feeling very much needed, and very successful in the way we were managing to work things out. Lying in bed one Tuesday, the early-morning sun just burning through the window, the kind of spring morning that makes you grateful for winter so that you have a bleak comparison for such loveliness, I was thinking of Amy, always the first to crawl into bed and say good morning and how rosy and warm and sweet-smelling she was.

The phone rang, and shook me out of my reverie. I thought it must be Stan, calling as he often did when he got to work just to say hello. It was my father.

"You know Raish hasn't been well." Raish was Lacey's seven-year-old son, and my godson. He had fallen at school a few months ago, and been oddly lethargic ever since. The image of him at the Barnum and Bailey Circus, where we had recently taken Stan's and my sister's kids, popped into my mind. Raish had sat for a while at the end of the row, not talking to anybody, just drinking in the activity under the big top. I moved over next to him, and he held my hand tightly through most of the performance. But in the car going home, he was his usual devilish self, a perfect match for Amy Rose.

"Yes, Lacey told me." My stomach tensed just a hair.

"He has leukemia." That was all he said. I was numb—I didn't need to ask what the prognosis was.

I called Stan. "Do you want me to come home?" But there was nothing that he could do, and he didn't have much to say either, just remembered, I'm sure, the day he first heard he had cancer.

All the springtime went out of the day, like air from a punctured balloon. I called my sister, and was glad that she wasn't home because I really didn't know what to say to her. I called my mother, because I thought I should. She was certain (erroneously, thankfully) that Raish would never come home from the hospital. Everyone was very stoic.

It was the first tragedy in our family. Always before the ills had been minor, the dying reserved for the old. I opened the desk drawer where we kept snapshots, and sorted through to find the few of Raish that I knew were there. I couldn't find the one taken the day he was born. A puckish face, a little crooked smile, and laughter in his wise eyes—there was a secret there.

I went down to the girls' room, left the morning before in its usual disarray, toys scattered, lumpily made beds. I straightened up the room slowly, remembering the millions of times in our short time together I had yelled at them, and I imagined how many times Lacey must have yelled at Raish in his seven years.

Does it really matter? I thought. What difference does it really make if they leave their stuff all over? As I sorted and boxed and organized the overflowing toy box, I wondered how I would have felt if the phone call had been about Leslie or Amy or Jennifer.

Raish went into remission and came home, and the perspective that his impending death had given to my more trivial woes faded. It seemed the minor annoyances that spring were always connected to Roberta. We had to leave about three one Sunday afternoon to get the girls home—they weren't staying until Monday morning this weekend—and they were nowhere to be found. As usual, they hated to go, and would do what they could to procrastinate. After a great deal of effort we finally located them playing inside the house of one of their friends. Stanley was as angry as I had ever seen him. (I found myself wishing that he would get equally incensed over some of the more burning issues in my life, like the typewriter.) He dragged them down the block, berating them for their selfishness and lack of responsibility, Jennifer in tears, Amy looking a little bewildered at this furious stranger, her father, Leslie just following along behind. Yet Stan's performance, while astonishing to us, was still so mild that no passing stranger would have taken the slightest note.

We loaded them into the car, and Amy further incurred her father's wrath by swinging over her head a miniature flashlight that she had gotten as a souvenir from the circus. He ripped it from her hand and threw it out the window down against the garden wall. I could see it shatter into pieces. For one of the few times in her life, Amy was still.

Unfortunately Stanley was discussing his daughters' obligation not to keep him waiting rather than checking in the rearview mirror as he backed up. There was a resounding crunch as he crashed into the stone stoop in front of the house. He began, quietly, to curse.

And so did I. By this time I was tired of his pointless tirade at the poor kids, who were disappointed at leaving earlier than usual. They couldn't understand why he should be so angry that they wanted to stay longer when normally he didn't get angry at them when they thought he should.

"You stupid jerk!" I yelled. "Why don't you look where you're going? Get the hell out of the driver's seat. *I'm* going to drive. Go on, get out." I jumped out and ran around to inspect the damaged left rear fender.

He didn't even get out to see what he had done, just slid over to the passenger side and let me get behind the wheel.

I pulled up, away from the porch, and made a textbook show of looking in my side mirror, determined to show him that with a little care, one did not have to back into things, no matter how angry one was.

The crash and the lurch that ensued almost immediately came as a complete surprise to all of us. We turned around, and there, crunched up against the right rear fender, was our neighbor's Camaro.

I looked at Stan, who was trying to look nonchalant, and I looked at the girls, who were trying hard not to move a muscle, afraid it might be the wrong one. And then we all began to laugh. And we laughed and laughed so hard that we cried.

I dropped Stan at a tennis court not far from Roberta's where he was to play a match with an old playwright/insurance salesman friend, and then went on to Bobbi's house. There was no car in the driveway, and no sign of life around the house, which wasn't unusual even though it was precisely the time she had been told to expect us. Roberta was rarely in evidence when I took the girls home or picked them up. She had, I'm sure, no more of a desire to see or speak to me than I to her, and it must have been even more painful for her to be reminded of Stan's future than for me to be reminded of his past. This day, though, was different. The front door was locked. Leslie and Amy rang the bell, peered in the windows, then ran around to try the back door. They came running up to me with big grins.

"We have to go back with you. There's nobody home."

Leslie and Amy sounded gleeful, but there was confusion in their eyes. It was hard for them to understand why their mother, who was expecting them, was not home. It was the first time it had happened to them. Not so for Jennifer, who had climbed into the front seat with me, watchful, her eyes filling up with tears. Several weeks before, the house had been closed tight on a Monday morning, and I waited more than two hours with Jenny for Roberta to show up. This time I didn't wait; I put the children back in the car and went to the tennis court to pick up Stan.

I was glad the ride was short, because I had a tough time fielding their questions.

"Why wasn't my mom home? Didn't she know we were coming?" Leslie was plaintive and wistful, twirling strands of her long brown hair around her finger.

Amy took her thumb out of her mouth long enough to answer in her direct and positive way. "She prob'ly went with Joellyn to one of those dumb meetings. She's probably just too busy." Hanging over the front seat, she turned and, speaking quickly, directed her next statement to me. "She's very busy, my mom is. She goes to conventions and meetings, and things like that, and we're going to march in a rally someday. She's very busy, Leslie. She's very busy, and that's why she wasn't there." Amy Rose sucked her thumb pensively for another moment, and then tried to entice Jennifer into a game of "My sister's name is Lucy . . ." at a level of intensity about three times above normal.

I watched Amy's face in the mirror, and could see an actual physical transformation in her features. When I had first met her in Bloomingdale's that fateful day, she had been more animal than child, but over the months she had gradually reversed that, and was more often what one would expect of a six-year-old tomboy. But when she was upset or frightened, as now, she would explode, shutting out everything but what she wanted to do or say. Right now her eyes were glazed, and she began to pull Jennifer over the seat into the back to play with her. Jenny hauled back and socked Amy's arm.

"Stop it, stop it. You're hurting me," Jenny cried. Leslie shrieked, "Amy!" because she was being shoved by Jennifer as she tried to get out of Amy's way.

As the full-blown three-way battle progressed, the little throb that had begun in my temples when we found Roberta away was now full circle around my head. The old joke about the kid who comes home from school and finds that his parents have moved ran through my head, and it didn't seem very funny. I felt sorry for them, but any second I was going to get an arm or an elbow, or conceivably one of Jennifer's feet, in my face. So, without saying a word, I pulled off onto the shoulder of the road.

Once they realized the car was parked, they stopped—the three raised voices and the six flailing arms ceasing in unison. They turned to me with trembling expectation, knowing from experience that stopping the car midtrip did not bode well. The magnitude of their warfare and the number of times that I screamed at them to shut up or cut it out were variables in the equation that could equal a smack on the fanny all around, and they weren't sure this time what I would do or how far they had gone.

To their great surprise, I didn't yell or raise my voice or raise my hand in their direction.

"You all must feel really terrible that your mom wasn't waiting for you, don't you?" Tears coursed down the cheeks of Leslie and Jennifer, and I gathered them to me with one arm and reached out to Amy, once again sucking her thumb, in the back seat. She stood stiffly, letting me circle her, but not yielding as the other two were so eager to do. And she was too brave to cry.

"She was just too busy. She didn't forget. She probably tried to call Daddy but he wasn't home. She'll be home soon." Amy's head was nodding up and down vigorously in agreement with her own analysis. I rubbed her shiny black hair that we had washed that morning, and gently pulled her thumb out of her mouth, holding her hand firmly in mine. Her palm was damp with fear and anger, and she made a tight, tense little fist, but she didn't pull away from me.

I was extremely uncomfortable, stretched in two directions, front and back across the car, but I managed not to let go of anybody, or push anybody away until each had calmed down. Amy I held on to after the others had started to straighten up and wipe their eyes and look for tissues to blow their weepy noses. Then I brought her up in the front seat with the rest of us. It seemed like a good time for us all to be together.

"I'm sure there is a good reason why she isn't there. You're right, Amy, I'm sure she just got busy."

"What are we going to do if she doesn't come home?" Leslie asked matter-of-factly. "Can we go home with you?"

"We'll see what Daddy says."

We picked up Stan at the tennis court, and when he got in the car he was greeted with a chorused account of the recent events.

"Mommy's not home, can we stay with you?" "Mommy's not home, she's busy at a meeting probably."

He called the house, and got no answer. "Let's all go get something to eat, and then we'll decide what to do." But the only one who could eat a McDonald's burger was Stan. The girls kept wanting to know if it was time to call yet, and could they come with us if Bobbi still wasn't home. When he finally called, there was still no answer. "Maybe she's there and just not answering the phone." We drove by the house again, but it was silent and dark in the dusk.

Stanley came up with one of his in-the-clutch ideas. He called his best friend, Adam Stone, and explained the situation briefly. Adam, a brilliant engineer and almost-architect from Princeton and Brown, lived with his lady in half of a chicken coop on a farm some indeterminate but not excessive distance from where we were. He and Sara were flower children of the seventies. Sara, whom I had never met, was a very close friend of Roberta's.

"We're going to Adam and Sara's. It's much closer than driving home, and then back in the morning." The girls cheered, and I cringed, because I didn't want to descend on one of Roberta's best friends out of the blue for an overnight visit; but the thought of hours of driving that night and the fact it would be me driving back the next morning finally convinced me. Adam was most friendly to me, as he always had been. Sara didn't even say hello. She arranged some blankets on the floor of Adam's office, then bedded the girls down with auntly hugs and kisses, and a show of familiarity which I read as saying, "I know these children better than you do, and know how to take care of them better than you do. Look what you've done to these poor kids, ruining their parents' marriage, taking their father." She glared at me when I made Amy go to the bathroom, and again when I went in, after she had left, to kiss them all goodnight.

We sat around on unmatched kitchen chairs drinking Almadén burgundy, and Adam, playing the gracious host, entertained us with stories and tried to ease the strain.

"Hey, Sara, you got any of that great bread you made today? What say we have some?" He was ignoring the fact that she hadn't said a word to anyone but the three children since we had arrived, now more than an hour ago. She cut thick slices of textured wheat bread, and smeared it generously with what looked like, from where we sat, real butter.

Hungry after not having eaten much supper, I quickly took a bite and almost choked. The bread was covered with a thick, greasy, sickening glue, and it was all I could do not to throw up. Stan was the next to take a bite, but he spit it out.

"Adam, I think your butter is bad."

"Impossible," said Sara. "I just got it at the co-op today. I know it's good."

Adam licked it gingerly. "Yawk." He got up, went over to the counter, and picked up the half-used package that Sara had left there.

"Is this what you put on, Sara?" Adam started to laugh. "No wonder it didn't taste like butter!" He held up a pound bar of lard. Sara, mortified at her mistake, collected our uneaten bread and threw it out in the yard for the chickens to peck at in the morning.

Dawn brought more bread, with jam this time, for breakfast, and steaming coffee. Sara still wasn't talking to either one of us. The morning also brought an answer, finally, from Bobbi in the form of a repeated busy signal. The phone was off the hook.

We piled the kids into the car amid quacks and crows and moos and honks, and drove off into the sunrise, dropping Leslie and Amy at school, and then pulling up in front of the house. Bobbi's new station wagon was parked in the driveway. Nuzzled against its rear bumper was a black Ford compact.

"That's Joellyn's car. She must be here too," Jennifer answered our unasked question. The house still looked asleep, even though it was eight-thirty. Jenny hugged us both goodbye and clambered out of the car. We watched as she went up the walk and tried the door. It swung open, and she went inside, waving as she closed it behind her.

It's sad that no one, not even Sara, considered the possibility that Roberta might have come to harm. We all knew she was just "too busy."

16

We packed into our first six months as a weekend family a lifetime of ground rules, traditions, and relationship-building. We tried to catch up to what we wanted to be, tried to be, from Friday afternoon until Monday morning—a "normal" family— even though we weren't, and we knew we weren't. Stan had his own fantasies about what he had wanted marriage and parent-hood to be. He had been exceedingly disappointed in the first respect, and exceedingly frustrated in the second. For him, our life together was an opportunity to do everything over and do it right.

The overpowering urge that I felt as a second wife was to bury the first, to lose the past in the frenzy of the present, and least of all to be reminded of anything that smacked of past intimacy, sex, loving devotion, or familial bliss. I refused to ac-knowledge that there had been one single moment of anything resembling happiness in his first marriage.

But Amy, our trouble-starter, was determined to bring up as many recollections as she could.

"Are we going to take two tents to the Grand Canyon, Daddy, so that you and Mary can have one all to yourselves, like you and Mommy used to do? Huh, Daddy?"

Or the time he brought me yellow roses, for no other reason this time than that he loved me.

"Gee, those are nice, Dad. They look just like the kind you

always used to bring Bobbi." Then to me, "My dad used to bring my mom yellow roses like that all the time."

"Daddy, tell me again about the time that I was born. Tell me how you took Mommy to the hospital, and waited for me to be born."

Even though I was sure Amy knew exactly what she was doing, there was always the off chance that I was wrong. So rather than confront her, I complained to Stan about it, with the gratifying response, "It's just your imagination. Amy couldn't do that." He began to listen for it, though, and then told me that Amy needed to be able to talk about the good memories that she had, that it was important to her to be able to work through her feelings about the divorce. But finally, he began to be as upset by it as I was, and in his mild-mannered, Clark Kent way, took her to task.

"Now, Amy, when you talk about things that happened between Bobbi and me, it makes me feel bad, and it makes Mary feel bad. As a matter of fact, I think that's why you do it, because you are angry at us, because of the divorce, and because we're so happy. Is that true?" She didn't look at either of us, but sat, unyielding, sucking her thumb. She nodded, almost imperceptibly, blushing prettily with guilt and embarrassment at having been caught.

"What do you have to say about that?" His tone was so reasoned that it must have infuriated her. "Hmmm?"

"Nothin'," she said sulkily.

"Well, I want you to think about it, and think about why you do it, and think about how it makes us feel. And if you're doing it on purpose to hurt our feelings, that's a very, very bad thing to do. It's okay for you to be angry at us, but then we should talk about it. You should never be deliberately cruel to anybody, and we think you sometimes are."

"What's 'delly-bratly' mean?" Amy inquired deftly, hoping to change the subject.

"It means doing something on purpose. Now remember what I told you, and if you don't stop it, I'm going to have to punish you." Stan ended the conversation with one of his unbelieved threats. But the fact that he had seen what I had, and talked it through, no matter how gently, was a breakthrough in the way he was beginning to deal with the girls.

Amy stopped teasing us for a while. But she would still do it to me when I was alone with her, and we often overheard her doing the same thing with her sisters. We finally talked to her about that, too.

"You have to stop teasing, or when you grow up people aren't going to like you or want you for a friend. You can be such a sweet and lovely little girl, Amy Rose, when you want to be."

The struggle with Amy, then and now, was to get her to feel good about herself, to feel that she was pretty, likable, smart, and capable, instead of ugly, stupid, and cruel. For a time she lived a self-fulfilling prophecy, more often than not exhibiting behavior that was unpleasant or unattractive, eliciting negative responses from those around her. I've learned that this is a trait common in children with dyslexia, and we have worked very hard to make Amy feel good about herself.

A lot of the problems that I faced in adolescence and even adulthood, the root of a lot of the neurotic actions that I have nurtured, are the result, I think, of being criticized, being told that what I was doing was wrong or foolish, rather than being given guidance or support in changing. Living with Amy was a constant series of flashbacks to my childhood, and I could finally understand why my parents often got so angry at me, because it was infuriating, exasperating behavior. So working with Amy— on Amy—became one of my missions, and at times a mission impossible. But in my quest to be a more insightful mother than I sometimes felt I had had, and a better mother than Amy had, I was undaunted, because I knew how very crucial it would be to Amy's life for her to change.

I don't think that spanking is necessarily such a terrible thing, especially when logic and reason and loving-kindness fail completely. Amy Rose was on occasion so incorrigible that sometimes the only way for me to maintain a semblance of sanity was to smack her rear end with what I hoped was not too much vigor. But usually discipline consisted of early bedtime or no TV or no dessert. Whatever the punishment, she took it with aplomb, and would be on her good behavior for at least a few hours, and often as much as a day. Stan never interfered and always backed me up, although it probably would have been a good idea if he had done more of it himself.

One weekend, however, when we were on an outing with another couple who were also friends of Bobbi's, Amy, testing and teasing, pushed me way beyond the limits of my patience. I finally resorted to a swat on her fanny to get her to behave. I should have had more sense than to do it in front of an audience.

The upshot of the weekend was that Stan got a telephone call from Roberta telling him that under no circumstances was I to continue "beating" the children, and that if I so much as raised a finger against any of them again they would no longer be allowed to visit us. He said she wouldn't listen to what had happened, and he didn't know what to do. Stan's attorney was less than no help. For the next few weeks, Stanley just shrugged uselessly. "What can I do?" he said. And Amy, knowing what had happened, tried my patience beyond my wildest expectations.

"You can't spank us anymore, you know. My mom won't let you." She taunted me unmercifully, having herself a fine old disruptive time. I screamed until I was purple, but she was oblivious to words. All the other punishments I might conjure up were totally fruitless, because Amy felt her mother had shackled me sufficiently to be powerless.

Stan was little help.

"You have simply got to *do* something, Stanley. I can't go on like this. Amy is playing *Gaslight* with me, and succeeding quite nicely, thank you, in driving me stark raving mad. Either you do something about her behavior, or she can't come here anymore, at least not while I'm around."

"What do you want me to do?" He really didn't seem to know.

"What she needs is someone to get through to her that the way she's behaving is definitely not okay. The only thing she understands is a wallop across her fanny, but I'm not allowed to do that. So maybe you should do it. Besides, it isn't fair to ask me to take care of them all the time if I'm not allowed to discipline them."

"Look, if that's what you think she needs, that's what she should get. And it's okay with me if you do it. Marila, the kids aren't guests when they are here, they are part of the family, and you're part of the family. You have to be able to handle them the way you think is best, and frankly, the girls have changed so much in just four or five months that whatever it is you're doing must be working. If you think Amy needs to be spanked, go ahead and do it. When she's here, she's your daughter as much as she is mine, and it isn't good for her or for you or for me if you have to come to me to discipline her for what you don't approve of."

"What about Roberta?"

"Roberta be damned. If she'd exercised more control over Amy from the beginning, we wouldn't have so many problems now."

I couldn't believe what I was hearing. I didn't know whether to hug him for supporting me now, or to punch him for not doing it sooner.

The next time that Amy was totally incorrigible, I decided to test his attitude.

"Amy, this is positively your last chance. If you keep teasing your sisters, you are going to feel on your little behind a very good reason to stop." She had spent the past hour taking her sisters' dolls and messing up the play houses they were so carefully constructing from tissue boxes and playing cards, and I had already been called in twice to mediate.

"You can't spank me. My mom won't let you." Those defiant little brown eyes!

"Want to bet? You're in my house, and when you are in my house you are going to mind me or take the consequences. You can't threaten me, young lady. I know perfectly well that your mother thinks it's okay for me to spank you when you're naughty."

164

Needless to say, she decided to test me, and I came through with a hearty slap on her behind. Amy went crying to her father, who told her the same thing that he had told me and that I had told Amy, all without prompting. She was taken aback at having her strategy blown up so completely, and things were quickly back to normal, with me meting out appropriate punishments for inappropriate behavior, like the wicked stepmother, while Stan sat placidly by, not interfering.

As for Roberta, we never heard another word about the dreadful way I was "beating" her children, and my sporadic swats turned out to be much less significant in the course of things than Joellyn's eruptions at the children, the effects of which they gradually began to share with us.

There were a few times during the spring when, for one reason or another, Roberta wouldn't let the kids come and spend the weekend. One was Mother's Day. This one I could understand, because while they were, I knew, becoming more and more attached to me as a mother figure, they loved their real mother and felt a tremendous sense of loyalty and devotion to her.

We had always told the girls that if they didn't want to come, they didn't have to. It had to be their choice. In all the years that the girls have been spending time with us, there hasn't been more than a handful of weekends that they have chosen not to come.

One weekend Leslie decided of her own volition not to come. When I arrived, one of Roberta's friends was there with the girls, waiting for me.

"Leslie doesn't want to go and see her dad this weekend," Judy said. Leslie was standing by the open door, waiting for my reaction. She looked scared, and I guessed that Roberta had told her we would be furious. I waved, and smiled.

I talked to Leslie for a few minutes, kissed her soundly and hugged her goodbye, and told her that we would miss her terribly, but if she wanted to stay home, it was fine. That was the weekend I began to realize that Amy was not always the disruptive factor in the girls' play I had come to think, because that was the first weekend that there wasn't a single argument between Amy and Jennifer. The peace was sublime.

That weekend's tension didn't come until I brought the girls back, on Sunday this time, Stan having another tennis match. Leslie came to the door lipsticked and eyeshadowed. What should have looked like a child playing dress-up took on a ghoulish air because the hall was filled with the sweet smoke of marijuana. I must have been visibly shocked, because she sheepishly pulled the little ones in and quickly closed the door. I drove to the tennis club and told Stan what I had seen, but by the time we got back there, Leslie's face had been scrubbed clean, and there was a cool breeze blowing through the house from front to back.

That was also the spring of our first Passover Seder, our first tradition. I cooked and baked holiday specialties for a week, brisket and chicken, two kinds of kugels, rugula and banana cake, *tzimmes* and *charoses*. It was a Jewish feast prepared by a shiksa, and I did my father-in-law proud. Twenty people, friends as well as relatives, came to that first Seder, held the second sundown of the holiday week. The house wasn't big enough, but God was with us on that warm mid-April night, and we set the tables in the garden with a hundred white candles for light. It fell to me to say one of the initial prayers, my first in Hebrew, and looking around the table at what was now my family and my friends I felt peace and contentment. But with a pang. Roberta had refused to let Leslie, Amy, and Jennifer be part of that evening, and I was surprised at how empty that made me feel— not so much anger at her for spoiling our celebration as real sadness at not having the girls with us. My sister was there with her children, Raish pale but cheerful, and Stan's sister was there with her children—it was frustrating that we, at this, our Seder, had to be without Stan's.

Just before summer started, we had a weekend to beat all, in terms of our anger toward Roberta. She wanted the girls on Saturday morning, and told Stan to pick them up at a New York City address about noontime. I was sitting in the garden, enjoying a respite before the weekend commotion began, when the car pulled up by the house. Stanley got out and slammed the door behind him with vengeance, the children sidling after him, trying to stay hidden. It was the angriest I had ever seen him.

The girls were dressed in grubby shorts and T-shirts that were emblazoned with slogans, and Leslie had a colored sash tied across her chest. They had spent the morning marching at a rally which included supporters of the more militant lesbian wing of the women's movement, where Bobbi and Joellyn's sympathy lay. Amy, who runs on and on and on, tripping over her words, when she is upset, told me how Roberta had spoken loudly through a horn, and led the cheers. But I could barely pay attention to her words, I was so shocked at the way Leslie looked.

We had spent six months growing hair, buying barrettes weekend after weekend so she could keep it out of her eyes, using the curling iron, tying bows on pigtails, being patient through the awkward stages. She had been so proud of her hair, by now always clean and shining, grown below her shoulders.

But all that effort, all that time, was now in vain. I was facing one of the shortest haircuts I had ever seen—not a scrap of hair to spare on her head. One look and I began to cry, and she cried with me.

Then there were the buttons. Across Leslie's sash were pinned buttons bearing such slogans as "I am a castrating bitch!" I was horrified. Stan took out of his pocket a crumpled poster he had pulled off the wall where he picked up the kids, an advertisement for an upcoming Coyotes rights-for-prostitutes rally.

Shortly after that incident, Leslie tearfully told us about a book that Roberta and Joellyn had given her to read that made her "feel funny." It was a comic book on alternative sex.

"I don't understand it all," she wept. "But it makes me feel really bad." Stan got the book from her about two weeks later, and it had things in it that I had barely heard of, a cartoon justification of "anything goes"—homosexuality, anal sex, sodomy, masturbation, as well as penis size, rubbers and abortion, and, incidentally, straight sex. We filed the book away, along with the buttons, for the custody suit that now seemed essential. As always, it was incredible to me, after consulting not only with Stan's present lawyer but with two other lawyers we checked with as well, that in the eyes of the law, none of this was an indication of an unacceptable environment—not when the alternative custodians were Stan and I, who were not yet legally married.

17

The first time I met Stan's second lawyer he was sitting in his office, a second-floor walk-up over a candy store. He asked his secretary to hold all calls—the only exception being one he took from his ex-wife, with whom he companionably discussed plans for his daughter's weekend. It looked like a setup to me.

I had fervently hoped that this lawyer would bring salvation, but one meeting convinced me that Jack was not the answer to our prayers. But my consort hoped that he possessed the talent and wisdom to handle this gruesome and interminable divorce because Jack had neatly handled several straightforward transactions for him in the past.

Jack pumped both of our hands with great vigor, telling Stanley with an exaggerated wink and a slap on the shoulder, "Heh, heh, Stanley old boy, you're looking like a million dollars, heh, heh. You don't look like you're suffering, things are going really good, heh? Heh, heh." He smirked at me pointedly.

I couldn't wait to get out of there, although it seemed the interview was too short and the notes which he scrawled on the single sheet of yellow legal paper too skimpy for him to get very far with the formal settlement agreement he was promising to have drawn up within a week.

"We'll get this thing wrapped up quickly, so you two lovebirds, heh, heh, can make it legal, heh, heh, know what I mean?" He pumped Stanley's hand as vigorously goodbye as he had hello.

"Stanley, are you sure this guy can help you?" We were walking down Main Street, on our way to a store which had been dunning Stan for payment on some merchandise that Bobbi had ordered and charged to him. Stan had showed Jack the latest letter from a collection agency, and his advice had been, "Pay it, Stan. We'll write it off as alimony."

"Well, I don't know. He doesn't seem quite as bright as I remembered. I'm a little bit nervous about using him, but I don't have much choice now. I hate to start all over again with somebody else I don't know."

So he didn't.

But after three months, still no agreement finalized, a close friend of Stan's convinced him that he wasn't getting the advice or the help that he needed. Roberta kept asking for more and more, and Jack kept saying, "Pay it, pay it, it'll all work out." Fed up, Stanley made some phone calls, and discovered that most lawyers don't want to be the third in a row to handle a case. But he finally got one who agreed to talk, and listen, and perhaps advise.

Although I pleaded that I had had enough of his lawyers and his legal problems, Stan insisted that I go along for moral support. I soon found out that the real reason was to brief me so that he could back out and let me handle it for him. He was tired of losing, and paying, and paying and paying, and thought that I, without his burden of guilt, would do far better than he was doing.

Joe Glavin was a big, easygoing Irishman with seven children. He constantly chewed on a plastic coffee stirrer to help him break the smoking habit, and we liked him right off the bat because he didn't tell us we didn't look as if we were suffering. He seemed sensitive, assessed the situation quickly, and told us clearly what he felt he could and couldn't do.

"It probably doesn't make any sense to let this guy go," he said. "You've spent a lot of time and money with him, and he's told you that he almost has the details worked out." Jack had called two days before, informing us we could meet the next week to go over the papers. "Why don't you go ahead with that, and I'll look it over once you have it, and recommend whatever changes I think would be helpful. *But don't sign anything.*" We left feeling more secure, on the right track at last.

The first draft of the settlement contained what Stan had carefully outlined to Jack as the maximum he could afford in terms of alimony, child support, a large life insurance trust, Bobbi's car payments, educational commitments, mortgage and loan payments, medical and dental obligations, and innumerable other little things. But Jack had taken this as Stan's basic position, from which there was nothing to give but more. The only thing Stan got without fighting for was liberal visitation, including three weekends out of four and nearly two months—June and August—in the summer, as well as other holidays.

"They will want some changes, of course. They've already indicated they want more child support, and some more bills paid. Let's see." He checked his notes from conversations with Bobbi's attorney. "They want you to guarantee private schools for all the children. And camp. And pay for a housekeeper for her. Of course they want you to promise that you'll never seek custody of the children. That's about it. What do you think?"

"I can't agree with these new demands," Stan said, irritated. "I told you what I could do, and I can't do any better than that."

"But, hey, Stan, that was just negotiating, right? You knew you'd have to give a little on some of these things, didn't you? Sure. This isn't so bad. We're pretty close."

"Jack, what I told you was my bottom position. They can take it or leave it. In good faith I tried to be as generous as I could, because I want my children well taken care of. But I can't afford another penny. Mary is going to have to work as it is, and that will disrupt our plans for a family of our own. I can't do it." He shook his head.

"Hey, look. Just like everything else, these things are negotiated. You give a little, you get a little. They don't expect to get all this. Come on, ya gotta be reasonable."

So they pushed and pulled, and massaged, and the papers went

171

back and forth from lawyer to lawyer, and I began to meet with Glavin, who was reviewing the drafts. We usually met in a Howard Johnson's on his way home from his office.

"This is really an extremely generous settlement—is Stan sure that this is what he wants to do?" I nodded, knowing how desperately he wanted to be finished with the haranguing and the paperwork so he could get on with a more peaceful life.

"There are two things you should insist adding. The first regarding custody. Don't ever give up the right to go after the kids or negate the possibility that they can live with you if they choose. Secondly, don't agree to pay all kinds of expenses for the kids unless you are consulted first. That way, not only will you have a little control over things, but you'll be more likely to know what's happening."

It took only two more trips to get the damned thing signed, sealed, and delivered. I made both trips. "Mary, I can't get away today, and you're getting the girls anyway. Could you stop at Jack's and pick the papers up on your way by?" It happened to be the last day of school for Leslie, and she was getting an award at the exercises. She had asked her father and me if we would go.

"I'll be the only one getting a prize without anybody there. Please, Daddy, Mary. Please come," she had pleaded. We were proud of her, and this seemed like something important we could do to help reassure her how much we cared about her.

Stan, not surprisingly, at the last minute found he couldn't make it. After much hesitation on my part, and persuasion on his and Leslie's, I went alone. I came a few minutes early, and was talking to her teacher about how delightful and precocious a child she was, feeling good hearing Mrs. Anderson tell me how often, and with how much affection, Leslie talked about her "other mother."

Suddenly there was a commotion down the hall, and the fourth grade went stampeding by, Bobbi bringing up the rear with Leslie. I looked at Mrs. Anderson, and she looked back, both of us paling. Leslie, the little brat, had done it again. Mrs. Anderson took me by the hand and introduced me to her math teacher.

"This is Leslie's stepmother. She is going to sit with us today." And I did. Mrs. Anderson took good care of me, sensing that I was in near shock. I didn't want to give Bobbi the satisfaction of leaving, especially when I was supposed to take Leslie with me, but I felt like an absolute fool. I tried to rationalize to myself that I had as much right as anybody to be there, since I had just spent half an hour registering her for the next term, and paying her tuition and the transportation bill that Bobbi had neglected. I was also the one she was going home with, and with whom she was going to be living for nearly two months, half at the beginning and half at the end of the summer as per the agreement I was about to pick up. But I still felt monstrously like an intruder.

We sat through the program, I with the teachers, dressed in a linen suit, stockings, and high heels, the way mothers used to dress when they visited the private school that I had attended. Roberta sat on the other side of the gym, alone, in jeans and a peasant blouse, her bare feet in sandals. Leslie would glance over her shoulder, first in one direction, then in the other, uneasy, and just a touch, I hoped, embarrassed. Later I realized that she had not engineered this meeting as she had the other; but that Bobbi, once she found out I would be there, had probably come to cause me discomfort, and to confound a daughter who she already felt was growing away from her.

When it was all over, and the two hundred youngsters broke ranks wildly for summer vacation, Leslie stood and waited, not knowing what to do with the mess that confronted her. I waved, Roberta just watched. Leslie came to me.

We hugged, and chatted, and I admired her prize. She called over a couple of her friends and introduced them to me, manipulating us around so that her back was to her mother and she wouldn't have to see any reproach.

"Shall we go? We have an errand to do, and then we'll pick up the little ones for the weekend." My arm was around her shoulder; I was selfish enough to want to make the most of my triumph.

"They aren't at home. Here's where we have to pick them

up," she said, giving me a scrap of paper with an address on it.

Roberta was standing now, still alone and off to the side, looking lost and insecure without the support of a champion like Mrs. Anderson or the victory of being Leslie's choice of the hour. She called over to Leslie, "I'm going," and turned to walk away. Leslie paused, ran and gave her a quick hug, then came right back to me without a backward glance at her mother. I saw Roberta's shoulders droop slightly in defeat, and I felt very glad that I wasn't in her shoes that day.

The paper Leslie had given me had on it a street address in Camden, an hour's drive south and in the opposite direction from where my appointment was with the lawyer. I would have to drive up an hour to get the papers, down two hours to get the girls, and then two hours back home. And I had no idea where we were going. Neither did Leslie.

"It's Joellyn's house and I've been there before, but I don't know how to get there." When we finally found it, it proved to be a substantial brick home, neatly lawned, like most of the houses in the town where I grew up. The girls came running to greet me, shoeless and filthy, having played all day in the dirt.

"Get your shoes and let's go."

"Can't. The door's locked." Amy and Jennifer were already climbing in the car. Amy continued, "They had to go to a meeting, Mommy and Joellyn, so they told us to wait for you out here. What took you so long? I'm hungry. We haven't had lunch yet." It was already midafternoon.

I blew the breath out between my lips, audibly. But it didn't seem to upset Stan when he heard about it—at least if it did, he didn't show it or do anything about it. Increasingly, he was removing himself from anything to do with his former life, refusing to talk to Roberta at all about anything. I tended to excuse him, knowing that he was under a lot of emotional pressure, feeling guilty and sad about leaving his kids, so I would do what was required, usually with a smile but frustrated and furious inside. I didn't yet understand his hidden agendas, which related to his feelings that I was competent in areas in which he was not—could not be—objective, and his desire to develop the relationship between me and the girls as quickly and deeply as possible. By now the only person that I wasn't dealing with directly was Roberta, and that was as much her choice as mine. She had very early dismissed me by saying to Stan, "As far as I am concerned, she is a nonentity, and doesn't even exist."

Glavin checked the agreement I picked up from Jack and said he guessed it was the best that could be done, but it took him over a week to get back to us. The same day, Jack called to say that if it wasn't signed and returned by the next day, Bobbi wouldn't sign it at all. Stanley, away on business, flew into Kennedy Airport, where I met him with the document. He signed it between planes and flew back to his client. I drove the papers down to Jack, feeling that finally we were making some progress, and perhaps I'd be getting married after all.

That early June day began Leslie and Jennifer's summer vacation. A week later Amy was to join us, and the day I picked her up marked the beginning of my active relationship with Bobbi. Adam and Sara, who had moved out of their chicken coop and into a smokehouse on another farm, were having a housewarming that evening, and I planned to drop the two older girls off early so they wouldn't spend a lovely warm day on the New Jersey Turnpike. I should have expected trouble, because there was a full moon.

Sara and I visited, friendly now, having seen each other often enough to be at first civil, then to come to like each other. Finally and reluctantly I left, assuring Leslie and Jennifer I'd be back later. They stood and waved goodbye forlornly, until I was out of sight.

The trip from Sara and Adam's to get Amy took longer than I thought, and I arrived at Roberta's with hardly any time to spare. The next leg of my journey was to be the long ride to Mrs. Unger for Amy's appointment, and there could be no slipups if we were to make it on time. But when I pulled up in front of the house, Amy was nowhere to be seen. The front door was standing open, so I went up and knocked.

Roberta appeared in the doorway, dressed in shorts and a red tank top, and to my complete amazement, she extended her hand. I took it and she shook hands firmly. I thought perhaps we were about to let bygones be bygones, and try to start fresh. She gave it a hell of a try, but it became too much for her.

"Come on in. Amy isn't here; she's up at the pool. I'm getting things together for the summer."

She led the way into Leslie's room, where the little plastic suitcase they all shared lay open on the bed. She folded Leslie's riding jacket and laid it carefully on top of a meager assortment of playclothes.

"I can't seem to find her riding boots. But they probably don't fit her anymore, she grows so fast."

I didn't say anything beyond "Mmm-hmmm," because we had decided that we couldn't afford, and didn't want, to send Leslie away to riding camp during the time she was supposed to spend with us. But I was moved by the sad and defeated way that Roberta went about the task of packing her offspring off to spend the next three weeks with someone who she was afraid would dilute her children's feelings for her.

I wanted to reach out to her, to touch her arm, to say, "I know you love them, and they really love you. And you're something to them that I can never be. I'm really not trying to take them from you." But she spoke before I could, and I probably wouldn't have been able to say those things anyway.

"Some of my relatives are coming today, and they'll be here soon. I think it's best if you aren't here when they arrive." I nodded, and picked up the suitcase she had zippered shut, then followed her out to the car.

I slid behind the wheel and turned the key in the ignition, wanting to say more, say something.

She got there first. "Don't you have a check for me?" For the first time a note of bitterness crept into her voice. And before I could answer, or give her the check I had forgotten in my nervousness, she exploded.

"What do you think this is, anyway, Rent-A-Family? You can just come around, free as you please, and take them whenever you want. But I have the responsibility for them all of the time, and don't you forget it. I'm their mother, whether they're with me or not."

Her voice had risen and the neighbors were beginning to take notice. It was also getting late, and I had to find Amy.

"This isn't getting us anywhere," I said. "We don't play Rent-A-Family and you know it. It was your idea for me to bring the check." She had told Stan I couldn't pick up the girls without it. "And we'd like the girls with us all the time. You know that." I gripped the steering wheel so tightly that my nails dug into my palms. I was determined not to cry, though the tears were filling my eyes, and I was equally determined not to get hooked into the strident and embarrassing scene she was creating.

"Sure you would, and so would I. Are you implying that I don't want my kids around? You just try and take them away, and see what happens. Just wait. One of these days I'm going to beat you up." She waved her clenched fist at me. "If you're so goddam hot on having kids around, why don't you have your own and leave mine alone?" She couldn't have said anything that could have hurt me more, but I just said woodenly, "Amy's going to be late for Mrs. Unger. I have to go."

"That's a lot of crap. You think you're . . ." I didn't hear what she said, I just backed out of the driveway as quickly as I could, and drove off in search of Amy. Out of the corner of my eye I glimpsed the still-shaking fist uncurl into an obscene gesture.

I found Amy wanting eagerly to show me the way she could dive into the deep end of the pool. Then she sat dripping wet, purple-lipped and shivering, as I looked through the suitcase for clothes. Besides the jacket for Leslie, there were shorts for Jenny, and a pair of jeans too small for any of them. The only things that fit Amy were a dry bathing suit and a T-shirt. There were no shoes. I decided she would have to go to her session in the

177

bathing suit and barefoot, because I wasn't going back to pick anything up.

I was driving out of town, feeling distraught and humiliated by our encounter, when I heard a fierce incessant honking behind me. I glanced in the rearview mirror, and saw it was the silver Pontiac station wagon, that finger following me as she held her hand out the window. Amy saw the car, too, and began to wave.

"That's my mom." I pulled over when the honking got more frantic. I hoped all she wanted was to say goodbye to Amy. No such luck.

"You little cheating twirp, where's my check?" I flushed scarlet and, mortified, fumbled for the envelope, while she spit fire and venom. She snatched it out of my hand, yelling at me all the while, and drove off screaming rubber.

It took the whole ride for us to calm down. I was trembling, from the shock of feeling such anger directed at me, and anger of my own at Stan for exposing me to the hostility he was trying so hard to avoid.

All things considered, it was practically a miracle that we arrived at Dorothy Unger's only twenty minutes late, but what I didn't need was her stern face and a pointed look at her wristwatch.

"Don't you realize that Amy has to get here on time? She missed her last class, and now her time is almost over." I didn't remind her that Roberta had been supposed to bring her the week before.

Then Dorothy took in my tears and dishevelment and turned to Amy. "Amy, you read one of these books for a few minutes, and let me talk to Mary, okay?" Amy, for once, did as she was told.

Dorothy listened to the account of my day, which so far had included more than six hours on the road, not to mention my encounter with Roberta. She didn't say anything inspirational, but she listened to me sympathetically, and that was what I needed most right then.

I spent the afternoon, during and after Dorothy, summing up

in my mind the insanities of the past four or five months. Today had been the last straw.

But that marathon day was the beginning of the end of it all. I vowed as I rode back and forth on the Jersey Turnpike, and hither and yon in the Jersey hills, that Stan was going to have to begin to take care of his own affairs. They were his kids—if he wanted to see them, he'd have to go and get them. It was his divorce, and if he wanted it he'd have to make it happen. I'd never again let myself be in a situation where Roberta could humiliate me by screaming bloody murder on a quiet village street. It was a new day for me, and a new day for Stan, but they were slow dawnings.

18

Summer was the first time that the girls would be with us for more than four days, and I was really looking forward to the weeks ahead of us. I planned to be a model mother, like the young woman I had seen in one of my continuing house-hunting expeditions. She had been sitting in a chintzed wing chair, framed by the leaded window behind her in the neatest den I had ever seen. She was impeccably dressed, casually and perfectly, with a toddler sitting on her lap listening in rapture as she read him a story; her house was immaculately kept. That became my ideal, continually frustrated though I was in attaining it.

The reality of our summer didn't exactly match my vision, although we did find time to do things together. Most of the time all three girls tried hard to please me. There were some delightful shopping expeditions for new summer clothes, and I was pleased that Amy showed as much interest in pretty outfits as her sisters. We went swimming at a nearby lake perhaps three times a week. I arranged for Leslie to be tutored in math, kept taking Amy to Mrs. Unger, and tried to keep Stan happy. And I was working besides. My assignment that summer from Stan's company was to write a series of training modules for supervisors on effective management of people and time.

I tried very hard to be organized, and to plan my days carefully. Up early to see Stan off, breakfast with the girls, clean up the kitchen, make our bed, straighten up around the house. I'd be all ready to sit down at my desk and begin to work when there would be a tentative knock at the door, and usually Jennifer (they thought I'd get least mad at her for disturbing me) would say, "Mommy, could we have a cookie?" or "Mommy, would it be okay for us to go outside?" or "Mommy, can we have some paper and pencils to play with?" So I'd get up to give them what they wanted or needed, and sometimes play a little bit with them, and then go back to working for half an hour, which brought us to lunch. I probably should have locked myself away for four hours a day, letting them fend for themselves or investing in a baby-sitter, but I didn't like to say no to them where my time was concerned. I wanted them to feel that while I insisted on limits with regard to their behavior, if they needed me they should always feel free to come to me. And they did, so if I didn't like the interruptions, I had nobody but myself to blame.

Once we'd had a particularly trying day, one in a long series of rainy indoor days, and everybody's temper was a little bit short. Amy had been teasing, Jenny had been whining, and Leslie had been bossing them at her shrillest and not listening to me as I pressed her to do her chores, nagged her about her assignment for the tutor, and told her to let her sisters play in peace. "It's time you did some things on your own, with children your own age. You're getting too big for their childish games."

"I'm going over to Meredith's." Meredith was our baby-sitter, and she occasionally invited Leslie over to listen to records, or meet some of her younger friends.

"You're not going anywhere until you fold the towels and do your math." I was very tired of mothering at the moment, and couldn't imagine why I had ever thought it would be rewarding.

"Oh, yeah? You can't tell me what to do!" She stopped just short of saying "You're not my real mother," then stomped out the front door, turning just enough so that I could see out of the corner of my eye that she was sticking out her pointed tongue at me.

I let her go, and yelled instead at Amy, who said, loud enough for me to hear, "Leslie, you shouldn't stick your tongue out at Mommy that way." And then she looked at me sideways, just to make sure that in case I hadn't seen it, I had heard about it.

"Stop tattling, Amy. It's none of your business." I stormed around the house doing Leslie's chores and some more of my own that I didn't have the energy to do unless I was angry. When Stanley got home, I was still worked up, sick of being cooped up in the house for days on end, baby-sitting for what I felt at least that day were ingrates, and ready for him. As he walked in the door, I walked out.

"Your dinner is in the oven, and will be ready when the bell goes off. Amy's already set the table, and I don't know where the hell your oldest daughter is." I started to go down the stairs to the car.

"Hey, wait a minute, what's the matter? Where are you going?" The poor man was so puzzled.

"I don't know where I'm going, and I don't know when I'm coming back. And if you want to know what the matter is, why don't you ask them?" I drove off, and once I was in the car, and away from the house, I began to cry. Partly tears of frustration, but partly because I didn't have any place to go.

I headed toward a nearby shopping mall with a triple movie theater and over a hundred stores. I should have been able to find something to entertain me for a while.

But none of the movies interested me, and neither did any of the stores. I wandered aimlessly up one side and down the other of the tree-planted walkways that radiated from the double-storied central lobby, not seeing anything I wanted to buy, feeling hungry, but only able to eat a bite of the pizza that smelled so appetizing and tasted like cardboard. I decided that yogurt might be better, but when that went down like chalk, I realized that it wasn't the food I was eating but the dour mood that I was in.

I turned to the bigger department stores, and began to walk

through Stern's, hoping to lose myself and my depression in the melee. But as I walked through the men's department, I remembered that Stanley needed underwear and shirts and bought him some, and passing the jewelry counter, with its prominent display of Timex watches, I recalled the difficulty Leslie still had telling time. So I bought her a watch as incentive. I couldn't go back with packages for Stan and Leslie and nothing for the little two, so I bought Amy and Jennie paper dolls and coloring books, so that if the rain kept up they would have something new to interest them. All three needed socks, so I stopped in Girls' Wear for those (I've still never been able to figure out how so many socks get lost between the laundry basket and the dryer). And in the Sports Department I picked up some of the things we needed for our Grand Canyon adventure.

Finally, I stopped in a coffee shop, and over a steaming pot of tea, tried to analyze the situation as best I could, and come to some conclusions. There I was, trying to get away from a family that wasn't mine, from pressures and restraints that had been dropped, unsolicited, at my doorstep. I had wanted Stanley, not all the baggage of his first wife and his children, but in my aborted attempt at escape I was thwarted at every turn, because this one needed this, and that one needed that, and they had all four become so much a part of my life and myself that I really couldn't separate myself from them.

It wasn't just me alone anymore; I'd left behind the self I used to be and I would never be quite the same again. And it wasn't just the two of us, because Stanley had his baggage and it was something I was always going to have to put up with. The girls were as much a part of my life now as they were of his—if I wanted him, I had to want them. And they were, for the most part, sweet, good, and at least learning quickly, trying much of the time to please.

It wasn't their fault that they had been born to some other woman, and it wasn't their fault that she wasn't the kind of mother that I thought children should have. It certainly wasn't their fault that we might not have children of our own. But I was resenting them for all of those reasons, as well as for interfering with the nice, pleasant, placid life I imagined I would have liked to have. There were more and more times when I was wanting to yell at them, "Go away and leave me alone. Don't ask me to play with you, or read to you, or bake cookies with you, or take you swimming, or wash your hair, or tuck you in."

But I realized, sitting there, packages piled high next to me as a reminder of my entanglements back home, that I was the one who had created all those expectations. I was the one who had led them to assume that I would do all those things and more for them, gladly, and that they could depend on me for love, support, and attention. When we had started out more than six months before, they had needed all of that, and I had jumped in, without checking the terrain, to prove to me and them, and my folks, and Roberta, that it really wasn't so hard to be a good mother. Now I was, and it was a cage, with no way out.

The lights flicked on and off, signaling closing time at the mall. It was ten o'clock, and I'd been gone nearly five hours. I sighed deeply, and decided that it was time to go home. I wanted to, at least a little—they had all succeeded in getting so under my skin that I could honestly say that I loved them. Then, too, I really had no alternative—there was no place else for me to go, no one else to go to. But mostly I felt I was in much too deep to back out.

By the time I got home it was after eleven. The porch light was on, and Stan was at the door before the ignition was turned off. He didn't say anything at first, just wrapped his arms around me and held me so tightly that I lost my breath.

"Marila, Marila, Marila. Don't leave us, we need you so," he murmured into my hair, a gentle pleading whisper. Leslie had tried to wait up for me, but had given up, and the little ones, Stan told me, had cried all evening. The dinner that I had so carefully prepared was untouched. "We couldn't eat without you," he said. I looked in on the chickadees, Amy and Leslie sleeping soundly, thumbs in their mouths. Jennifer stirred when

I brushed her forehead, and opened her eyes. She reached up her arms and mumbled sleepily, "I'm glad you're home, Mommy. I knew you'd be home," and drifted back to her dreams with the trace of a smile on her face.

19

Roberta never had called the girls when they were with us on weekends, understandably so, I guess, because she would have been most likely to get me or Stan. She couldn't have had any more desire to talk to us than we to her, and it must have been painful for her to hear the girls sounding so happy. After all, it used to bother us a little when we called them at her house and they sounded as if they were having a terrific time.

But it always upset the girls that she didn't call, and they would ask us why. They also constantly wanted to know why we always drove them back and forth, and not Roberta. They began to see it as a lack of love on her part, that she didn't care enough about them or miss them enough to want to talk to them, or want them around badly enough to come and get them after they had been with us. We've never been able to convince them, though we tried, that her passivity has nothing to do with her feelings toward them, but has more to do with her relationship to Stan and her nonrelationship with me.

That whole first summer she called twice—one time I could have kissed her, and the other I could have killed her.

It had been a beautiful summer day, and I had packed my three up with bathing suits, dolls, and lunch, and we had spent a day at the lake with Lacey. The kids had a wonderful time, Leslie and her cousin Dana sunbathing like sophisticated ladies, Amy foregoing her usual porpoise activities to play instead quietly with Raish, who was home again after his second siege and who somehow Amy knew needed gentle companionship. Jenny paddled and played, building sand castles patiently for Amy and Raish to knock down when they felt rambunctious.

Other than that it was heart-wrenching to know my nephew was so ill, it was a lovely day, my sister not parroting one of my mother's lectures, and I not sharing any tales of woe. (I was learning.) The girls behaved like paragons, and I was, as I was more and more often, very proud of them. Late in the afternoon we set out for home, sunburned and glowing, stopping on the way for a Dairy Queen.

They each got gooey strawberry sundaes to go, and were eating them with gusto, chattering and giggling, when I put on my blinker to make a right-hand turn off the country road. Suddenly the front end of a Ford was imbedded in the left side of my Chevrolet, and a network of cracks had appeared in the windshield in front of Amy. The three girls all began to scream at once. I was too shocked to do anything but sit there, staring down at a wrinkled, white-haired man who sat in his car, looking just as stunned as I.

Once I got the girls out of the car, and calmed down, we realized they seemed unhurt, so I turned to contend with the police, and the half-blind old man who was saying over and over again, "But the car in front of me stopped at the stop sign. I thought I could just go ahead." A young policeman called for an ambulance when it was discovered that the cracks in the windshield had in fact been put there by Amy's head, and a dent in the dashboard by Leslie's; and they went off in it for X-rays.

At the hospital, I came head to head for the first time with the legality of my position—or rather the lack of it. When I got to the part of the admission form that said "relationship to patient," I was stumped. Mother was a lie. Stepmother was a lie. Stepmother-to-be was too complicated. The clerk at the desk noticed my hesitation and asked what the problem was.

"Well, I'm sorry, ma'am, but if you aren't the children's mother, or their legal guardian, you can't give permission to have the children treated. Can't you locate their father or mother?"

"You mean that you won't treat them if I'm not their mother? That's crazy."

"I'm sorry, but those are the rules."

"I can if I'm their guardian?"

"That's right."

"Okay, I'm their legal guardian." I signed the paper that way. "Now where's the doctor?"

So Amy and Leslie had their first experiences with an X-ray machine, and Jennifer, clutching my hand tightly in hers, cried as her sisters were wheeled on stretchers down the shadowy linoleumed hallway. Amy and Leslie thought it was a real lark. And the pictures were negative, neither girl having the slightest visible or invisible bruise or bump (it didn't surprise me about Amy, but I expected Leslie to have damaged more easily).

Once home again, we decided on tea and toast to sooth our shattered nerves. The kettle rattled, from my shaking so much with relief that we were all home safe, and I still had three intact little girls present and accounted for. The phone rang, and I was glad I'd be able to tell Stan that I hadn't damaged, even unwittingly, one of his children.

It wasn't Stan. It was Roberta.

"Hullo?" I said, fully expecting to hear his calm voice.

"I'd like to speak to the kids, please." It was a flat, even, nonhostile tone, and I jumped at it, because it suddenly dawned on me that I had to answer to her for their safety as well as to Stan.

"Jesus, am I glad you called!" She couldn't have missed the relief in my voice. "Before you talk to them, I want to tell you, I just had an accident. They're all right, they've been checked over, but Leslie and Amy each hit their heads hard enough to have headaches for a week."

"Is Jennifer okay?" She was calmer than I.

"Yes, she was in the back seat. Amy cracked the windshield, but didn't get a scratch. There's a slight possibility of concussion but the doctor didn't think it likely."

"Are you okay?" My dream had come true. We were having a civil conversation, though it had taken mayhem to do it.

"Yes, I'm fine. Just shaken, and worried about the kids."

"Well, as long as nobody was hurt. That's the important thing. Let me talk to them." And she did. They delightedly told her of the examining rooms, the X-ray machines, and the finger puppets they had gotten from the nurse for being such good patients. After a while, they said goodbye and hung up, and we went back to our tea and toast.

The only other time Roberta called that summer, I was trying to get the girls together to go to Mrs. Unger's, because I couldn't get a sitter. Leslie, as usual, was able to take care of herself, only requiring my presence once, not for assistance but rather to show me the seven pubic hairs that seemed to have sprouted overnight. She was a delightful mixture of grownup bravado and childish embarrassment when she informed me she could no longer take a bath with her sisters, because now she would need her privacy.

Amy and Jennifer bathed together, calling for help. I found them perching like frogs, their fannies barely skimming the top of the water.

"It's too hot," Amy said. "We can't even sit down."

"Do you want us to wash our hair?" Jennifer was trying to get the instructions straight.

"Here, I'll fix the water, and yes, wash your hair. And be quick about it, because we have to leave soon. We can't be late." My tone was less than loving. It had been another one of those mornings in which, no matter how brightly the sun is shining or how sweetly the birds are singing, nothing is right with the world. Nobody wanted to go to Mrs. Unger's, me included, so there was no cooperation from anyone.

"Amy! You got soap in my eyes. Now I can't see," wailed Jenny. I could hear them arguing two rooms away.

"I did not. You fell. Don't hit me, Jennifer." Amy struck back, connecting not with her sister, but with the open shampoo bottle resting on the edge of the tub. I got back just in time after the first shriek to see the whole thing in slow motion, as the bottle fell, not inward into the tub, but outward onto the thick bathroom carpet that was firmly cemented to the floor. The viscous liquid oozed out in huge orange droplets, and spread into pools before disappearing into the pile.

That was when the phone rang, and the sound jolted me into action.

"Goddammit, Amy Rose, can't you be more careful? Look what you've done!" I tried vainly to mop up the rug, as Jennifer began to cry, and Amy squeezed the soap too hard and it squirted out of her hands onto the floor right in the middle of the shampoo. I decided to wash them myself.

Leslie appeared in the doorway. "Mommy's on the phone, and she wants to talk to you," she said to her sisters, giving me such a smug look as she walked by that I was sure she had been listening with half an ear to my troubles.

Amy jumped out of the tub and raced to the phone, immediately bursting into terrible tears. I had rarely seen Amy so dramatic.

"I want to come home. Won't you come and get me? Mary hit me." I could have throttled her. I wanted Roberta to have an image of me as calm and cool and collected, always in control, enjoying loving obedience from her darling children at all times. I wanted her to find me maddeningly perfect, not the over-whelmed ringmaster in a three-ring circus, so I set out to recoup what I could.

I wrapped up naked Jennifer in a big towel, rubbed her dry, teasing a smile out of her, and quickly dressed her in her favorite sundress.

She was ready in five minutes, and more important to me, in a cheerful mood, partially bribed by a promise that I would take them to the beach later on. Amy was still sobbing into the phone, enumerating the many ways that I had wronged her.

"Amy, you have to get dressed now. Let Jenny talk," I coaxed, not wanting Roberta to hear me struggle with her middle daughter. She jerked away from my hand which was on the receiver and began to cry with renewed vigor.

"*Amy.* Let me talk. You had your turn. It's my turn. She's my mother, too." Jennifer's four-year-old logic prevailed, and Amy finally, reluctantly, handed over the phone to her younger sister. I whisked her away with the towel, and repeated my routine, trying to eavesdrop on Jennifer.

"Oh, Mommy, you know *Amy.* She just wet her pants, and spilled the shampoo, and stuff like that. How's the cat? We're going swimming . . ." And on she went, chattering her childish chatter, and not tattling on me, or the role that she had played in the morning's misadventures.

We got to Mrs. Unger's without a moment to spare, and, as I'd promised, I took them swimming when we got home.

The only time Roberta came to pick them up that summer was over the Fourth of July weekend. July was her month with the girls. The day set for their departure was the first of July, my birthday, the sort of rainy summer day when the sky wavers between shades of black, and is only brightened by an occasional flash of lightning. When I was a child it was the kind of day in which I used to play outside, splashing barefoot through the puddles and squishing the mud and the grass through my toes. It was a beautiful day.

The girls put on records and made up a show for me, singing the songs to *Grease* and pretending they were John Travolta and Olivia Newton-John. Then we took all the plants and set them out on the stoop so they could drink in the rain, and we moved upstairs to the porch outside my bedroom and listened to John Denver records.

Leslie was leaning over the railing, catching raindrops on her tongue. She rolled over and leaned out backward, letting the steady downpour fall on her face.

"Did you ever wash your hair with rainwater?" she asked.

"No, but it's supposed to be very good for it because it's so clean." By now Amy was copying her older sister, and hanging out. Jenny was too short to reach. "Can we do it?" They all turned expectantly, expecting me to say no.

Of course not, I thought. "Why not?" I said.

With gleeful exclamations and clapping, Leslie ran to get the shampoo, and I went to get a bucket that we filled with summer rain in no time.

We did Leslie first, then Amy, and finally Jennifer, but they weren't satisfied until I did mine as well. The four of us were sitting Indian-style on the balcony towel drying when Stan chugged up in his little red Volkswagen. It was only three o'clock in the afternoon, but the lights were already on against the darkness of the thundery day. He got out laden with packages, and waved at our shining heads and faces smiling down at him. He smiled back, but sadly, as the girls jumped up and tripped over each other in their rush to see their daddy. I wondered what he had bought me.

First came a yellow rose and a birthday kiss. "Are we eating early? They're coming around five." That was why he had looked sad. Damnit. Today, I didn't want them to go. On the beautiful, close days I wanted them to be mine.

"Thank you. What have you got for me?" I tried to peer into a bag he had under his arm, and then shook a big ribboned box he laid on the table. "Unless you want spaghetti, I can't have dinner by then." He wouldn't let me look.

"Let me see. Let me see!" Little hands and lilting voices clamored to be part of the party, and Stan finally gave in.

"Okay, okay. Here. Open this one first." He handed me the box. I noticed a smaller one on the chair, same white gloss, same red satin ribbon. One tug on an end, and the bow dissolved, so I could smooth it out neatly as I wound it around my fingers to save, the way my grandmother had always done.

The tissue paper carefully swaddled a gleaming, black-brown leather man's briefcase, with the name Stanley Silverzweig emblazoned in gold under the front flap. It was a beautiful bag. I didn't know what to say.

"Now this one!" He was chortling with delight at something as he handed me the smaller box. Inside was a very tailored, very boring briefcase, the color of a brown paper bag. Just like Christmas, I thought.

"Isn't it beautiful?" he exclaimed. "I thought it would make you look older, more professional." Someone had recently asked him if I was his daughter, and mortally wounded his ego. "And look. Look at this!" He opened up the flap, and pointed proudly. "Mary Zenorini Silverzweig." Tears began to sting my eyelids.

"Thank you," was all I could say as I hugged him, and traced the beautiful name on the dull leather. "Thank you." It portended a part of my future, I thought. Stan had been talking more and more about our starting our own business and working together someday.

"But I'm not done!" Now he was laughing outright. "One more!" The girls were awed and silent, standing on the periphery of something important, watching it, and only partly understanding as Stan pulled a little box out of his pocket. "Here. I love you, Marila." There were tears in his eyes, too.

It was a little square box, unwrapped and unribboned. "I hope you like it. I didn't spend too much. I knew you wouldn't mind."

I opened the box slowly, and nestled on the bed of cotton was a chamois sack. I felt the shape of a ring as I picked it up.

And a beautiful ring it was. Florentine gold, hand-wrought by an Italian craftsman, a touch wider than the one he'd bought for me several months before, with nuggets of white gold where mine had diamonds.

"It's just like yours, Marila. Look. Can you imagine that I found one that's such a perfect match to yours? Marila," he whispered. "I really love you. Will you marry me, Marila? Please?" Together, we put the ring on his finger. "You know in the Jewish religion, when you exchange rings, you're married." He looked at his hand admiringly, satisfied. It was evident that our getting really married was as important to him as it was to me.

My last present was an ice-cream cake from the Carvel down the road, and that was what we ended up having for supper, because we all lost our appetites when Stan reminded the girls that they were leaving very soon. It was a gloomy end to a glorious day.

A car pulled up in front at dusk, as the rain was ending, and the clouds breaking scarlet and gold to the west. Sally and Jimmy, Joellyn's children, stumbled out of the station wagon and ran up the steps, excited at seeing their sort-of sisters again. "We have to go to the bathroom," Jimmy announced. Amy ran charging to throw herself at her mother; Leslie and Jennifer held back almost shyly, waiting for their restrained, perfunctory hugs.

I was peeking surreptitiously out the window, glad that I could catch a glimpse in the fading light of Roberta and her lover, Joellyn, whom I had never seen before. Much taller than Roberta, as blond as she was dark, Joellyn had features that were set impassively even when she spoke to her lover or her children, and she moved tightly, with pent-up energy and tension. The girls often giggled to us that she was called "The Beast" behind her back.

Seeing Bobbi ne was one thing. Seeing her with her paramour was different. I was fascinated by my first look, firsthand, at avowed lesbians. My naively sheltered life had barely included the word in my vocabulary, and it was almost surprising that they didn't have horns and weren't covered with warts. Watching through my lace curtains, I reaffirmed my intellectual position that Bobbi and Joellyn could do whatever they wanted, and live whatever life-style they chose. But I prayed that my little ones would grow up unscathed. Before all five children were collected and deposited in the back of the station wagon there was a minor skirmish on the doorstep between Roberta and Stanley about the month's alimony check (it was in the mail). Joellyn and Roberta finally drove off with their brood, leaving us alone to finish celebrating my birthday in bed, with a bottle of champagne.

20

The time for the promised trip to the Grand Canyon arrived, the last two weeks of the summer, and I was in despair. The journey had been planned as most of our life was planned, with too many things to be seen and done in too short a space of time, too many things to do before we left, and Stan's most important meeting of the summer scheduled for the day after we returned. (That was his boss's way of making sure that he came back when he said he would.) Stan was enthusiastically throwing himself into preparations for the vacation, giving me long lists of things to do, to get, and not forget so we would be overprepared for any contingency. He was also going to be away on business almost the entire two weeks before departure.

"Come on, Mary," he said once, getting a sense of my reluctance, "it'll be great fun. We'll really get close to the kids, and just think—no work for two weeks!"

I didn't bother going into the boring details of why I couldn't get too thrilled over a "vacation" that covered two weeks in time, too many car miles to count, at least one thirty-mile hike to the Colorado River, all in a rented Maverick with three children, five backpacks, five sleeping bags, and a tent, not to mention other miscellaneous camping equipment, and the suitcase for the city clothes that Stanley needed for his business trip. He was going to meet us in Oklahoma City, where the trek would start and end. It was up to me to assemble and pack the people and paraphernalia, and get me and his daughters out there.

The first day of each weekend or visit that the girls were with us was always the toughest for me. It usually took me that long to adjust to their presence in my already too hectic life, and for them to settle down to our way of doing things, which, as Amy always said, was much more strict. But once that was over I found myself ready to enjoy the more delightful and rewarding aspects of having growing children around.

In the two weeks preceding our vacation, however, I found nothing redeeming or rewarding at all in motherhood. I was angry at Stanley for leaving me with his children, and I was trying to meet a project deadline that coincided with our departure date. I had little time or energy to spare for three hyperexcited, impossible children, and not an ounce of understanding or tolerance for their behavior, even though I knew that it was largely due to the fact that we had made a promise to them in the raging days of March, and were about to keep it.

That the four of us lived to see the Grand Canyon is nothing short of miraculous, given the last week we went through after Stan had kissed us goodbye, and flown gaily off to Houston. There were fights morning, noon, and night, and whining, teasing, tantrums, and pouts in between. Amy wet her pants an average of three times a day, not counting wetting her bed, and I didn't know what to do. I spanked her and scolded her, hugged her, and told her that it was okay, she couldn't help it. I finally threatened her, telling her she couldn't come if she didn't stop. That worked a little bit, cutting her accidents down to one a day.

The very worst day of all came, of course, the day we were to leave. It was a microcosm of the most exasperating and horrifying moments of the past seven months, culminating with Amy's throwing rocks at a neighborhood boy. The girls' excitement was uncontrollable, and by an hour before we were supposed to leave so was my temper. I unleashed all my pent-up fury and frustrations of the last few weeks, and perhaps months, in a brief but loud explosion that left me hoarse, Leslie and Jennifer subdued, and Amy with a sore behind.

A few minutes before we were to leave, I heard Jennifer on the porch, scolding in a singsong high-pitched voice.

"If you aren't a good dolly, you can't come to the Grand Canyon with us. You are a naughty, naughty dolly, and I am very mad at you." She was sitting in the sun, slapping her baby doll rhythmically on its fanny. I didn't know whether to laugh or cry.

"What's the matter, Jenny? Have you got a problem with your doll?"

"My dolly is very naughty today, and I have to spank her so that she can come to the Grand Canyon." It seemed perfectly logical to her, and I realized in a way I never had before how powerful my example was. We discussed it for a few moments, then Jenny decided to give her baby another chance, maybe trying to tell me that I should do the same with them.

It was done. We were on time, ready to go, clean, packed, and polished. I stuffed the packs and paraphernalia into the car, tucked the girls into the remaining spaces, locked the front door of our little house, and we were off.

As we boarded the plane for Oklahoma City I was pleased to be part of the "parents with small children first" group, too exhausted to fight the crush of a fully booked 747. Amy was full of questions, about how planes fly, the airport activities, where we were going, what we were doing—a child's boundless curiosity about things she didn't know as well as endless other questions, most of which she knew the answers to.

I sat between Jennifer and Amy, who had pleaded for the window seat, with Leslie, grownup, across the aisle by herself.

As the plane began to taxi out, Amy had her nose glued up against the window, giggling a deep excited giggle as she felt the plane move beneath her.

"We're goin', we're goin'—oh, oh!" The plane pulled onto the runway, and the engines began to roar. Jenny squeezed my hand tightly, startled at the noise but quiet, and Amy began a crescendo of "oohs" as the airplane gathered momentum that ended in a shriek when she realized that she was no longer firmly on the ground.

197

"Oh, oh, oh, ooh, ooh, *ooooh!*" I reached over and clapped my hand over her mouth as she reached high C.

"Quiet down, Amy," I hissed. As she turned to look at me, reproach in her brown eyes now luminous with tears, I realized exactly what was wrong. Brave Amy, bold Amy, daring Amy, was a very frightened little girl. I felt awful.

"I'm sorry, Amy Rose. Why didn't you tell me you were afraid?" She just shrugged, and wiped her tears with the back of her hand, turning once again to look out the window. Now safely up in the air, she was fine.

The children were delighted and distracted with their airline trays, confiscated salts, peppers, and the stirrers from the Bloody Marys I thought I needed to get through the day. It seemed to be another case where my level of anxiety and anguish far exceeded what the situation required. With the exception of Amy's terrified takeoff, all three were marvelous, sitting prettily, amusing themselves quietly, in direct contrast to another family several rows behind, whose children were running up and down the aisle and shouting across the plane at each other. Even Amy noticed the difference.

"Aren't those kids noisy? We're not noisy like that. Aren't we good? You wouldn't let us get away with that. You're strict!" She grinned at me, and I thought about the day before. I think she might have been thinking about it, too.

21

Two days of driving through country I had never seen before, and watching the flat Texas plains first become rolling hills, then the rocky mountains of New Mexico, was calming and brought me a sense of peace. We stayed an extra day at our first campsite, next to an energetic icy mountain stream, because I was violently ill for twenty-four hours, waking the next morning weak but purged of the final bit of sourness from my soul.

The five of us finally had the opportunity to be alone with nothing but each other. We had reduced our life to its most elemental state, so that we could be without distractions and interference. At this point in our history we had never done that—there were school, friends, Roberta, the divorce, business—always something. Perhaps we even created some of the diversions rather than have to deal directly with each other. But for most of this whole vacation we had no choice, and it's probably been the most important two weeks of our lives together.

The second morning in Taos I awoke to the sun filtering through the trees, the sounds of breakfast and the smell of coffee, everyone trying carefully not to disturb me. When I peeked surreptitiously out of the tent, I saw Leslie deep in conversation with her father, Amy trying to skip stones across the stream, and Jennifer chirping and flitting about. I had one of my flashes of pride and gratitude, and rose to meet the day and our life feeling renewed.

It was a long hot drive through Arizona and around to the North Rim of the Grand Canyon. The road gave evidence of death and life—a carcass by the side of the road, or buzzards circling over a heap out in the pasture, but a mile away, or in the next field, a mother nursed her young, or nudged her newborn colt to stand on wobbly legs. Yet the girls were too overwhelmed to enjoy the fantastic scenery around them. They would raise their heads for an occasional peek at an animal, but refused to look at the mountains and the gorges that followed one after the other.

There were no campsites left in Grand Canyon Park when we arrived, and it took five tries to find a ranger who would arrange for us to hike the fourteen miles down the trail from the North Rim to the Colorado River, two adults, three young children, and all their camping gear. We made our reservations for a campsite at Cottonwood, seven miles down Bright Angel Trail—seven miles straight down. Moreover, we could only get the site for one night, two days later.

"How are we going to make it down to the river if we only camp one night?" I said. "That means we'd have to hike twenty-one miles the second day if we're to get down to the river and back out to the top. We'd be dead before we made it."

But nothing as simple as a logistics problem ever fazed Stanley.

"Don't worry. We'll figure something out." And he went on making arrangements for the first available space.

We spent the interim camped on the edge of a cliff overlooking the canyon and the winding snakelike ribbon of a river that had slowly cut through the layers of rock and shale. The mornings were hazy, and then the sun would burn off the mist, leaving a hot cloudless sky until the midafternoon rain showers.

"Daddy, Mommy, I want to talk to you about something that's been bothering me." It was Leslie, who had seemed slightly uneasy and restless the last day or two. "It's pretty private." Amy, with her unerring sense of knowing when she is not wanted, joined the group.

"Hi." She traced lines in the dust with a stick, and didn't look at any of us directly.

"Go play with Jenny," I said, pointing over to where Jennifer was not quite dangerously close to the edge. "Go ahead." I patted her rear gently, and pushed her in the direction that I wanted her to go.

"But I want to stay here," she whined.

"Leslie wants a private talk," Stan interjected, "so you go play with Jen for a while."

"I want to talk, too," she said, eyes still dropped. "I have private things to say."

"Well, we'll talk with you later, Amy, okay? About whatever is on your mind. But now it's Leslie's turn." She sulked away, and positioned herself so that she could keep an eye on us.

"I don't know how to tell you this." I couldn't imagine what Leslie wanted to say. She picked up the stick that Amy had dropped and traced circles over Amy's lines.

"It's about my mother." We waited, and watched her eyes fill up with tears.

"I mean . . . I mean . . . well . . ." Neither of us wanted to push her into saying anything, nor were we really sure what she wanted to talk about. "You see, I don't think my mother really loves us. Or cares about us. She doesn't do all the things that you do for us, Mommy, you know, make us breakfast, or teach us manners . . . and . . . well, she doesn't seem to have any time for us anymore." She was trying hard not to cry.

"Is that since she's been friends with Joellyn?" Stan probed a little bit deeper. She nodded.

"She never did, but it's more now. That's another thing that bothers me. A while ago they had a party, and they were dancing together. But not disco, you know? And I've seen them kissing and holding hands." She began to sob. "I don't understand it, Daddy. What does it mean? Isn't that a bad thing to do? Sometimes we think she loves Joellyn more than she loves us. But that's not true, is it?"

For one of the few times in our lives, we were both at a loss for words. I reached out for the crying Leslie, and left the rest to Stan. We had been so foolish to imagine we could leave the more troubling and difficult aspects of our life behind.

"Of course she loves you, Leslie. I'm sure she loves you. But that's something that has always been difficult for her, showing people she cares about them. And loving one person doesn't mean you don't love someone else. I spend a lot of time with Mary, and I love her very much, but that doesn't mean I don't love you or Amy or Jennifer."

"But that's different. You're a man, and Mary's a woman. Mommy and Joellyn are both women. And I think it's awful. So does Carolyn." Carolyn was one of her closest friends in school.

"Carolyn? Did you tell Carolyn about it?" I was appalled that she would share this with a fourth-grade friend.

"She was there the first time I noticed it. She asked me why they sat so close on the couch, and slept in a bedroom with only one bed. I said they were good friends, and my mom could do whatever she wanted." She squared her shoulders and stuck her chin out the way she must have done that terrible day with Carolyn.

The tears came again. "Then one day I saw a letter from my mom to Joellyn. I couldn't help it, honest. It was right out on the dresser. I didn't sneak around to see it. Honest." Leslie eyed us nervously, expecting chastisement.

"We know that, Leslie. But what upset you so much?" I hoped I sounded reassuring.

"It . . . it . . . it said . . . 'I love you, Jodie'—that's what Mommy calls her—and it was signed Bobbi. Daddy . . ." She had regained her composure by now. "Daddy, is my mom a lesbian?"

Stan in his wisdom launched into a gentle dissertation on homosexuality, not condemning it, not supporting it, but presenting it as an option that some people choose because they are uncomfortable with conventional relationships. I thought it too much for a ten-year-old, but Leslie drank in every word, and seemed to understand. She even offered some childlike insight of her own.

"Is that one of the reasons why you and Mommy got divorced?"

"That's right. That had a lot to do with it." He spoke sadly of the years, even before Leslie was born, when he had had fantasies of what love and marriage should be, and tried vainly to make them a reality. "I really wanted it to work, Leslie. I really tried to love her enough. It just wasn't what she wanted."

Leslie was leaning up against me, so I couldn't walk away, although I wanted to. It was extraordinarily painful to listen to my love speak with such feeling about the years he had spent with another woman, trying so hard to create the kind of life and love that for all its ups and downs we had slipped into so easily. I felt very lonely as I sat gazing at one of the seven wonders of the world. Millions of years had carved out this great gorge and left the ledge on which we found ourselves discussing some of the harsher realities of life with a frightened, confused child.

The appointed day for our big venture came, and we savored every morsel of breakfast in preparation for the freeze-dried diet of the days ahead. We adjusted packs, repacked, and readjusted packs, procrastinating under the guise of careful preparation. Stan refilled the water bottles we had filled two hours before, and I checked shoes and socks to make sure that three pairs of sensitive feet wouldn't blister. Finally came the point when there was nothing left to do but set out on the seven-mile trail to the Cottonwood campground, halfway between the North Rim and the bottom of the Grand Canyon.

It was a strenuous descent—ten grueling hours—and when we finally reached the campground we were hot, sweaty, and too exhausted to be hungry. The camp ranger showed us to our site, where the three girls sank to the ground. They looked as if they never wanted to move again. Neither did I. But Stan persuaded us to wade to our knees in the stream of mountain water that was rushing down to meet the mighty Colorado below, and that revived me enough to hydrate our sumptuous feast of freeze-dried chicken and minute rice, with blueberry cobbler for dessert. It also revived my family enough to eat it.

The ranger arranged to let us have the campsite for a second night; we were all convinced that the girls needed a day's rest before hiking back up to the rim. Stan and I spent that day trekking the fourteen miles to the muddy Colorado and back while the girls regained their strength.

The next day was a slow hot climb up the winding trail out of the canyon, and we vacillated between exhaustion, bickering and gaiety, but cycling our moods among ourselves so that there was always somebody cheering the rest on.

Amy, without a doubt, got the prize for courage. Her complaints were few, and it was our problem that we let her pace frustrate and irritate us. She deserved a medal for letting herself be pushed beyond what could fairly be expected of a six-year-old.

Jennifer entertained herself by babbling in squirrel, or kitten, or puppy, or bird, and actually skipped along the path. Once, when we were halfway to the top and I was almost afraid to hear her answer, I asked, "How are you doing, Jennifer?"

"Oh, I'm fine, Mommy, I'm fine. My feet hurt and my tummy hurts and my head hurts and I'm veeeery tired, but that's all." And she skipped again, this time pretending that she was a baby lamb.

Leslie was our Sakajawea. As we began to peter out two miles from the top, she ran ahead to the next marker, doubling back to lend encouragement. She, too, never complained.

Stan carried Jenny from time to time, and all the way by the last mile. We could see angry thunderheads building up, and we wanted to reach the top before the rains came or the sun set. I was the last one off the trail, and we beat both the rain and sundown, but barely. Stan offered to carry my pack the last half mile, but I wouldn't let him. I had come this far, and I had to finish—without help.

We had made it. Dinner at the lodge was our only "fancy" meal of the vacation, steak all around. Stan had two. We ate hungrily and triumphantly, having accomplished what we set out to do, and having kept our promise to the girls to their satisfaction. I gazed over Stan's shoulder out the window at where we had been not too long before, watching the wind-whipped rain and the lightning brightening the sky like a network of electric nerves. I wondered what it was like now on our narrow little trail.

The last adventure of our vacation was a backpack excursion into the San Juan Mountains of Colorado. It was the most horrendous twenty-four hours of the entire trip, and worse in fact than any we had had before we left home.

Amy was at her worst, or at her best if one was evaluating her ability to be provocative, derisive, infuriating, belligerent, obstreperous, and recalcitrant. She wet her pants while she was awake, and she wet them while she slept. She knocked the dinner off the camp stove and dropped a pair of gray woolen hiking socks into the burning embers of the campfire.

I was grateful when the blessed peace of the mountains and the starry night finally settled over the meadow where we had pitched our tents.

But nine hours of sleep refreshed her more than me, and she started off the day by pushing Jennifer into the water (for which she got spanked), calling Leslie a "fuck-face" (for which she almost got her mouth washed out with green biodegradable soap), and asking a dozen tortuous, tormenting questions over and over.

Stan and I were both struggling with facing the reality of dealing with Amy and her problems, or what was worse, finding ourselves unable to deal with them. We seemed to have been making much headway, but since the days before our vacation started—except for her efforts on the Canyon trail—she had been slipping farther and farther back, and neither one of us knew what to do. Stan for the first time seemed acutely aware not only of the way Amy behaved, but also of the probable impairment of her social growth and adjustment if he couldn't help her change. I knew that physical punishment wasn't the answer, and screaming at her only gave me a sore throat and made her sullen; yet loving her—well, she often interpreted that as a license to do what she pleased.

We escaped for an hour's hike, needing a respite, trying not to think of what havoc Amy might be wreaking in our absence. We approached camp silently, catching the girls unaware.

"You just wait till they get here, Amy. Are you going to get it!" Leslie was barely audible over Jennifer's crying.

"If you tell, I'm really gonna punch you out, Leslie. I'm gonna give you an Indian burn, and maybe break your arm." If I didn't know Amy for big brown eyes, roses in her round warm cheeks, and a little two-pint body, I'd have expected a black leather motorcycle jacket and a switchblade knife.

"*She* won't let you get away with that. And you know it." I heard a slap. We entered the clearing just in time to see Amy slug Leslie after Leslie slugged Amy after Amy had given Leslie the slap we heard.

"Amy Rose, go inside the tent, and wait for me until I've talked to Leslie and Jennifer," Stan said tightly. "Then, and only then, maybe I will talk to you. I promised you this morning if you misbehaved you'd be in trouble. Get in there!" Amy ran to her tent, casting fearful glances over her shoulder.

Leslie and Jennifer tripped over each other, jumbling their words and sentences, in an effort to recount their trials of the past hour. Stanley listened intently to their tearful story. I had more than half tuned out their tale of woe. It was an old familiar story to me anyway. By the end, the girls were exhausted, having drained their frustrations on a new and very attentive audience. They were also a little nervous, because they could see a look of resolve and determination on their father's face the likes of which they had never seen before. Stan got up and slowly walked toward the Jansport tent, the tent that Amy never missed a chance to remind me he had used when he camped with Roberta. Amy was lying on the ground peeking through the flap to try to puzzle out her fate.

We couldn't hear his words from where we sat, but the sound of his voice was illuminated by fiery fingers of electricity in the air, and Amy's cries of anguish were drowned out by hollow rolling thunder. The coincidental and sudden storm brought a violent whipping rain, with lightning lighting up the sky and resounding cannon booms, like the finale of a good old-fashioned Fourth of July fireworks celebration.

The rainstorm probably didn't last ten minutes, but for each of those ten minutes, under the cover of nature and the tent, my gentle, tolerant Stanley let his middle daughter know exactly how it made him feel to see her go out of her way to make people angry at her, how it made him feel to see her hurt other people, and how much he wanted her to change. He was as angry, I believe, with himself for fathering a child who had so much trouble dealing with life, and not fathering her enough to help her overcome her difficulties, as he was with Amy Rose for being so difficult, and the Doomsday chorus that God was providing from above was a fitting accompaniment to a momentous occasion.

All her short life Amy had been pushing and testing the people closest to her, as well as strangers, because she was looking for response, attention, affection, and not getting them. She needed people to like her and love her in spite of her problems; she needed to feel that someone really cared about the kind of person she was, and the kind of person she would grow up to be. Stanley had told her how much he loved her before, yelled at her and swatted her before, but never really communicated the depth of his concern for her. It must have been terribly important to Amy to finally realize that her father, whom she was afraid she might lose entirely through the divorce, cared so much about her. The wild hunted look began to leave her eyes, and the two storms that happened that day are as bright in my memory as the sunlight that followed the rain.

The rest of the vacation was anticlimactic, and the few days of summer that remained were peaceful and serene. Stan had assumed a new stature in all his daughters' eyes after his concert with the Almighty, and he had in mine as well. My ability to tolerate, care for, and deal with his daughters was enhanced just by the fact that I was no longer operating in a vacuum. Now when I bitched and ranted and raved about this or that childish transgression, Stanley would at least listen to me, and, on occasion, even be less tolerant than I.

The summer ended with our having reached a milestone in familial understanding, but nothing else had changed. I had visions of Fridays down to Camden, Saturdays to Mrs. Unger, Monday mornings back to school, and still no divorce in sight. I had tried to wangle a private Labor Day weekend with my love to recoup from the trials of the summer before the trials of the winter began, but without success. The girls begged to stay until the very last day of their vacation, with wide eyes and tears, and Stan thought it a perfect way to end the summer. I didn't have the heart to burst their balloons.

22

Early in September, Stanley and I moved into our first "together" house. I decided to rent rather than sell my house in Mount Tabor; keeping it was like an insurance policy in case things didn't work out, and helped me maintain my sense of independence. Our new home was a lovely eighteenth-century farmhouse in central New Jersey, on a secluded acre not far from the center of the village. I don't think Washington ever slept there, but he probably rode by it on his way between camping out in Jockey Hollow and crossing the Delaware during the American Revolution.

Mr. Partekamp checked it out, and his pronouncement on this house, which came within our budget because of a new employment agreement that Stan signed with Barry, was much more favorable than that on the white elephant. The columns on the porch had a little bit of dryrot, and the gabled roof looked soft in a few places, but it was basically sound. And beautiful. The yard had enough space for Jennifer to ride her Wheelie safely, Amy to ride her bike, and Leslie to play with her friends. The town school system was good, an essential, as Stan was certain he would pursue custody someday and it soothed him to know that there would be lovely bedrooms for the girls, and the ivy-covered schoolhouse for grades one through eight was close enough for them to walk to should it ever come to pass that they would live with us.

Over the course of the summer, "coming to live with us" had become the stock conversation, replacing "why Daddy and Mommy got the divorce." Stan told them always how much he wanted them to be with us all the time, how much I wanted them to be with us all the time. And I didn't argue the point. Despite the fact I cared deeply for the girls, I wasn't really ready to devote myself to them on a full-time basis, and wasn't sure if I ever would be. But I knew if Stan really wanted to bring them into our home on a permanent basis, absolutely nothing, including me, would stop him.

The girls would say, when he asked them, that they didn't know where they wanted to live—or with whom. Jennifer once told me that she wished we lived in a big apartment house, and her daddy and I could live in one apartment, and her mommy could live across the hall. Then the kids could just go back and forth as they pleased.

"Or you and Daddy could buy a great big house, and we could all live there together. But not Joellyn. That would be best of all." How blissfully naive childhood can be. I patiently explained that it wouldn't work, and why. She sadly seemed to understand.

Leslie was afraid that to come and live with us would make Roberta feel that they didn't love her anymore, and would make her so mad at them that she wouldn't love them. Amy seemed on the whole to prefer to keep things the way they were. "My mom's not as strict as Mary. I don't like it so strict."

The purchase of our house created a subtle change in our relationship with my parents. Before the closing, we invited them to see the house and then have dinner with us to celebrate our good fortune at finding such a jewel. They found us sitting on the front steps as they drove up the winding driveway. I could see their eyes widen in surprise at the very substantial clapboard house, with its neat shutters and gracious columns on the full-length porch, shaded by Japanese maples and spruce. An honest-to-God home rather than a place to shack up.

We didn't have the key yet, so we just let them peek into as many windows as they could, while we extrolled the attributes

and virtues of the two-hundred-year-old beauty. They didn't
say much, but I sensed my father was impressed. He carefully
avoided the question of whose house it actually was, though
wondering, I'm sure, whether or not our situation was simply
going to reverse, with me living in Stanley's house instead of
Stanley in mine. Always (well, almost always) sensitive to other
people's needs, Stan sensed his future father-in-law's uneasiness,
and in that way that only he can do, went right to the heart of
the matter, no prompting, no preamble.

"The house is in Mary's name, too, Joe, not just mine," Stan
assured him. "We plan on getting married as soon as possible,
but even before that, I want to make some visible commitment
to Mary, so that she—and you—know just how serious I am. I
think she knows." He turned to me and smiled. "But you might
still have your doubts. I hope this will put them to rest." Both
my father and mother colored slightly, but my father muttered
gruffly that he didn't have any qualms about Stan's sincerity,
he was just concerned about how hard the wait might be on
me.

It was one of the first times I ever heard my father clearly
voice his concern about me. I had always known deep down
that my father loved me, and he had, in the best way he knew
how, been a good father. But I was only beginning to realize
how important it was for parents and children to *share* feelings,
and how much pain and misunderstanding he and I might have
spared each other if we had done so earlier.

Although the episode with Amy on our last backpack marked
the beginning of the end of Stanley's passivity about the care
and discipline of his daughters, his growing assertiveness did not
yet extend to his dealings with Roberta.

I was still elected to do the ferrying that I dreaded, although,
to my amazement and pleasure, Stan often accompanied me either
going or coming; the hour and a half of quiet time we thus had
together became another of the cherished interludes in our relationship. The move to our new house should have brought us
about twenty minutes closer to the girls, but Roberta's move

into Joellyn's house in Camden actually increased my net trip by half an hour. Moving into our new old house, as well as Stan's effort to keep me company, had made me feel benevolent toward him, however, and I cheerfully performed the taxi duty that he so detested. (It wasn't the long ride he hated, but the fact that it usually resulted in some kind of exchange, vituperative on her part, exasperatedly patient on his, with Bobbi.)

During this glorious fall I watched the leaves on our Japanese maples turn purple and flutter to the ground like feathers, and watched my "daughters" romp in the hot Indian-summer sun. I ran a sleepover party for six ten-year-olds who came to me at two o'clock in the morning to ask for the facts of life their own mothers thought they were too young to hear, but which Leslie had assured them that I, different from "other mothers," would be delighted to impart. I planted tulips and daffodils for the coming spring and played at being mistress of my new house, always feeling a little bit like saying that my mother wasn't home when someone came to the door. And these were the same glorious fall days during which Roberta and I cemented for all time our nonrelationship.

We had come back from the Grand Canyon expecting to hear good things from Jack, who had told us early in the summer that he was going to proceed with the filing of the divorce. We anticipated a smooth and rapid execution, considering that he and Bobbi's lawyer were friends. What we came back to instead was indeed the innocuous no-fault decree that Stan in his generosity and decency toward Roberta and natural reluctance at airing dirty linen had had Jack file. But what was also awaiting us was a lengthy diatribe in the form of a countersuit, charging Stanley with adultery, mental cruelty, desertion, and a few other things as well. Roberta, too, had switched lawyers, this time on principle hiring a woman and leaving us with a twenty-five-hundred-dollar bill from her first lawyer and God knew what from the second.

Stan was his usual silent, stoic self, but I was absolutely livid, since it looked as if things would now drag out interminably. I vowed that I would no longer give my parents any possible timetable, no matter how much they pressured us, because it was too embarrassing to keep telling them that things had changed again. The worst of it all was that we still weren't getting married, not because we so chose but because Roberta seemed to be doing everything possible to prevent it, with all the venom of a woman scorned.

But finally even Stan had his fill of delays. He fired Jack and hired his consultant lawyer, Joe Glavin, who had helped him muddle through finalizing his separation agreement several months before. We were both hopeful that this would move matters along.

Insulated somewhat from the never-ending tumult in which we seemed to live, the children were absorbed in their own activities. That fall Leslie was a cheerleader for her school's soccer team, and every weekend was filled with endless practice of leaps and jumps and chants and cheers, not to mention splits and flips. She conducted weekly classes in the driveway, teaching Amy and Jennifer and any neighborhood children who cared to join, "Hey hey, what do you say . . ." with the accompanying gyrations.

Her first soccer game was on a Wednesday afternoon after school, and she wanted us to come. When I found out that someone other than Roberta—Leslie didn't know who—was to come by to pick her up at four o'clock after the game, I decided to attend and play mother to my quasi-daughter's cheerleading debut.

The team lost the game six to nothing, and the five girls on the squad were as disorganized and unsynchronized as only ten-year-old cheerleaders can be. I sat on the sidelines with Mrs. Anderson, her teacher, and she introduced me to the other mothers as Leslie's mother. "That's the way she thinks of you," Mrs. Anderson said conspiratorially, "and it's easier that way." It was certainly easier than "stepmother-to-be," as I characterized myself, and I liked hearing my new name even if it wasn't yet mine.

Four o'clock came and went, Leslie and I sitting on the front steps of the locked school, all the other children gone, and Mrs. Anderson visibly relieved that there was someone besides herself to wait with Leslie for her ride home.

"I know someone is coming for me. My mom told me so. She said she was busy, but one of her friends would come." Leslie's eyes were worried, though, and she was twisting her hair around her index finger nervously, glancing down the driveway, and avoiding my eyes.

"Someone will be here soon, I'm sure." I put my arm around her shoulder and squeezed her reassuringly, although I wasn't reassured myself.

Five o'clock, and no sign of a living soul. Six o'clock, and it was too dark and too chilly to sit around outside any longer. But I wasn't about to drive Leslie to Camden. "Let's go," I finally said. "It's too late to wait—I have to get home, and you are going to come with me, because you can't sit here in the dark alone. We'll stop on the way and call." Leslie called at the first pay phone we came across, but the line was busy.

We stopped at a diner and had a cheeseburger apiece. The line was still busy. It was after nine by the time we got home, and the first thing I did was call Stan, who was in Boston overnight.

"What else could you have done?" He sounded understanding. "I'd have done the same thing. And besides, Leslie sounds really happy, and is having a good time. Don't worry about it."

She *had* had a good time. So had I. We'd talked about school, and her girlfriends, and Jack, the boy in her class whom she liked, and who she hoped liked her. She talked about the clothes she needed, and what she wanted to be when she grew up. And she talked at great length, and with great maturity, about her mother and Joellyn and their relationship, and how that made her feel.

"I can't bring people home—it's too embarrassing. I don't want my friends to know. They tease me on the bus.

"And some of the kids won't play with me. Their mothers won't let them play with me, because they are afraid that I'm a lesbian too. Am I? Will I be? How do I know?" She twisted the strand of hair tighter and tighter.

By the time we got settled at home and she'd talked to her father she was in jolly spirits again, but when she finally spoke to Roberta she wasn't prepared for the telephone tirade that her mother directed, first at her for coming with me, and then at me for taking her. Once again she threatened to beat me up. "I'd like to kill you," she said. It was never clear through her rage whether or not we were supposed to have waited together on the cold marble steps for the friend who never came, or whether I should have left Leslie there alone. So once I realized that I wouldn't be able to cut through her irrationality, I simply hung up.

Maybe I should have stayed on the phone. The next day Stan got a call from Glavin informing him that Bobbi had accused me of kidnapping, and would have pressed charges had Leslie not been in school the next morning. Her attorney had also informed the headmistress in no uncertain terms that under no circumstances was I to be permitted to pick up Leslie.

I was furious. Furious that she would and could exercise such control over my activities, and furious at Stanley because once again, he shrugged it off with a "What can we do?"

On the other hand, I was delighted that I now had an ironclad excuse for not doing what was becoming more and more tedious: going to Camden on Fridays to pick up the kids. And I didn't.

23

Christmas turned out to be the best of times and the worst of times. We had planned a Christmas around the girls, and began a family tradition by going to my aunt's Christmas-tree farm in South Jersey. With much consultation and examination, Leslie, Amy, and Jennifer finally decided on a gargantuan specimen, which took up a third of our twenty-foot-long dining room. It never got decorated.

Roberta decided that the children should not be allowed to visit us over Christmas vacation.

"Christmas is a family time, and Joellyn and I are their family. I won't let them go," she said, despite the fact that visitation rights in the separation agreement (more aptly titled a separation dispute) clearly called for split holiday times.

Glavin sympathized with Stan and told him that he could initiate court action to enforce the visitation, but by the time it could be settled, he counseled, school would be starting again and there would be no vacation to share. We were at a loss what to do.

Stan had some of his first genuinely hard-headed clashes with Bobbi over that Christmas, but she wouldn't budge an inch.

Roberta's attitude increased the distance between her and the girls because they couldn't understand her anger and hostility. From where they sat, Daddy was happy with Mary, and Daddy and Mary both loved them and wanted what was best for them and made them happiest. Roberta seemed happy too, with Joellyn, so why was she so mad at Daddy? "And why," they would say, with insight, "does it always feel like when she won't let us see you, it's because she wants to hurt you, Daddy? She makes us stay there, and then she goes away and leaves us with a baby-sitter, or else they have parties that they say are for kids and only invite grownups." Even at their young ages, they were most articulate in expressing that it didn't feel to them as if their mother really loved them. They wanted her to, and they hoped she did, so they would pretend it was so because otherwise it was too painful.

When it became clear to us that we had no hope of seeing the children without the heated argument that Stan always avoided and the house began to echo with their absence, we made hurried plans to go away right after Christmas. We took a bargain flight to Luxembourg and ended up in Paris, in a twenty-six-dollar-a-day three-room suite, at the Hotel Colbert, two blocks from the Seine, and through the gabled window of our eight-foot-square sitting room we had a clear view of the rose window in Notre Dame Cathedral. It was a cold, blustery, and rainy two weeks that we stole, walking the streets, the Tuileries, and the Jardin du Luxembourg, finding none of the French's arrogance toward Americans that we had expected to encounter.

It was also two weeks of exploring each other in new and different ways, a time very different from our hectic Haiti trip when we had almost frantically tried both to develop our relationship and avoid each other at the same time. In Paris we were tranquil, sleeping till eight, making love until ten, then walking the few blocks to a café on the Boulevard St. Michel. Two cups of café au lait and a few croissants later we were ready to face another day exploring and sitting in cafés or on park benches reading books we bought from Shakespeare and Company. We'd end the day at Deux Magots imagining Simone de Beauvoir and Jean-Paul Sartre sipping café or apértifs at a corner table.

We celebrated New Year's Eve at a Vivaldi concert in the oldest church in Paris, and inspired by the Louvre and the Jeu de Paume, spent a rainy, dreary, happy day painting and proving to ourselves that our attempts at creativity would never hang with the masters.

When it was finally and regretfully time to go home, we hired a car and drove through the French countryside north to Luxembourg, past concrete pill boxes, and fields once again fertile after the ravages of the war. Icelandic Airlines cooperated with mechanical failures, and God with a blizzard, so we managed to stretch our vacation out another day. We walked in the soft snowfall on that gift of a night, and I began to recognize the tension building up in my muscles and my gut as the time approached to return to the minor and major inconveniences of our existence. I realized how truly glad I had been to have these two weeks alone with Stan, away from his demanding daughters and his still-not-quite-ex-wife. And it delighted me no end that her attempt to ruin our Christmas backfired, providing us with one of our sweetest times of all.

It took another two weeks and several tough calls to Roberta's lawyer before we saw the girls again. The lack of visitation took its toll of Stan, who missed them terribly, and took its toll of the children, who are the ones who suffered most from Roberta's plots to keep them from seeing or talking to their father. On the other hand, I selfishly enjoyed every moment of my unexpected freedom to the fullest. It was always a joy to go through a weekend without having to do laundry or plan regular meals or referee juvenile spats, while pretending that Stan and I were alone and unfettered. But then I began to miss the girls too, and was looking forward to celebrating Amy's seventh birthday with a cake that, at her request, would be in the shape of a ballerina.

Several times that January I went with my sister Lacey and Raish to Columbia Presbyterian Babies' Hospital in New York, for his transfusions and chemotherapy treatments. Only six weeks away from his seventh birthday, his body swollen from disease and medicines, Raish still tried to appear placid and reassuring to those around him.

He was lying on a stretcher in the clinic, plasma IV dripping into a needle inserted in a vein in the bruised crook of his elbow. It was lunchtime.

"I want some cereal." It was a whisper, and an effort to speak.

"What kind?"

"The kind with the sugar that crinkles."

"I'll go and get you some," I volunteered, wanting to go anywhere to get him anything.

"You don't know what kind I mean," Raish said with mild exasperation. "You won't get it fast enough."

"Sugar Frosted Flakes with Tony the Tiger, right?" I smiled as brightly as I could, and was delighted at the answering lopsided grin.

"How did you know?"

"I just did. See you soon."

It took me longer than I thought to find a supermarket and then to get through the express lane that was so slow, but I came back with his Frosted Flakes and some Yankee Doodles, another favorite. Lacey went to get him some milk.

"How are you doing, babe?" I asked, catching the worried expression in his sick eyes, half-hypnotized by the drip-drip movement of the life-sustaining plasma.

"Fine." I was reminded of Jennifer in the Grand Canyon, only Raish's struggle was not to get to the top of the canyon, but to survive. I don't think anybody had talked to him about what he was facing, or about death, but he knew.

Lacey didn't want to celebrate his birthday early, hoping that by going about life as usual she could postpone the inevitable.

"But, Mommy," he said to her one day, "I have to have my birthday presents now. My birthday's too late. There isn't any time."

He was right. The last weekend of his life was gray and somber, like my mood. We had the girls with us, but I couldn't stand the sound of their voices. On Saturday I went into New York alone; he had been readmitted to the hospital.

There were a lot of people there, my parents, and some of Lacey's in-laws, some of her friends. Lacey was sitting by Raish's bed. My cousin, Father Henry, a Jesuit priest, dropped by. We talked for a few moments about unimportant things, until at last he stooped to give my nephew the sacrament of the dying, as he had given him the sacrament of baptism just after he was born.

I came to the side of the bed, and held Raish's hand as Henry prayed what are supposed to be comforting prayers, and anointed his head with oil. The room was dim, and through my tears, I saw the nave of St. Joseph's Church where nearly seven years before, as his godmother, I had held Raish in my arms as Henry prayed and anointed him with the first sacrament of life.

When I got home, I couldn't even talk to Stanley. I couldn't look at his kids, not when we thought it was practically impossible to have our own, and my godson, the closest thing to a child of my own I might ever have, was dying. I stayed up all night cleaning and scrubbing and waxing and polishing. Sunday I was still toiling away, feeling more and more frantic, more and more helpless. I called my mother, and she said there was no change, but I was too agitated to stay home. I told Stan I was going back to the hospital, and he insisted on taking me in. We got a baby-sitter on the third try, and drove to New York in the cold January drizzle.

There were hardly any visitors at all, and Lacey was, I think, glad to see us. The nurse just shook her head at Stan and me when we met her in the hall, and after spending a few minutes with Lacey and her husband, Stan left to pick up the girls and drive them to Camden. Raish's breathing was getting more and more labored, and the doctor gave him oxygen. He pushed it away.

"No," he said. "I don't want that. Please. I don't want that." And they didn't try to give it to him anymore.

One time he reached out to his mother. "Mama, Mama. Help me." She held him close, and the tears rolled down her cheeks, onto his head. "Don't cry, Mama. Please don't cry. I love you."

"What? What did you say?" She hadn't been able to hear him clearly, his voice muffled against her breast.

"I love you." They were the last words I heard him speak.

Stan had been gone not quite long enough to have gotten to Camden when my sister and her husband came out of Raish's room. Their drained faces told me Raish was gone. Lacey told me I could go in to see him if I wanted. He lay curiously peaceful, as if grateful that his ordeal was over. I touched his hand, still warm, and glanced about the room at the array of toys, cars, games, and posters that he had wanted, that people had felt he needed to distract him from his reality. I wanted to take something as a keepsake from my godson, but I didn't. I just left, and prayed all the way home I'd never have to watch one of my own little chickadees suffer as he had suffered.

In the depression that followed Raish's death, some of the doubts my parents had generated over the last year and a half began to lurk in the recesses of my mind, and I grew more and more fidgety as the months went by.

Did Stan really want to marry me? He had now assumed control of all the interactions with his attorney. Was this because he was changing, and taking charge, or because he wanted to prolong his freedom, and the wedding, as much as possible? I had no way of telling. He was always sweet, tender, and caring toward me, and as always, I thought, a little too considerate of Roberta, given the way she had treated him, and me. But he always denied vehemently ever wanting to go back and resume life with her again. There was little I could do but believe him until he proved otherwise.

The first hearing for the divorce was set, wonder of wonders, for the first week of May. Roberta had it postponed.

The second hearing was set for May 21. Roberta had that postponed too.

The third hearing was set for the second week in June, just before we were to pick up the girls for the summer. Once again, Roberta postponed the hearing.

The judge went on vacation until August.

I was as close to a nervous breakdown as I ever want to get.

I was getting angrier and angrier at Roberta for the control that she was exerting on my life, and more and more nervous that, once the divorce actually took place, I would have to, God forbid, get married. I realized at last that the past two years had been a wonderful continuation of my history of getting involved but never committing myself. For two years I had been able to say, "Well, of course we want to get married, but his divorce isn't final yet." Once the judge swung that gavel, I would have very little choice but to go through with it.

Angry and ambivalent, I decided that I wasn't going to do anything to make Roberta's life easier while she was making mine so miserable, and that included baby-sitting *her* kids all summer so she and her lady love could go gallivanting around the country on Stanley's alimony. And I told Stanley so in no uncertain terms. "No wedding, no summer visitation."

He tried to soften me up with a camping trip along the craggy coast of Maine, where we were captivated by the lobster-fishing village of Cutler and purchased a home on the harbor that was aching to be loved. "We'll retire here someday, it's an investment in our future," he persuaded me, and since we'd just sold my house in Mount Tabor, having found it impossible to rent, I agreed. But I didn't change my mind about the girls.

We fought and we argued and I cried. "There is no way I am going to take care of her kids all summer. You'll have to think of something else."

"But, Marila," he said and sighed, "they are my children too."

"I don't care," I said, beside myself with frustration. "If she only lets you see the kids when it's convenient for her, I'm not going to do anything to help her out. She calls me a nonentity, and I'm not good enough for her precious darlings, but when she wants to go off cross-country all summer, then I'm mighty convenient. Nothing doing. You make other arrangements, because those kids aren't coming here until after the divorce."

"Marila, you're upset," he understated. "I love my girls and I want them with us. You don't know what you're saying. You don't mean it."

"Oh, yes I do. You have to decide whether you want those kids around or me. Take your choice."

Being Stanley, and therefore being sure he could work anything out that had to be, he showed up one sunny June afternoon with all three girls in tow. He obviously hadn't told them that for the time being I couldn't stand the thought of them, let alone their presence in the house, and they rushed to hug me and kiss me and tell me how glad they were to be with us, and how happy they were that it was summer.

When three faces are turned upward in the utmost trust that they are a welcome part of your life, what can you do? I gave Stan a look that carried a complete arsenal, not just daggers, but I opened my arms to the three little girls who had done nothing for me to be angry about but be born to the wrong mother. Stanley smiled his sweet smile and wandered away whistling, knowing that I would be as affectionate as ever (most of the time), as giving as ever (most of the time), and that the girls would have nothing but pleasant memories of the summer.

And it turned out to be a pretty good summer after all. We did a lot of things together, the kind of model-mother things that as usual I had wanted to do, but could never quite pull off. There were excursions to the Statue of Liberty, a visit to the World Trade Center, and jaunts to Long Island to visit their grandfather. We went swimming, and to the zoo, and to a museum or two. They had a wonderful time.

I didn't have such a bad time either, actually. I'd awaken with a splitting headache and wander down to the kitchen, where I'd fix my morning pick-me-up, six ounces of orange juice on the rocks, diluted half again with vodka. By the time I'd fixed the girls' breakfast, I would be feeling no pain, and the world would have taken on an orange glow.

I'd work for a few hours, have another screwdriver as a late-morning snack, and be ready to play the perfect mother. The girls couldn't get over their good fortune at having me be always in good spirits. Around five o'clock I'd start again, now with vodka on the rocks, preparing myself for the ordeal of Stan's homecoming. I transferred my hostility from the daughters to the father, and the only way that I could even talk to him that summer was to be half-tanked.

Toward the end of July he began to meet frequently with Glavin, and I caught him often making secretive phone calls. When the bill came, I scrutinized it carefully, and found any number of calls to Roberta.

"What are you calling her for?" I screamed. "What do you have to say to her?"

"I . . . I was calling the kids, I guess," he stumbled.

"But the kids are *here!*" I shouted, outraged, enraged, petrified that soon I was going to be married and have three part-time children, and there would be no escape, no way to walk out.

One morning he called me from a client's office. "It's set for the ninth of August. If they postpone again, they'll default. So hell or high water, it's the ninth." He sounded a kiss and hung up. I poured myself another drink, even though the sun was barely up.

Those next nine days were torture. We didn't fight because we barely spoke. We didn't make plans for the wedding because we didn't want to be disappointed. We didn't tell anybody because we didn't want to jinx it. And we didn't have much sex.

It was a hot, humid, hazy midsummer day, that August ninth. Stan dressed to go to the Morris County Court House.

"It shouldn't take long, Joe said. He thinks we'll be through by lunchtime." He kissed me goodbye, and drove off with a wave, leaving me to my vodka and his children. I couldn't bear to hang around and wait, so I manufactured an errand, left the kids with a sitter, and went off to be alone.

I got home around two, and he pulled in the driveway right behind me.

I sat down on the front porch, waiting, not wanting to see him, not wanting to hear what he had to say, wanting only to know that it was over and I could be his wife, and wanting more than anything to hear that I could stay single.

"Leave me alone with Mary, kids," I heard him tell them in

the hallway. "I'll talk to you later." He came onto the porch, his collar open with the heat, his jacket slung over his shoulder. "That's that." He grinned sheepishly.

"Really?" I could feel a lump in my throat and couldn't swallow.

"Yup." He put his arms around me, and kissed me, as tentatively as he had the very first time. He rubbed his hand over the back of my head, and kissed me again, not quite so tentatively. "I love you, Marila. Will you marry me?"

This was it, the first legal proposal he could make. All my ill-founded doubts vanished, and the yes I gave him in response was this time more than a lover's ritual. The waiting was over.

My joy was short-lived, when I found out the results of the day in court. I also discovered the purpose of all the phone calls to Camden. Stan had traded for a no-fault divorce what, for us, amounted to a small fortune.

"You agreed to that? How could you have? We don't have that kind of money. How could you have done that?" I tore away from him, and ran upstairs to our bedroom, the tears beginning to flow. I slammed the bedroom door behind me, I hoped, in his face, but to my dismay the door, nearly as old as the house, splintered into three pieces, and hung from the hinges like an effigy. He peered at me through one of the gaping holes, trying to look appealing and apologetic.

"How could you?" I cried again.

He shrugged. "I thought it was more important for you that the grounds not be adultery. I was worried about how you'd feel, Marila." His voice became tinged with wonderment. "It's all over."

"Oh, Stanley, I love you! But . . . well . . . I'd rather have the money." We began to laugh, and laughed and laughed, and then we cried. It had finally happened. We were going to get married.

That evening we had a serious conversation with the girls.

"I went to the judge today," said Stan seriously, "and he signed the papers which mean I'm no longer married to your mommy. Now Mary and I are going to get married."

"I thought you were married with Mary already. So what?" said Amy bluntly, apparently not upset. But Leslie began to cry, and Jennifer followed suit.

"I always hoped that you would go back with Mommy," said Leslie woefully. "I never really thought you'd get a divorce." That made two of us.

The wedding plans were awkward, to say the least, but we set out to make it a wedding to remember. First the rabbi. Stanley called up the Union of American Hebrew Congregations in New York to find a rabbi who would marry a shiksa to a Jew. The phone was answered by Rabbi Charlie Greenspan, who turned out to have been a college acquaintance of Stan's until one drunken night when Stan and his cronies had thrown all of Charlie's furniture out of the window as testimony to what at the moment they considered was his obnoxious personality. But Charlie was above grudges, and connected us with one of the very few rabbis who would make us legal.

Stan wanted the reception at the Tavern on the Green in Central Park, and we set the ceremony for the United Nations chapel. It was going to be a real wedding, and I was going to be a real bride.

My parents seemed silently appalled. My father hates New York City. He couldn't imagine why anybody would want to go there for anything, let alone to get married. "What about traffic? What about parking? Why don't you do something simple?" I couldn't be sure but I think what he had in mind was a quiet ceremony by a justice of the peace, a quick glass of champagne, and back to business. We didn't see it that way. After all, it was my first wedding.

Invitations were a problem. I sent notes from Stanley and me to the people we invited, rather than formal invitations from my parents. It seemed awkward, but we never had the feeling my father fully approved or wanted to get involved, although he gave me away and generously footed the bill for the party, which surprised (as well as pleased) us both. Later I realized he might have been waiting for me to ask him to assume the full and traditional father-of-the-bride role. In any case, as on so many other occasions, we probably should have talked things through, for then there might not have been the sense on my part that my parents thought even a modest wedding bash was not exactly in good taste.

My wedding dress was also a problem. Stan wanted me to wear a traditional fluffy white wedding-cake gown, while I felt that something off-white (off-color?) would be more appropriate. It was tacky, my mother and convention communicated silently, to dress as a bride when in the virginal sense of the word, I wasn't one. I shopped with my mother fruitlessly, at Bergdorf's, Saks and Bonwit's, but ended up feeling that the whole thing was a sham and a farce and it didn't matter what I wore. I finally settled for a Mexican dress that was pretty but not special, and one that Stanley didn't especially like.

Our wedding day was the hottest, most humid day of the year, a Wednesday with the temperature above ninety before noon. I had spent the night at my folks with the girls, determined that Stan and I should be apart on the eve of our wedding. I was caught up in the superstition of our not seeing each other on that day until the ceremony itself, so to sleep together, I was afraid, would have portended disaster.

I got up early and dressed all in black, even to my underwear, and tied a black kerchief over my hair, looking more like a grieving widow or a novice about to take vows of chastity than a bride. I was mourning the loss of my freedom. My mother made me a fried egg and a piece of toast for breakfast, neither of which I could eat, and for lunch she gave me five milligrams of Valium. I was a zombie all day. The world was moving and floating around me, and I could hear and see things, but I wasn't part of them. And it wasn't the Valium. It was my wedding day. I was scared to death.

The wedding itself, a seven-thirty P.M. candlelit affair, is a fuzzy memory—Beethoven played by an organist who wanted his twenty dollars before the ceremony; my father nervously walking me down the aisle; the *chupa*—wedding canopy—tilted over our heads, because my nephew, Len, one of the *chupa* bearers, was only five feet tall. We were married in Hebrew, and I think I promised to love, honor, and obey. At last we drank the wedding wine from a sterling-silver cup without spilling a drop and Stan smashed a crystal glass under his foot with gusto. There was much hugging and kissing once we got out of the chapel, and we had gotten a parking ticket.

The procession to the Tavern on the Green was not as complicated as my father had expected, no one getting lost, everyone finding parking places. Stan and I entered the restaurant, he carrying Amy and I Jennifer, while close behind were Leslie and our nieces and nephews, giving us the appearance of a newly married family of eight.

The reception was in a glittering crystal palace, with candlelight reflecting off the chandeliers, and our honeymoon was a memorable week in Vienna, Venice, and Verona. I was Mrs. Stan Silverzweig, and there was no going back.

24

All of that seems years ago, lifetimes ago. I can no longer remember when I wasn't with Stan, or how empty and unfulfilling my life must have been without him. And whatever my current frustrations, they don't match my current joys, and they are, in the final analysis, much less significant than whatever they would have been had I married Frank or Michael or Don and lived in suburbia in a two-story colonial with two cars, a lawnmower and a snow blower in the garage, two children in the playroom, a dog on the back porch, and a dishwasher, food processor, and garbage disposal in the kitchen.

I think if I had done that, I would have been hopelessly bored and remained hopelessly focused and narrow. I would have achieved "success," would have "made it" in the conventional sense—and would have been ashamed to admit how tense and miserable I really was. I'd have drunk a lot of vodka, read a lot of books, and been a model mother and homemaker. But I wouldn't have changed as I have: my outlook on life, my perspective, my ability to deal with people and situations, my sense of self-worth. And changed I have.

The time flips by so quickly, a collage of laughter, tears, anger, and peace, with dashes of resentment for spice. The wedding changed things—it *is* different once you're married. A subtle social pressure slips away, you no longer feel that touch of righteous defiance. "There's nothing wrong with our living together." There are probably many women who cope with the silent reproofs better than I did, perhaps don't really feel them; but reared as I had been, I suffered the indignities of "living in sin" both real and imagined, because I wanted to be with Stan.

We had hoped—anticipated—that marriage would bring us peace and tranquillity, some breathing space, a respite from the hectic pace we had always kept, at least in part to cover up our insecurities and cram lifetimes into years. We planned to relax.

We returned from our Italian honeymoon, as always when we returned from vacations, full of resolutions to spend less, save more, and write books; and took the girls for a relaxing weekend visit to my parents at their farm in southern Vermont, where they had moved for good right after the wedding. It was the epitome of rambling old New Englandia, with added-on ells, five fireplaces, and a big old country kitchen. Their land was rambling too, a spread of field and mountain, forest and the bursting stream that marked their property line. The first barn was on the drawing boards, the tractor in the garage to prepare the earth for planting in the spring, the first ten cords of logs waiting to be split and cut for firewood.

We lay in bed that Saturday night, the unpolluted air drifting in the open window, talking about our house and theirs.

"Remember when we first moved in? All those rainstorms?" I snuggled closer to the warmth of Stan's body, recalling the night we had been awakened at three in the morning by a steady drip, drip, drip to find four square yards of the white bedroom ceiling dark and blistered, the floor beneath it a puddle.

"These people here that sold you this house, well, lady, it looks like they sold you a turkey," the roofer had told us kindly. "This here ceiling was covered nice like with some thick white paint, but you're gonna have one hell of a mess here with this leak. 'Cause I can't *find* it!"

Stan laughed, remembering. "And the pipes that burst last Christmas when we were in Paris. The boiler in the cellar here looks older than ours. I don't envy them the fuel bill."

"How would you like to plow Dad's driveway?" It was about

twice as long as ours and we were always getting snowed in; by the time we got dug out, it was usually too late to get where we had to go. We fell asleep smiling over the adventures my folks would have with their antique haven, which they had already dubbed "Costly Acres."

It was a lovely interlude, walking in the woods, playing Frisbee with the girls in the fields. My parents were at their best—perhaps because we were now respectable. But as we left, I felt a knot tighten in the pit of my stomach, the knot that grew whenever we were away from home. I wondered what catastrophe awaited us this time—bedroom ceiling on the floor again? The bathroom leaking into the hallway? The birds that had found their way into the attic—would they have discovered the living room?— the way the squirrel did?

"Stan." We'd been driving in silence for a while. "Stanley, let's sell our house." And as I said the words, the muscles in my stomach relaxed, and I knew it was a smart idea. Critical repairs were getting more frequent, the fuel bills higher, and the wallpaper in the living room was starting to peel. It was beginning to turn into another white elephant.

We turned it upside down, and inside out, and couldn't find anything wrong with the idea. We decided to build when spring came, on land that we had yet to find.

By the time we arrived home we had not only mentally sold the house we were once sure would be ours forever, but we had, also mentally, purchased several acres of wooded land on a southern slope, and designed and furnished a no-maintenence passive-solar-energy home that could be expanded if and when the girls came to live with us permanently. We decided to postpone for a while the peaceful and stable existence we had planned when in Venice and Verona, and immediately set out to find the perfect piece of land. But our new venture was unexpectedly thwarted.

Management consulting isn't an easy way to make a living, with financial security only as long-lived as the duration of the contracts one can sell. Barry had always been good at selling and Stan at getting good enough bottom-line results to justify six-figure investments by major corporations in the less quantifiable area of employee motivation. But because consulting in human relations can be labor-intensive, Barry was trying to create a widget, a program he could sell over and over again. So based on interest but very little commitment from a prospective funder for the development of such a program, he had concentrated ninety percent of his staff toward this end for the last six months.

It turned out to be the wrong widget. Shortly after we returned from our weekend of decision in Vermont, Barry called a staff meeting.

"The Four Star Manufacturing Company has decided they aren't ready to subsidize the program beyond the preliminary development." He didn't look at anyone, just the wall over our heads. "Obviously this will affect all of us." He cleared his throat and went on, but I didn't hear what he was saying. All I could think of was that Barry was a millionaire, and we only had two thousand dollars in the bank. It seemed as if we would be a lot more affected than he.

After the rest of the staff left, there was a heated argument between Stan and Barry. The arrangement Stan had with Barry was profit sharing after overhead, spelled out in detail in Stan's employment contract. But over the last two years the overhead had nearly tripled. With Four Star out of the picture, the contracts left in-house wouldn't cover expenses, let alone leave anything over as profits to be shared.

Barry was sympathetic, but firm. The contract called for profit sharing, and that was that. He assured Stan that within three or four months the business would be back, and Stan would be drawing income again.

We spent two weeks discussing alternatives, and looking for strategies to get through the next few months without any money coming in. The more we talked about it, the more we felt that we'd rather be penniless and independent than penniless and tied to Barry Fields. Stan's reputation as a consultant was impeccable. If it got Barry business, why shouldn't it get business for us?

Once we gathered our courage to take the plunge and set out on our own, the only thing in our way was the employment contract that Stan had signed more than a year before, that contract which he had counted on for financial security. It took several weeks of negotiation, but it finally happened—Stan and I were partners in a corporation as well as in life. We were restricted from working with certain companies for a period of time, and we were required to sell our house and revert the proceeds to Barry. But we were free.

The first few hours felt terrific. Until we realized we were actually in business for ourselves, with no clients, no income, three children and an ex-wife to support, a too-large drafty house to sell in the slow winter market, and no money to buy another one.

Then Stan took to his bed for the first two days of the existence of Silverzweig Associates, too nervous to call the people we knew, afraid of rejection. I cleaned house in a frenzy, scrubbing windows and waxing floors, running upstairs every hour or so to see if Stanley was still alive, and to ask him when he was going to get up and begin to support me.

I was thrilled when our first contract came through two months after that fateful staff meeting, because we had been living on the tin boxes of change I had hoarded for years, and the cashiers in the supermarket were getting to know me by the fact that whenever I came in, I paid for the week's groceries with pennies, nickels, and dimes. It was a happy accident that a former client of Stan's called him at Barry's office, and a part-time secretary gave this company president our phone number instead of asking him what he wanted. His already successful supermarket company was opening a new type of store in New England, and he wanted Stan to develop a program that would build morale and help solve some sticky training problems. Stan agreed gratefully, and we've been working with them ever since.

Also by some stroke of good fortune, Citicorp decided we were a good credit risk (little did they know!) and gave us, without our asking, fifteen thousand dollars in unsecured write-a-check credit. The change I had saved put food on the table, but Ready-Credit paid the rent, the alimony, and the child support. Our regular checking account had a please-overdraw-and-pay-interest clause, so I was free to borrow on that, and then there were those old reliables, Master Charge and BankAmericard. If it weren't for plastic and the facile economic system of the seventies, we could hardly have survived.

I had never run a business, but I learned. I made Stanley, as he wanted to be, President, but I kept Vice-President, Secretary, Treasurer, and Chairman of the Board for myself. I made sales calls, typed letters and proposals, borrowed from one account to pay another. And prayed.

The first eighteen months after we were married were all work. Eighteen hours a day, six, even seven days a week. We would promise the moon to sell a client, and then deliver not one but three or four moons, so the client would be satisfied, and a good reference.

We did assessments, going into a company that had problems in productivity, absenteeism, waste, sales, union relations, or whatever, and finding out why, leaving behind a detailed plan of attack for implementing the solutions we would recommend. And of course we always made ourselves available to help if, as was usually the case, the client so desired.

We wrote training and orientation packages, developed news-letters, and established internal Human Resource departments in companies where only paper-pushing personnel departments existed. We set up a video studio, and began producing motivational training and communications tapes. In short, we did everything that anybody asked us to.

Starting the business was hectic and exhilarating, but the timing was bad for the girls. One of their greatest fears was that after the wedding, things would be different; they wouldn't be quite so welcome; they wouldn't be quite so tolerated; we would only have time for ourselves and really not want them around.

Stan didn't want his daughters to feel that he had forsaken them, so he took great pains to explain to them what had happened between us and Barry Fields ("I didn't like him anyway," said Amy, wrinkling up her nose). We told them how hard we would have to work now, and how much we needed them to understand that when we didn't see them at all, or that when they were with us and we had to work, it didn't mean we didn't love them, but that because we loved them, we wanted to be sure to be able to provide for them. They could sense that we were working with a feverish intensity that meant something very different from a lack of love.

All through that time, all three girls continued to express more and more articulately their desire to live with us. We would talk about it, what it would be like, what it would take to make it happen, on their part and on ours, and how Roberta would react. That was what scared them the most.

Amy was blunt. "She'll kill us. And so will Joellyn."

Leslie was more practical, more interested in the mechanics. "Do I have to talk to a judge? What do I have to say? Will Mommy know what I say? Will I ever see her again if I come with you?" She never let a visit pass without bringing up the subject.

Jennifer, now in her sixth year, was quiet and often tearful, clinging to us silently, and when we asked her how she felt, she would shake her head slowly from side to side. "Sad," she would say. "I feel sad." But she couldn't say why. She just cried every Monday morning.

"You know, if you want to live with us, it won't mean that you won't see your mother," Stan reassured them. "Things would just be reversed. You'd be with us during school, and visit her weekends. It wouldn't be much different at all."

"Daaaad." Amy sounded exasperated. "You know she wouldn't come to get us. You always drive to pick us up, and then you always drive us back. You know she wouldn't want to do that."

Because of the incredible pressure of getting the business off the ground, a custody suit was the last thing we could handle right then. But we kept telling the girls that if they chose to live with us we would do everything within our power to make it happen. They needed to know we wanted them very much.

Within six months half our business, including our major client, was located in Philadelphia, so we took an apartment there, finally getting rid of the house. Philadelphia was closer to Camden, which cut down on the driving, and there was a swimming pool in the building, so we were often able to do our weekend work around the pool while the girls swam. They were delighted.

"If we lived with you, where would we sleep?" Amy again, naturally. The bedroom that they used on weekends was occupied by a boisterous, officious secretary on weekdays; their coloring books and Leslie's Nancy Drews were tucked in among volumes of Drucker, Maslow, and Levinson. Gone were the canopied beds and the dressing tables with dotted-swiss skirts, the closets and dressers full of playclothes, the trunks full of toys, the rooms that had been their own in our just-sold house. And never once, from any of them, was there the slightest murmur of complaint, the slightest sense of reproach. They knew that times were hard and times were different, but that it didn't change the way we felt about each other.

Sometimes, I felt like crawling into a black hole and disappearing, I was so tired. There were other times, though, when I wanted to come out slugging, and a frequent target was Roberta. I had managed to reduce my active contact with her to zero, but her presence was always there, making for problems, and excluding Stan from the more important issues of his daughters' upbringing.

Like Amy's school. When Roberta moved to Camden, Amy had transferred to an elementary school with open classrooms. For an average child it could have been a stimulating experience. But for Amy it was a situation which encouraged her hyperactivity. She was one of very few white children in her class, and earmarked for racial taunts, which she responded to as belligerently as they were proffered. Increasingly she was becoming a behavior problem for her teacher, and we discovered by accident that her school was attempting to place her in a public school for neurologically impaired and emotionally disturbed children. Roberta had never told us.

"The child is being tested to death, and tutored too much. She needs to be able to lead a normal life on weekends, not have special classes," said the principal when we came to find out what was happening. This was the first we had known of any special attempts at helping Amy with her learning and behavioral difficulties in school. We had had to discontinue Amy's Saturday sessions with Mrs. Unger after we moved to Philadelphia.

A place finally opened up for Amy in the special school, but before we let her go there we wanted to be sure that it would be the kind of place that would help her, not hurt her. We went to meet the social worker, school psychologist, teacher, and principal who would be responsible for helping Amy catch up scholastically and socially so she could be mainstreamed back into the public school system, a process they predicted would take about two years.

We all met in the library of the elementary school, and gathered around a round shellacked pine table, sitting on low chairs designed for little bottoms. The walls were hung with finger-painted scenes of sunsets and sunrises, paper cutouts of fruit, crayoned drawings of families, a parade of nursery-rhyme characters carrying phonics symbols.

We were a motley crew. Stan and I looked, we hoped, professional and parently. Mr. Johnson, the principal, was so small he was proportioned for the furniture. There was the psychologist, Miss Fisher (all "her" children called her Patti, she told us proudly), who was warm and human, and assured us she would meet with Amy on a regular basis. The social worker, Mrs. Frack, barely taller than Johnson, looked to me as if she weighed in at about one hundred and forty pounds. She was middle-aged, with thinning blond hair and blood-red lipstick. She seemed tense and hostile, this woman who helped decide the fate of so many special children in Camden.

"You are trying to hamper the progress we plan to make with

Amy," said Mrs. Frack thinly. "She is being pulled in too many directions by too many people, and her mother informs me that you really aren't interested in her education. Well, we here at the Admiral Perry School are concerned, and do care." She spit as she spoke, and Stan, next to her, brushed off his knee.

"Miss Frack—" Stan began.

"Mrs."

"Excuse me, Mrs. Frack. You have only heard one side of the story, and before we continue, I think you should know all the facts." As only Stan can, he painted his perception of the eight years of Amy's life that had culminated in this meeting—including a seemingly mild rebuke of an evaluation system that omitted to consult with the father of the child in question; of a social worker who accepted the word of one party as truth without attempting to communicate with the other party in Amy's life. "It doesn't seem very thorough, does it?" He finished with a smile, having cast his darts very close to home.

"We are here to talk about Amy's attendance at the Admiral Perry School, Mr. Silverswish." Instead of getting red with anger, she had gotten pale, accentuating her lipstick and the circles of rouge on her cheeks.

The conversation turned to the evaluation results, and the class in which Amy was going to be placed. They had shown it to us before we came to the library, without labeling it, and our first reaction had been one of horror. The room seemed jammed— a standard-size classroom with only six students and a harassed teacher, but the children were all over the place. Amy was like a docile little lamb in comparison with them. Now Mrs. Frack told us it was an E.D. class, and that was where she felt Amy belonged.

"She is not emotionally disturbed," I said tightly, thinking back to the scene in the classroom, imagining how frightened Amy would be inside, and how tough and wild she would act in order to overcome her fear. "She has dyslexia, and needs special tutoring. But she is not like those children you showed us, and you know it."

"Mrs. Silverzwag, you must realize you do not have a normal daughter. Do you understand that? Your child is not normal, and you must learn to accept that fact. We know what's best for her."

The people and voices around me oozed together and lost all definition. I felt my blouse grow wet under my armpits, and my face flush hot, as everyone around me shrank. I kept hearing that voice, that voice that seemed so barren, and I wanted to lash out at her.

It was terrible to listen to the "expert" tell me she knew more what my Amy needed than I did, all the more frustrating and agonizing because there was nothing that I could do about it. She wasn't my child, and all the confidence and intuition I had that Amy would prosper with us didn't mean a damn, because it wasn't legal and Roberta wouldn't let her come to us.

I slowly drifted back into the discussion, heated now, Stan picking up where I had faded. Patti Fisher joined our side, stating firmly that Amy's hyperactivity would probably be exacerbated, not controlled, by being put in that class. Johnson was silent. I had a sense he was waiting to find out which side would win before he jumped on the victory bandwagon.

"There's room in the class for N.I.s," said Miss Fisher, in response to a statement by Frack that "Something *has* to be done."

"What's that?" we asked.

"Neurologically impaired. They are children, like Amy, who have learning disabilities of some type. It's also a class of children closer to Amy in age, and there is one other girl in the class." The E.D. class had been all boys. It seemed that this was the first time that this particular option had been discussed, and we seized on it as a compromise. The more we saw and heard the more reluctant we were to have Amy come here to school, but there wasn't much we could do, and that was where Amy ended up.

25

It took nine months before we felt secure in our business, with a few small contracts securely in our pockets, and a two-year contract with Food Fair in Philadelphia which we thought would really make life easy. Until, that is, we discovered they were in worse financial shape than we were.

First we fought to keep Food Fair out of Chapter Eleven, and then we fought to keep the Philadelphia Region alive. We've never worked so hard in our lives, and it was tough on the girls. I had only so much energy and dedication, and too often I didn't have enough left over to give them.

Being married was demanding in itself. Stan had a great need for love and caring, and I had a great need to give it. Sometimes I'd feel we got too wrapped up in our work, too distant from each other's thoughts and feelings; but then he would catch my eye across a room, or touch my hand in passing, or kiss me gently in the elevator on the way to a meeting, and my heart would fly.

Then there was the business, which, as I got better at it, and more confident, and not least began to see it as successful, gave me a real sense of fulfillment and accomplishment. But it took so much out of me. It was a long time before I realized that it was the pressure of having a business that depended as much on ingenuity as on skill that kept me from giving as freely as I should have the support and attention that the girls craved.

I would often dread the moment when they would arrive, and that two-hour interlude to myself when Stan went to pick them up became one of the highlights of my week. But they would show up at the door, looking sad, depressed, and dirty, reaching up to me, silently pleading with me not to let them down. I couldn't help but feel for them, hug them, and tell them how glad I was to see them. I felt very guilty and selfish, because these three little girls felt no one loved them but Stan and me, and they clung to me more and more, following me, copying me, wanting me to reach out and touch them.

The house we'd bought in Cutler, on the coast of Maine, had always been just ours, a private place that no one knew of. We didn't get there very often, but when I needed a respite I could close my eyes and watch the icy whitecaps smash against a tyrannosaurus-like boulder, or hear the gulls squawk as they swooped to dive for their dinner. It was the only house we'd ever had that was just ours, without dolls and TV or an office, without breakfast, lunch, and dinner on schedule, where we could make love in the living room in the middle of the day, secure that no client or child would pop in unannounced.

But now Stan planned to take the girls down to Cutler for Christmas. I swore I wouldn't go if they did.

"Can't we keep something just for ourselves? Everything is always business or kids, and I need a break." Despite my deep feeling for them, I sometimes still fought the fact I'd married not only Stanley but his children as well. And he had already told his daughters, before this discussion, that we were going to Cutler for Christmas. He'd told them all about the beach we went to, and our neighbors, the beauty of the ocean, and the harbor at sunset, the raging squalls, and the succulent lobsters. And he had told all three not to tell me that he had told them.

As Christmas approached, I discovered that almost every time I walked into the room, conversation would come to a dead stop, and the four of them would look around guiltily. Stan had carefully primed the girls, telling them I had to work over the holiday and I felt very bad that I wouldn't be with them.

"Don't talk about it in front of her—she really wishes she could come." And the pact of silence was sealed.

Christmas came, and they tearfully begged me to go. "Please, Mommy, it won't be Christmas without you." So I went. And as we drove the fifteen hours to get to what was now our only real home, I finally realized I was going not because I had to, but because I chose to. After all, it wouldn't have been Christmas for me without them.

Throughout all of this tumult and my often unreasonable moodiness, the three little angels never gave up on me. They felt I loved them whether I hugged them or hollered at them, and because I'd always told them I wanted them with us, they took me at my word. They refused to believe I had changed the way I felt about them, and treated it as a phase I was going through.

It was. I was struggling, belatedly perhaps, with the end of my adolescence, the fearfully cold reality that life was a battle nobody fought for you, but which you couldn't fight alone.

Leslie, Amy, and Jennifer were waging their own private war on the Camden front, and they turned to us for support. They talked constantly about living with us. Leslie began to ask Amy's questions. "Where would we live?" "Who would stay with me?" "Where would I go to school?" "Would I get to see my mother?" And underlying every conversation, every question, was the over-riding one "Do you really want me?"

I knew what she wanted to hear, and I knew what Stan wanted me to say. And I said it. Sometimes I felt it—yes, I really want you with me, with us, I really want you as my daughter full-time. But there were the other times when my juices curdled at the thought. Then I'd be vague, or silent, and let Stan fill in the space. But I have never been able to bring myself to say—to myself, let alone to anyone else—that I didn't want Leslie, or Amy or Jennifer, for that matter, to live with us. None of us wanted a full-blown custody fight. The girls wanted Roberta to realize on her own what they realized even in their innocence, and what Stan and I felt in our limited wisdom, that the three of them would be healthier emotionally, and happier, with us.

"She just stands by and watches while Joellyn hits Amy, or yells at us. She doesn't care about us. She only loves Joellyn," Leslie observed one Sunday over the french toast, which, feeling benevolent, I had been inclined to make. Whenever I was in a reasonably good mood they included me in their discussions and analyses of their complicated little lives.

"But I love Mary, and you don't seem to mind," responded Stanley.

"Yeah," said Amy, "but you love her differently than you love us, and you love us too. And Mary loves us. Right?" She gazed up at me questioningly, wanting desperately to be right, and taking the dollop of maple syrup that I poured on her breakfast as a visible sign of the words I spoke.

"Of course I love you, Amy. Very much." And I meant it.

"Jodie scares us." Jennifer, nearing seven, was becoming verbal, experimenting with participation in what she might perceive as a grownup conversation. During these philosophical discussions about their futures and their fears, she often just sat silently on my lap. Not today. "She yells so loud."

"But so do I!" I said. "You tell Daddy and me that you're frightened of me, too. Why is it different?"

Amy tried to answer, but Stan hushed her up so Jennifer could continue.

"Well, sometimes you have angry eyes, but Joellyn—her whole body gets mad at us. And she doesn't really care about us. You do. You yell at us, but you love us too." It was one of her longest speeches ever, and she couldn't look at anybody. She just sat picking at a baby hangnail.

Stan's eyes would meet mine during these conversations, over the heads of our brood, and we would signal each other in exasperation and despair. They weren't happy, that was clear. They were not in the kind of scholastic environment that was satisfying their needs, let alone stimulating them. They were "parented" by two women, one of whom they hoped cared about them, the other of whom they were convinced didn't. And yet we weren't sure they would be better off if they were wrested forcibly from that environment and plunked down in another, with two parents who loved them but a sense of guilt at betraying their natural mother. Leslie was actively experimenting with her feelings about living with us, since she was approaching the age where the choice could be hers. She transferred her allegiance from one parent to the other, embarrassed at what she feared would be interpreted as fickleness.

"Mommy. Daddy. I have something to tell you." It was another Sunday, and I had made fried doughs for breakfast. The sections of the Sunday *Times* were scattered on chairs and on the floor, Stanley and I absorbed, he in the Book Review, I in the crossword puzzle.

"Dad, Mom. Can we talk about something?" Leslie's voice was firm, but her hands were trembling.

"Are you gonna tell them?" Amy was panting with expectation, and Leslie wanted no part of her interference.

"Bug off, Amy, and mind your own business." There was a definitiveness to her tone that I had never heard before. Amy slithered away, abashed, to bother Jennifer.

"If . . . if . . . it's okay with you, I want to come and live with you. And this time it's for real. I mean, I'm really going to do it, no matter what she says. Can I? Please?" It was at once a pathetic plea and one of the strongest statements I ever heard her make.

So we talked it through, as we had many times before. "I'm not going to change my mind this time. I'm not. I have to leave. Don't say I have to stay."

We had always made it very clear to all three girls that we would welcome them with open arms whenever they chose. But Food Fair had folded in Philadelphia, and our business was suddenly back to ground zero. Stanley spoke first. "Well, of course you can live with us, Leslie. But . . . well, things are unsettled now, because of the business. So . . . that if you live with us, you'll have to live in Cutler. That's the only stable thing in our life right now, and the only place we could put you in school without your having to change in a year or two. What do you think?" It was a mark of our unity that I had almost precisely the same thought at precisely the same moment, though we had never discussed the possibility before.

Her eyes sparkled like the water in the harbor on a sunny day. "Oh, can I? Really? There's no place I'd rather live," she squealed. We all began to cry—Leslie from relief at her decision to take the biggest step of her life, Stan from joy that his daughter had chosen for herself what he felt was best for her, and I from a mixture of joy that Leslie had chosen me for a mother and a selfish sorrow that our private, independent, somewhat self-centered but totally delicious life was going to change, and never be quite the same again.

Neither was Leslie's. She went back to Camden, and did something we never thought she'd have the guts to do, something which I don't think I would have had the strength to do at thirteen. She told Roberta that night she was coming to live with us, and she didn't waver an inch from then on.

According to Leslie, the pressure Roberta and Joellyn put on her was formidable: raging battles that stopped just short of physical violence, with the child reaffirming her decision to leave, to be part of a more normal household, and the adults verbally abusing her for being selfish, ungrateful, and hateful.

She described sneers, and jibes, and contempt. She responded to their queries of "How can you do this to us?" with "How can you do this to me?"

Stan answered Bobbi's telephoned rantings and ravings about "What had he done" with what was, to Bobbi, an infuriating "It was her idea. I've told them if they're happier with you, that's where they should be, but if they want to be with us, well, that's okay too." She slammed the phone down screaming, "I'll take you to court."

Leslie worried about the possibility of having to meet with a judge, even privately, to denounce her mother if she had to, but even that she seemed willing to do. Our fruitless pursuit for a good lawyer produced what we felt was a brilliant solution to the court situation Roberta was threatening. We decided that since Leslie was the one who wanted to move, and was of an age where her opinion carried a great deal of weight, Leslie was the one with whom Roberta had the issue. So we began our search to hire an attorney for Leslie, in a sense to let her fight her own battle.

It never came to that. In one of Leslie's shouting matches with her mother, when Roberta was raging about the expected attack from Stan and blaming Leslie for what was happening, Leslie calmly informed her that it wasn't Stan who would be taking her to court, but Leslie herself.

Roberta apparently couldn't tolerate the rejection of her lifestyle by her daughter as a public issue. She might also have feared that a suit by Leslie would have affected her custody of Amy and Jennifer as well, and she wasn't ready to risk that. Whatever the reason, Roberta told Leslie she could leave if she wanted to. "School gets out on the fourteenth of June, and that's the day I want you out of the house. And once you're out, you're out. We don't want you back."

Leslie told us her last three months in Camden were a combination of the silent treatment and an attempt to make her feel that she was treating her mother, her sisters, and Joellyn in the most unfair way imaginable.

Tearfully, she would talk to us about her sense of isolation, and her anger at her mother's reaction. "Doesn't she care about me or what I want and need? Doesn't she want me to be happy?" Every day put more distance between mother and daughter, and persuaded Leslie with increasing certainty that she was doing what was best for her. "She wouldn't act this way if she loved me."

I knew what she was going through, and I realized I was not the pillar of strength that I could—and maybe should—have been during that difficult time. But I was having one hell of a difficult time of my own.

My weekends of what often felt like compulsive mothering I envisioned stretching into daily permanence, without respite, because Leslie would have nowhere else to go. Our intimate dinners for two would become dinners for three, our periodic honeymoons would be family vacations, the late-morning interludes in bed would have to be cut short. In the back of my mind would be school, homework, the dentist, and where she was at ten o'clock at night.

Saying that I didn't want Leslie—or any of them—wasn't and never had been an option. While I might not actively encourage them, I didn't have the right to deny the kids access to our life, especially if it meant their salvation.

So during the months that Leslie was struggling to keep her resolve, I went underground. It was the last time in my life I would be relatively unfettered and free, and I decided to savor every last moment of it. Under the legitimate guise of moving out of Philadelphia, relocating our business office in New York, settling our household lock, stock, and barrel Downeast in Cutler, Maine, and courting and consummating deals with new clients to take the place of Food Fair, I managed to keep my contact with the girls at less than minimum, and didn't feel the least bit guilty about it. I felt rather as if I were taking my last gulps of air before I drowned, taking my last look at spring before I went blind.

It was a beautiful spring in Cutler, the first one we had ever seen there. The wild pear trees were rampant in the meadows, and the wild rose bushes blossomed in profusion. If it hadn't been for Leslie, we couldn't have made Cutler our home so early in our life, and I was grateful to her for that before she ever got there.

26

Stan picked up Leslie the day after her school ended, a hot and muggy June Friday that was begging for a thunderstorm. She brought a few clothes, some books and posters, and a quilt. When I met them in New York (having stayed behind to relish the last few precious moments of my freedom) she was nervous. So was I.

This was going to be different, this life with a full-time teenage daughter. No weekend child, who I knew would be returning to another world come Monday morning, releasing me back into my own life until Friday came around again. Instead, Leslie was an almost-adult whose childish and grownup needs all had to be satisfied.

The first six months were the hardest, beginning with the tears that she couldn't stop shedding as our plane took off from La Guardia for Maine, leaving behind her mother, her sisters, and the familiar life she had known. She felt she had betrayed them all.

All summer long she drove me to distraction. She was always moody and often insolent, usually at her worst after the phone rang and it wasn't her mother calling to ask, "Hi, how's it going?" or after the mail arrived and there was nothing for her postmarked Camden. The calls and the cards never came, except for one brief note in July. Ecstatic, Leslie wrote right back, then was more hurt than ever when there was no reply.

But by August, when Amy and Jennifer came to spend their usual summer month with us, there were stirrings of subtle change. The magic of Cutler was stealing through her, and she was beginning to find some peace in waking up every day to the sun glittering on the blue Atlantic, or Sandburg's fog, moving on its cat feet over the water and across the road, then up the lawn, onto the porch, and through the open windows. She was starting to make friends, trying to carve out a niche for herself in a small town where, if you aren't born into it or don't marry into it, you almost never quite belong.

Amy and Jennifer were astounded at—and upset by—their new big sister because for the first time that's what she was, rather than their surrogate mother. They came to me in tears when she closed her bedroom door and refused to let them inside to share her nearly fourteen-year-old life.

"But she never did that before. She always played with us," they whined. "She's mean."

"You have to remember that Leslie's a big girl now, and has more grownup interests. But she loves you just the same as ever, even more because she doesn't see you so much," I'd say gently. "Wait and see how you feel when you're her age."

And Leslie would come to me, also in tears. "I feel so guilty when I want to go with my friends or just be by myself. I don't always *want* to play with them. Does that make me selfish?" She seemed haunted by the accusations Bobbi and Joellyn had made before she left Camden, ridiculing her for wanting to be an "only child," for wanting to put a distance between herself and her much younger siblings.

"No, Leslie," I sighed. The last thing this already overburdened adolescent needed was more guilt. "No, Leslie," I repeated more emphatically. "There's nothing wrong with telling your sisters to bug off. You're so much older that it's natural you should want to do things without them. But it's not what they're used to from you, and it will take time."

"They say my mom and Joellyn won't even talk about me. They say they're terribly mad at me for coming to live with you and Dad." She traced circles with a long manicured fingernail on the countertop where I was preparing dinner. "Mama, do you think my mom loves me?" The circles widened, and I didn't answer for a moment. I knew she wanted me to tell her the truth.

"I'm sure she loves you, Leslie. I don't think it's possible for a mother not to love a daughter."

"Then why in all this time hasn't she called me, and only written to me that once? If she loves me, why doesn't she want me to be happy?"

"She may be angry at you, or hurt that you decided to live with us, but she'll get over it. And some people aren't as demonstrative as others. Some people aren't good letter writers. She might have trouble letting her feelings out, and letting you know how much she cares about you."

"Well, I don't think she cares at all." Amy's abrupt entrance ended that disturbing conversation, but the reason for Leslie's summer slump was clear: She was struggling with Bobbi's apparent rejection for an action that Leslie felt was not only justifiable, but essential.

The end of the summer meant a tearful parting for the little ones, but Leslie, while she hated to see her sisters leave, was eagerly anticipating school, trying out for cheerleading, and starting our life together as a real family without the distractions of summer and sisters. She yearned to enjoy her new life to the fullest, so she pushed down the nagging thought that perhaps she had had no right to change her destiny.

She talked to Bobbi a few times that fall when Stan would call to talk to the little ones. Once Leslie told us that Bobbi called her. Around Veterans Day, Leslie wanted to visit Camden for the long weekend, but it couldn't be worked out. It shook her badly.

We didn't see Amy and Jennifer much between September and Thanksgiving, although Stan talked to them nearly every day. With Leslie in Cutler, that was where we spent most of our time. We had a live-in housekeeper who stayed with her the few days a week that Stan and I were away working, but Leslie needed us, and we felt more complete when we were with her. We were a family now, and we were learning to live together.

Right after Thanksgiving, Leslie's mood began to darken and her school work began to slip. There were tantrums and tears, and sometimes despair. One night I heard her scream out, and ran to comfort her. She was sitting up in bed, crying.

"They were chasing me, and Joellyn was hitting me, and then she started to shovel dirt on me. She was burying me alive, and my mother just stood and watched." Leslie clung to me as if she were four and not fourteen.

I hugged her tightly until she was calm enough to talk, and then she explained a growing fear she had of going back to Camden. We had all assumed she'd spend Christmas vacation there. "Don't make me go," she pleaded. "Don't make me go back."

She didn't. We spent Christmas together, the three of us, but after the holiday she turned moody and sullen. At first we worried about her, trying to be understanding, but our irritation grew as she cast a gloomy pall upon our life. Stan finally confronted her head on at dinner one evening.

She sat silently through a lecture on her noncontribution to our family happiness, twirling a lock of hair, her long lashes sweeping the peaches in her creamy skin. When he finished, she sat silently.

"What in God's name is the matter with you?" he asked.

"Nothing," she muttered.

"*Something* is bothering you. And I've had about all I can take of your attitude. What's wrong? Is it Bobbi?"

Her only response was a slightly more downward turn of her mouth.

She was only able to tell us what was on her mind gradually, in conversations that continued sporadically for many weeks and articulated her sense that she was a fifth wheel, that she'd intruded in our private life, that she wasn't lovable or wantable.

"How can you want me when my own mother doesn't want me?" she cried, pleading with us to reassure her that she was welcome and belonged. She turned to me. "Why should you want me around? You and Daddy could have a much better time if I wasn't with you. I just mess everything up!"

I tried to convince her then and later that she doesn't mess things up for me, she changes things. She's always in the back of my mind; I'm always wondering what she's doing and if she's happy. I worry that she's been hurt too much for me to help her, and that she doesn't wholly believe me when I tell her that I love her and she's important to me.

We don't seem to have the blowups, the shouting matches that I hear other mothers tell me they have with their teenage daughters, or that Leslie's friends have with their mothers. She and I try harder than most to work things out, perhaps because neither of us is altogether free of fear; she at times that we'll send her back, I that she might decide to go. I almost never think that she wants to leave us. I know that I want her to stay.

Still, despite her ups and downs, Leslie enjoyed her first year as an only child greatly, though she had to steel herself for the possible advent of her sisters to spoil her utopia. But even more than that, she feared the birth of a baby.

"Are you and Daddy going to have a baby?" I was giving her a Toni and couldn't see her face, hidden behind the hand that proffered a pink plastic waving curler.

"We would like to." When she had asked this before, I had been able to answer with a comforting "Probably not," but we had finally called the fertility doctor.

She didn't respond, except to drop her head a fraction of an inch closer to her chest. I realized she must have seen the books on motherhood and birth that Stan had given me for a fertility present, and Leslie probably thought I was pregnant.

"But we aren't yet, Les. You'll be among the first to know, don't worry."

"Oh, I'm not worried about it." She sounded worried.

"And it won't change the way I feel about you."

"Well, I am afraid that you'll love a new baby more than me, because after all, it'll be yours and Daddy's. That'll make it special."

252

"But you'll always be my daughter, and always be very special to me. Besides, I have enough girls. If it isn't a boy, I'm sending it back." She giggled, and handed me another roller.

"It must be hard for you, being reminded of Roberta all the time when we're around."

"Not all the time. Only sometimes. Especially when you girls look like her."

"I don't look *anything* like her," Leslie replied vehemently.

Stan spent the week before Thanksgiving working in Boston and New Jersey, leaving Leslie and me in Cutler to truss the turkey and bake the pies. He also picked up Amy and Jennifer and brought them home for the long weekend. They were clinging and cranky, and at first I attributed it to the long trip and discombobulation because we hadn't been together for a long time. But their behavior persisted, and after two days, we found out what was wrong.

Just past dawn, Stan and I were sipping from mugs of steaming coffee in the living room curled up peacefully under the picture windows watching the scallop draggers that had come into the harbor during the night, and the few hardy lobster fishermen who were preparing their traps to go out on the cold winter sea. There were only vague stirrings from the bedroom above, and we hoped that Amy and Jennifer would amuse themselves for a little while longer.

No such luck. Their door opened and Amy knocked on the door leading up to our attic bedroom. "Mom. Dad. Are you awake?"

"Down here, Amy," Stan called softly, and in a second Amy was halfway down the stairs, peering through the banister.

"Jenny's crying and won't stop."

"What's the matter?"

"I don't know. Maybe she had a bad dream or something. She got out of bed, and now she's lying on the floor crying."

Our eyes met and we sighed, expecting some childish sisterly quarrel. "Go get her."

But when Amy led Jennifer tenderly downstairs by the hand we could both see that this was not the result of any teasing that had backfired or a fight over who was going to play with Barbie's Ken. Jenny was bent over, hands clenched into fists she pressed against her eyes as if to stem the flow of tears. She was sobbing desperately. I pulled her onto my lap and drew the comforter around us both.

"What's the matter, Jen?" She shook her head from side to side, and shrugged in silent sadness.

"I didn't do anything, Dad. Honest." Amy was sitting close to her father, wide beautiful brown eyes, spring roses in her cheeks, feeling intensely the distress of her baby sister.

"I know that, Amy. You just tried to help." He hugged her, and held her close.

"She just started to cry. In a ball on the floor. She got all curled up and cried. But I didn't do anything."

We waited the endless moments it took for Jennifer's crying to ease, and then the eternity until she could bring herself to answer our questions about why she was so upset.

"I'm sad because I want to commit suicide."

"What?" Stan's voice was strangled.

"Sometimes I want to commit suicide."

"Do you know what that means?"

She nodded. "It means to kill myself. Sometimes I want to kill myself, and not live anymore." I shivered, spiders crawling up my back.

It wasn't easy to get to the root of Jennifer's feelings. But as we talked and talked and talked to Jennifer, Amy, who was popping in and out, began to share some of her own emotions and frustrations. Jennifer was able to say at last what was driving her to such an extreme.

"I want to live with you and Mary and Leslie," she said to her daddy. "I don't want to live in Camden anymore." The voice that had been so choked with sobs was firm at last.

"So do I, Dad. I want to live with you too. Can we? Huh? Can we?" Amy pleaded.

We hadn't expected this quite so soon, or with quite such conviction. But they showed remarkable maturity in their perceptions of their Camden home life, and we were compelled to listen. We also had to take Jennifer's threat of suicide seriously, as an indication that some aspects of her life were more unbearable for her than we could imagine. Balancing that was the knowledge that if we did as they asked—began proceedings to transfer custody to us—this time there would be no relatively easy acquiescence from Bobbi as with Leslie. This time it would be war.

"Think about whether it's what you really want, girls," Stan ended that fateful conversation. "We'll keep talking about it, and if you still feel the same way in a few months, then we'll do something about it. Okay?" Both girls nodded and smiled, certain that their father wouldn't let them down.

Amy and Jennifer remained steadfast throughout the year in their determination to live with us.

"I know why you left, Leslie," said Jennifer one breakfast. She began to count on her fingers. "Eight, nine, ten, eleven, twelve. Do I have to be thirteen? That's five years. Daddy, that's too long." Given the depth of their feelings, we concurred.

They knew, even at eight and ten, what the consequences of this choice might be, because they had seen Bobbi's relationship with Leslie deteriorate from the day she first expressed her decision to leave the Camden house to the point where she and Bobbi never saw each other and rarely spoke. They had also seen Leslie flourish and come into her own, and they wanted the same for themselves.

Their feelings about Bobbi were ambiguous, compassion and anger both, but they couldn't understand what seemed to them her irrational attitude about allowing them freedom of choice.

"You and Mary always told us we could live wherever we wanted as long as we were happy," Amy said to Stan. "Why doesn't she feel that way?"

"And we'd visit her a lot, just like we visit you," Jennifer chimed in. But she knew getting Bobbi to agree was a lost cause. She told us about the day she had asked Bobbi what she would do if Jenny decided to live with her dad. "She got so mad at me. She yelled and yelled." Jenny was afraid to mention it to her ever again.

The first week in May we met with a New Jersey attorney who had been recommended to us by someone who had been recommended to us by a friend. We had gotten a good reference.

"There are only two attorneys in the state that I would consider if I were you," said a kind, disembodied voice on the other end of the telephone. "If you think you're going to get to court, though, you'll need a good litigator. And that's just one guy. Paul Rowe. Tell him I told you to call."

A name from a name. We crossed our fingers.

That first day in the sophisticated law offices of Greenbaum, Greenbaum, Rowe and Smith, we waited on the cranberry couch in the reception area that was at the center of two arms of offices and conference rooms. The men and women passing back and forth were a blend of young and old, hip and sedate, sharp and casual. But they all looked savvy, and they all looked as if everything were under control.

Paul Rowe, senior partner, Greenbaum, Greenbaum, Rowe and Smith. The river of neutral commercial carpeting that flowed throughout the halls and offices stopped short at his doorway, and was replaced by thick off-white shag. Instead of a standard desk, he had a pedestal table, and the sofa and chairs were leather, the color of butternut squash. Here was comfortable opulence, a room very different from the rest of the office suite.

His slim and smiling secretary ushered us into his sanctum, Paul barely glancing at us, leaning back after only half rising to shake hands.

"Tell me what you've got." He locked his hands behind his head and crossed his legs. "I have to be out of here by five, and it's almost four. Will that do it?" Our appointment had been for three-thirty.

Stan, willing as always to please, took out the one-page outline he had carefully prepared. "Sure, Paul." Since Stan can take five minutes or five hours to say the same thing, the deadline didn't faze him in the slightest.

The pictures on Paul's walls were of his son and daughter— an impish blond toddler and a dark-haired pre-adolescent version of Paul who gave promise of becoming a dynamite lady. And there was one framed photo of Paul, on a camel. He was thinner then, with dark hair and a mustache that did him no favors. The Paul who sat across the desk was suave, hair almost white, mustache gone, much more in his element among legal trivia than Arabian transportation. I hoped that he was taller than he seemed behind his desk, because I have a dread of Napoleon complexes.

Paul interrupted Stan's monologue now and then, asking a question, making a point with a pencil or an unbent paper clip, eyes often focused on the ceiling, always listening. By the time a tiny digital clock tucked among law books on a shelf showed five-fifteen he was leaning forward intently, eyes down now, fingers playing with the paper clip.

"Well, what do you think? Do we have a case?" Stan finished.

Paul sat back again, laid back. "If you're saying you think Bobbi is an unfit mother because she's a homosexual, you haven't got a chance." He waited for Stan's response.

"That's not the issue. I've known that for a long time. But it's only recently that the kids have been talking about wanting to leave—and why. They say they hate Joellyn, and feel Bobbi doesn't give them the love and care they want. I've given you dozens of examples, things the kids have told me themselves. It boils down to that the kids have told us they want out, and that's why I'm here." He smiled embarrassedly. "If the truth be known, I'd rather all three of them were happy there." Stan reached out for my hand. "Selfishly speaking, we'd have a lot more fun if it were just the two of us."

"If the things you've told me can be corroborated by Amy and Jennifer—and believe me, they will have to be—then I think you'll have a case and a chance to win."

When pressed, he put the odds at fifty-fifty. That was fifty percent better than the odds anyone had given us before, and I knew that would probably be sufficient to sell Stan on Paul and whatever power Greenbaum, Greenbaum, Rowe and Smith could hope to muster.

"I really do have to go now. I have to pick up my kids." It was Paul's turn to be embarrassed. "I'm divorced, you see, and tonight my kids spend with me."

"How about cost?" Stan, for once, was up front about money.

"These things are hard to judge, but I'd guess in the neighborhood of twenty-five thousand dollars if it actually gets to court. It could be fifty. Who knows? We charge on a time basis, so there are no guarantees."

He walked us to the point where shag turned to office functional chic. I was comforted by the fact that he was taller than I had feared.

"Think about it and get back to me. If we can start within the next week or two, we'll probably have a hearing sometime in early fall. The only other thing that I can say is that—well, if they were my kids, I'd do it."

We didn't interview another lawyer. Stan was convinced that Paul liked us immediately, and that he would have our best interests at heart. Besides, on the same day in 1936 Stan had been born in Brooklyn and Paul had been born in Budapest. Even more improbably, for much of their adult lives they had lived within blocks of each other, and had once almost bought the same house in New Jersey. It was karma through and through.

Now we could talk to the girls with more insight into the legal ramifications, what the process would mean to them. On two successive weekends with Amy and Jennifer we tested their commitment and pressed them.

"You have to talk to a court psychiatrist, to a probation officer, and then finally to the judge. As long as you tell them what you really think and feel, it should work out the way you want it to. But if you can't talk to them the way you've talked to us, and tell them *why* you want to live with us, as you've been telling us, it won't work and you'll probably have to stay in Camden."

They convinced us that they were up to it, although they were frightened of Bobbi's and Joellyn's reactions. "Joellyn will kill us if we say we want to live with you," Amy said, shaking her head.

"I know!" exclaimed Jennifer. "Let's trick everybody. We won't tell Mom or Joellyn, or anybody else, except the judge and the doctor, and that 'bation lady. We'll trick them all! Then on the last day the judge can just let us come with you!" She was very proud of her solution.

"It probably won't happen that way, babe," Stan said. "It would be better if you could tell everybody, including your mom, what you want to do. But if you can't, that's okay. Remember it's the judge, the psychiatrist, and the probation officer who count the most."

They solemnly promised that they would tell "everything" when they had to, and trusted us that it would not be too terrible an ordeal. Stan gave Paul the go-ahead, and that was the end of whatever semblance of normalcy we had been able to establish in our lives. Our whole world shattered, and we began first to be ruled and then consumed by this monster called a custody fight.

27

It had taken only two months for Dr. Hembree of Columbia Presbyterian Hospital to solve Stan's problem of retrograde ejaculation. The answer turned out to be little pink torpedo-shaped capsules, an over-the-counter remedy for hay fever and asthma. They cleared his nasal passages, revved him up so he was always out of breath, and made his reproductive system work the way nature intended it to by stimulating certain critical nerves and muscles.

When I first began to suspect I might be pregnant, I didn't dare believe it. It wasn't until we had begun to try in earnest to start another family that I let myself admit how important a baby of my own was to me. I loved Stan's three daughters dearly, but I needed to see a reflection of *me* in a child who called me Mommy, not the face of another woman. I wanted the chance to create my own struggles and troubles in raising a child, not try only to solve those of some other mother.

I knew I would be able to deal tranquilly with whatever horrors the custody action would bring as long as I had that little pocket of peace inside of me. And on the day that Bobbi was served with an Order to Show Cause why custody should not be transferred to Stan, my pregnancy was confirmed.

Thirteen months and fourteen days passed between the day we first met Paul Rowe and the day we sat in the Morris County

Courthouse to hear the final outcome of the case. The toll that the process took is incalculable, rocking and tossing everyone involved like dice in a tumbler. But the process is designed to serve justice and cannot be circumvented or ignored.

Custody trials are not jury trials; the verdict is arrived at by a judge, based on testimony that he hears from one party requesting the change, and the other who seeks to maintain the status quo. The burden of proof naturally fell upon Stan, to show not only through a factual basis that the transfer of custody was really in the best interests of the children, but also that there had been a significant change in circumstances since the initial custody arrangement was agreed to.

In a case of this type, with emotions so intense and bitter, the subjective evidence supplied by each side is often not sufficient to provide the judge with a true picture of the existing situation. Additional "fact witnesses" who testify generally don't carry much weight either, because it's only natural they will support the respective "fitness" of each parent.

Thus the "expert" witnesses—medical and investigative professionals either appointed by the court or hired by each side to present their interpretation of the facts—become critically important. The court usually requires a comparative investigation of each home environment, and often evaluation of all parties by an independent psychiatrist; almost always the parties are permitted to hire their own psychiatrists or psychologists.

The final perspective that the judge is given on the situation is derived from interviews with the children in private sessions, to explore their preferences, if they have any. Very often children will be happy with their existing situation, and that will override any factors which might otherwise have indicated a switch in custody.

But ultimately the outcome, the determination of what will become of a child's life, depends on the way one person only, the judge, assimilates the evidence that is presented, processes it internally, and draws his conclusions. It is very very scary.

It sounded, as Paul described it to us, simple and straightforward. Like everything else we've ever done, it turned out to be anything but.

Once the decision to proceed was made, Paul and Stan spent weeks preparing the initial affidavit seeking a change in custody. It outlined in eleven succinct pages events the children had related to us, and statements they had made to us about their feelings. At Paul's direction, homosexuality was noted as an issue only insofar as the children articulated their distress over certain specifically relevant occurrences.

We had, of course, expected a reaction to Stan's single affidavit, but what we got was overreaction. Bobbi presented forty-three affidavits in response to Stan's one, her intent clearly being to inundate the court with every imaginable (and unimaginable) accusation against Stan, and to paint a portrait of Roberta that combined the attributes of Wonder Woman, Carrie Nation, and the Blessed Mother. Her game plan appeared to be not to play at all—to convince the court that there wasn't any basis for a case, no change in circumstance, no reason to transfer custody, not even the children's articulated preference.

Most of Bobbi's affidavits were from friends and acquaintances, but there were two that were objectively disturbing. One was from Dr. Frances Seidman, a psychologist, the other from Dr. Richard Green, a psychiatrist. Both "experts" recommended on the basis of their interviews with Amy and Jennifer, whom they saw within days of Bobbi's being served with the Order to Show Cause, that the children's best interests would be served if they were allowed to remain with their natural mother.

Paul was outraged and nervous as we literally weighed the bulk of their defense against Stan's few pages of complaint, and it was the expert affidavits that caused him the most concern. Each child had told Dr. Green that she wanted to stay in Camden and live with her mother.

"They should have waited for the order from the judge before they took the girls to see anybody, but we can't do anything about it now. That affidavit from Green is going to hurt us, though." He shook his head and blew out his breath from between pursed lips. "We'll just have to see what the judge does. He may just see it as some kind of smokescreen. The lady doth protest too much and all that. There will be a hearing on the third of July to decide the merits of having a plenary hearing—that means the actual trial. We should win that, but from then on it's all uphill."

Stan was naturally optimistic, and never even considered the possibility that we would do anything but prevail; I was more inclined to Paul's pessimism. But we both wished we had something more on our side going into that hearing on July third than Stan's skinny affidavit, which contained much information about life in Bobbi's household that we had gotten over the years from Leslie, Amy, and Jennifer rather than firsthand knowledge. We were shooting a lot of bullets that the girls had given us, and we had no way of knowing whether or not they were blanks.

The week before the hearing was intense with activity reviewing the hundreds of pages of accusations, denials, and opinions in the affidavits and preparing for every contingency.

All everybody wanted to talk about was custody: could we get it, would we get it, how would we get it, and how miserable would the whole revolting process be. It was as if nothing else in the world existed. All I wanted to do was revel in the miracle that was happening in my belly, but everybody was too distracted to join me. Day by day I compared the little thing in me to the appropriate microphotographs of fetal development, transfixed by a book that Stan had given me for Mother's Day. It was the most exciting prospect I had ever faced, and I was savoring it.

The week we spent in Cutler before the hearing was bleak. I woke up Monday morning and the fog on the harbor was smothering and chilly. Stan spoke to Paul half a dozen times, but I had had custody up the kazoo and couldn't stand to listen to another word of it.

A few times I wandered out to the back of the house, where we were building an addition—including a nursery—but it was cold and the hammers were noisy, so I went back inside.

Tuesday was my birthday. I was thirty-three. I sat in the living room in one of the mission rockers, reading about my five-or-six-week-old fetus, wishing as I gazed out the window that the wind would shift to southwest and blow the fog out to sea.

"What's the matter, Marila?" Stan was reorganizing his burgeoning custody file. "How's the little mother? I thought it would be fun if we went to the Lincoln House tonight to celebrate your birthday. What do you think?"

"I don't feel like doing much of anything, but if you want to, it's okay with me."

My head was beginning to throb, so I took a Tylenol, despite my worry that it might have an adverse effect on the baby. I surveyed the construction again, and John, the contractor and our dear neighbor, chased me back inside. "You shouldn't be out here on a day like this in bare feet. You can't catch a cold now!" I decided to escape in sleep.

I'd been dozing for an hour or so when Stan came to find me. "Are you okay?" he asked solicitously. He lowered himself onto the bed and gathered me in his arms, and I slept again with my head on his shoulder.

When I woke up this time I found I was bleeding—huge red rushes of blood that filled me with grief, not fear. I wanted to keep my legs crossed and my thighs tightly pressed together so the little life couldn't wash away. I cried silently all the way to the hospital.

Sometime before dawn the bleeding slowed to a trickle, and in the morning the doctor confirmed what in my heart I already knew. There wouldn't be any baby this time.

The most amazing thing of all to me was how quickly the process of creating life takes over your body, changing it in such subtle, almost imperceptible ways. I tried to recall the sensation of fullness, and couldn't. I was just flat and empty and felt very much alone.

Stan didn't go to New Jersey for the hearing on the third; he brought me home from the hospital instead. Paul called, satisfied.

"We got what we were entitled to," he said. "I thought for a moment Bobbi's lawyer was going to cry. Her voice actually quavered when she realized she would lose. But as a matter of law there was no way she could have won."

He recounted the court proceeding to us with great delight, and we hoped he would prove half as brilliant over the long haul as he had evidently been that day. He secured for Amy and Jennifer their right to a full hearing and an evaluation by a court-appointed psychiatrist, as well as an evaluation of both home environments by the Morris County probation department, the equivalent of Human Services or Health and Welfare in many states.

It was, Paul assured us, cause for tightly reined optimism. "Maybe you *will* get a fair shake. But remember, judges don't like to find that a mother is unfit. And the fact that she's a lesbian isn't going to work in your favor necessarily; as a matter of fact it might even work against you."

We knew that only too clearly, because as Stan had been preparing to file his suit, Joellyn's ex-husband was facing her in court in a custody fight for their children based on that very issue. He lost before he began, in a three-day hearing that swept away his feeble protests in a tide of gay-rights power.

"We can't take the girls to be evaluated by your expert, whoever that will be, though," Paul continued, "until after the court psychiatrist has made his finding. That's because the judge was annoyed that Bobbi had rushed the kids out to Seidman and Green. They were both involved in Joellyn's case, by the way."

"That's not fair, Paul. We should have the same chance Bobbi does," I said.

"Don't worry, Mary. You still have the option—you just have to wait to exercise it, that's all. He doesn't want the girls put through any more stress than necessary. And if it turns out the shrink he appoints decides in your favor, then you won't even need another expert."

"How about the visitation this weekend?" Stan had been unable to see his daughters, and had barely spoken to them, in the three weeks since Bobbi had been served with the Order to Show Cause.

Bobbi had been successfully keeping them incommunicado by leaving her phone off the hook, hanging up when she picked up on Stan, or telling him that the girls were "asleep" or out playing. Part of the proceeding that day had been to ensure Stan access to the girls.

"You can pick them up tomorrow," Paul said. "And Bobbi was there in the courtroom and heard the judge order that she couldn't interfere with visitation as it was spelled out in your separation agreement, which is three out of four weekends. So we won that too. All in all, Stan, we had a very good day."

Neither Stan nor I wanted him to go away that weekend. I needed him with me and he wanted to stay. But we both knew that he had no choice.

Stan called Bobbi and told her he'd be picking up the girls in the afternoon, after taking an early-morning flight down. She spared the time for a scornful "They won't be here, so don't waste your time," and hung up. She was apparently ignoring the outcome of the day before in court.

But Stan went down anyway, and, as Bobbi had predicted, nobody was home when he arrived at the Camdenites, as we had begun to call Roberta and Joellyn collectively. He was angry and frustrated, growing more so because it took two weeks thereafter for Paul to get a consent order allowing Stan to see Amy and Jennifer.

All in all, six weeks passed before we saw the little ones, weeks that had left their mark on the childish faces that greeted us with a mixture of fear and delight. Jennifer's arms encircled my waist so tightly it hurt, and she buried her face in my chest. "She cried all the way home," Stan said to me.

But Amy's eyes were twinkling and a smile was tickling the corners of her mouth.

"They said we'd lost, but Dad says that isn't true. It isn't, is it? I mean, we haven't lost? I'm really gonna get a chance to talk to the judge? Why did they say we lost when we didn't? That was mean. They said that so many people were writing affidavits that we couldn't win. They said you only wrote one,

Dad, and that it was all lies." She was breathless, but in her Amy way she forged on, relieving the pressures that had been building up during her enforced separation from us.

"Are you sure we won? They got all those affidavits, Dad. And my mom's lawyer is a good one, Dad. She won Joellyn's case. They say Paul's no good, and you lost."

According to Stan she had been rattling on in the same vein for the last hour and a half, petrified that her battle was over before it had begun, wanting desperately to hear that wasn't so.

"We tricked Dr. Green," Jennifer contributed once during the weekend. "You said we only had to tell the probation officer and court psychiatrist and the judge, and Dr. Green was a friend of my mom's and Joellyn's. If we told him we wanted to live with you, he would have told them and then we'd have been in trouble."

It was a long and difficult weekend, trying to convince the little skeptics that it wasn't the end of the line, and we were in a lot better shape than they thought.

"Don't you worry, Amy Rose. You're going to have the chance to tell the judge what you want and what you feel. I promise." And because they had such faith in their father, they finally believed him.

The girls spent August with us as usual, and the main topic of conversation this year was, of course, custody. They decided that they had to be up-front with Bobbi about where they wanted to live.

"Mom doesn't talk about it with us," they said. "She just tells us we lost. She never asks us what we want."

"And you haven't said that you want to live with us?"

The two heads shook in unison. "We're afraid of what they'll do. Joellyn gets so mad at us."

They called Bobbi on the phone several times to convince her to let them start school in Cutler in September.

"We'll visit you a lot," said Amy kindly. "And it doesn't mean we don't love you, Mom. It just means we want to do what's best for us. It's *our* lives, you know." But Bobbi refused to discuss it, and finally, in the middle of August, she had her number changed and unlisted.

The week after Labor Day, Stan, Leslie, and I came down to Morristown from Cutler for our interviews with the probation officer, having been given hardly any notice. We had no idea whatsoever when she was going to see Amy and Jenny. Once they went back to Camden after summer vacation we lost touch with them again, with almost no calls getting through and visitation made impossible. Stan was unable to tell them the probation officer, Mrs. Kaszerman, was their friend, and they should be open with her.

It was Mrs. Kaszerman herself who told us that she had seen Amy, Jennifer, Roberta, and Joellyn in Camden just a few days before. Middle-aged and fidgety, she spent a great deal of time telling us how very pleasant Bobbi and Joellyn seemed, and what a shame it was that all of this was happening. Still, Stan telephoned Paul later with confidence.

"I think she liked us. She told me not to worry, everything would work out for us."

"Those were her exact words, Stan?" I could visualize Paul in his office, eyes focused on an imaginary spot in the ceiling as they had been that first day we met him.

"Well, not exactly. But that was the impression I had."

"Stan, I've never met a client yet who thought he or she did poorly on a probation investigation. Don't count on anything until we read that report. But I sure hope you're right, because if she goes the other way we're in trouble. All we have left is Buxton." Buxton was Martin Buxton, the child psychiatrist the judge had named as the independent court psychiatrist.

"Don't worry, Paul. I'm sure the girls did fine."

They didn't. The report from Mrs. Kaszerman, distributed the last week in September, was a real blow. Despite the many pages describing an environment in Camden that at best could be considered way outside the norm of American culture, the paragraph of conclusion was clear.

The house was clean and neat; the Camdenites were concerned

268

and caring "parents"; Amy said moving to Maine with us would be a "disaster," and Jenny refused to commit herself until she spoke privately to the judge. There was not, in Mrs. Kaszerman's opinion, any reason whatsoever to transfer custody.

Stan was sick, Paul offhand. "You win some, you lose some." But we knew he felt the defeat almost as deeply as we did.

While we had been waiting for the probation report and dates for the interviews with Dr. Buxton to be set—the next logical step in the process—a side issue was heard in court: visitation and telephone access. Paul once more proved his worth, reestablishing the thrice-monthly weekend visitation and obtaining an order for daily phone calls.

The more important victory that day was Leslie's. Her mother had counterfiled a motion which would require Leslie to visit Camden every weekend, an extraordinary request since in the more than year that Leslie had been living with us she had only seen Bobbi once, when Stan had taken her to Camden, suggesting that she try to work out her relationship with Bobbi. After that hour-long visit, Bobbi said, "We'll have to stay in touch," but nothing ever came of it.

"If she wants to see me she should call me, or invite me, or write me. Not ask some judge to make me see her. I'll run away if I have to go," Leslie said angrily.

Primarily on the basis of an affidavit that Leslie wrote describing her feelings and her perception of her relationship with Bobbi, the judge determined that Leslie was free to visit her mother only if and when she chose.

With the harassment of our inability to see and talk to Amy and Jennifer seemingly over at last, Stan dedicated himself to encouraging the girls to tell the truth to Dr. Buxton. Paul had already advised us to drop the whole thing if the interviews with Buxton were a repeat of those with Green and Kaszerman.

"You're sure they aren't just telling you what you want to hear, aren't you? You really believe they want to live with you? They're not making this stuff up? Remember, you and Bobbi, Stan, just cancel each other out. It's the professionals who will make the difference, and right now you're not doing well." We were sure in our hearts, but that wasn't getting us anywhere.

"Tell Dr. Buxton what you feel, girls, tell him what you've told us, and tell him what you feel. You don't have to be afraid to tell the truth, or to talk about your feelings."

"Don't worry, Daddy, we'll tell him," said Jennifer seriously.

"But you didn't tell Mrs. Kaszerman," he answered.

"Daddy," she informed him righteously. "I didn't know that was the probation lady. I thought she was a friend of my mom's. Besides, my mom and Joellyn could hear. That's why I didn't tell her. But I'll tell the doctor and the judge."

"Will they find out what we say to Buxton?" Amy was facing some of the harsher realities of the situation. " 'Cause they'll sure be mad."

"They probably will, Amy Rose," Stan told Amy. "But if you can't tell Dr. Buxton, then I think we'll lose. Right now we've got a good chance to win," he exaggerated, "but if Dr. Buxton thinks you should live with Bobbi, that's probably what will happen."

"We can try again next year though, right?" asked Amy hopefully.

"I'm afraid not, honey. It's so expensive that we might not be able to do it again." We were approaching Paul's original estimate and there wasn't even a trial date yet. "This is it, Amy. You've got to do it now if you really want it. I know it's tough, but there isn't any other way. Think you can do it?"

"Well, I guess. But they're gonna burn!"

Bobbi bought them each a five-speed dirt bike the week before they saw Dr. Buxton. "It's a bribe," Amy whispered on the phone when she told us about it. "But don't worry, it didn't work. I haven't changed my mind."

Six weeks passed before the results of Dr. Buxton's methodical, comprehensive interviews were released, six weeks of terrible tension that was compounded by three events: The court transferred the case to another judge, Bobbi hired a new lawyer, and we were informed that for several months our telephone calls with Amy and Jennifer had been taped.

We didn't get just *another* judge, we got a *new* one. Judge Newman had been succeeded by Judge Shelton when he returned to private practice at the end of the summer, so not only was this Judge Daniel Coburn our third judge, but we were one of his first cases.

"I don't know why this happened," Paul told us. "It could be that Shelton's calendar was so backed up this was the only way to get the trial going before spring." He didn't know anything more about Coburn beyond that he was young and had a reputation as a high-powered tough attorney.

After not faring well in any of the skirmishes that had so far brought us to court, Bobbi must have decided that she needed an attorney with enough clout to match Paul, who was, I'm sure, a much more formidable opponent than she had ever anticipated Stan would retain. She replaced the lawyer who had been adequate for Joellyn's custody suit, a not unattractive, rectangularly shaped and featured woman, with Annamay Sheppard, a diminutive wisp of a lady with wispy hair. But she was a professor at the Rutgers University law school who had a history of involvements in various causes, a civil libertarian who would fight for what she saw as someone's rights, and who had a reputation for not losing. She gave up her sabbatical to fight for Roberta.

One of her first interactions with Paul concerned "the tapes," ten hours of cassettes containing more than four hours of intermittent recorded conversations between Stan and/or me, and Leslie and Amy and Jennifer.

"What have you been telling those kids? Annamay just told me she had listened to these tapes, and they were 'hair-raising.' Did you know they were taping you? They say you've brainwashed the kids, threatened them, and bribed them."

"Paul, all we've ever said was that they should say what they feel. Is that so terrible?" Stan was calm, but I was furious. The idea that someone had been eavesdropping on my conversations for months was too much to bear.

The tapes became an issue in the case, but not for some time. More pressing was Buxton's report and opinion, because as Paul kept pushing the court to set a trial date, the other side was trying to prevent it altogether. "The probation report was in our favor," Bobbi's lawyer said, "so if Dr. Buxton comes to the same conclusion there's no point in proceeding." Privately, we agreed with her.

As we waited those weeks for Dr. Buxton's all-important report, Amy and Jennifer were feeling the tension too, bearing the brunt of Joellyn's short temper and Bobbi's indifference.

One Saturday we picked up the girls, and Amy looked as if she'd been caught up in a tornado and set down in a mud hole.

"Joellyn threw me out of the house this morning, and wouldn't let me back in," she sobbed. "She grabbed me and spit in my face, and told me how mean I was to my mother. I hate her." Amy vowed she had done nothing to provoke Joellyn (as we knew she often did) but was in her bedroom practicing songs for her school Christmas concert. We didn't know what to think.

"And look at this. Listen to what they said." She pulled out of her pocket a piece of yellow ruled paper, covered with comments in her childish print-writing, written with varying degrees of legibility at various angles. She read them aloud, like a roving reporter, then handed it to me.

"What *is* this, Amy?" The paper was covered with run-of-the-mill jibes and epithets, nothing we hadn't heard before.

"I sat at the top of the stairs in the dark and wrote down what they said. They were talking about you and Daddy and Paul and saying bad things."

Sunday morning, Amy sat at the end of our bed, arms wrapped around her knees.

"What's that, Amy?" Stan asked, pointing to her arm. "Let me see."

There were four clear marks resembling fingerprints, three on the top, one on the underside of Amy's arm.

"Is that where Joellyn grabbed you?" The thought had come to both of us at the same moment. Amy just nodded.

Stan was on the phone in less than two minutes, and a minute later had Paul on the other end.

"I'm not sending them back there."

"You have to."

"I can't. What if something else happens?" I knew he was thinking about the times that Leslie, Amy, and Jennifer had told us that Joellyn had beaten Amy with a belt.

"Let me think about it. I'll call you back."

Paul did his thinking quickly. The phone rang ten minutes later.

"First I want you to know we aren't going to win this motion. No judge, especially one who doesn't have his feet wet, is going to transfer custody on a temporary basis in a case like this. It's too hot. So don't be disappointed if we lose this one." We didn't believe him.

Monday morning Annamay was informed of our emergency application to transfer custody, and Paul was informed by Judge Coburn's office that Dr. Buxton had recommended that custody be awarded to us. The judge said he had tried to call Paul Saturday, but had been unable to reach him.

Bobbi was in court that afternoon, but Joellyn didn't show.

Judge Coburn examined Amy's arm in chambers. He read the affidavits. He didn't listen to any testimony, talk to the kids about what had happened, or take any oral argument from the attorneys. Motion dismissed, as Paul had predicted.

What Coburn did do was tell Roberta in no uncertain terms that she had a responsibility for the safety of her children, and an obligation to control her paramour's temper. Then he appointed a "guardian ad litem," whom Amy and Jennifer were to call every day until the trial was over.

Neither Amy nor Jennifer had spoken to Bobbi when they saw her, and she hadn't spoken to them. They had stood behind me, worried, silent, preparing to face whatever wrath awaited them for having exposed in black and blue a side of Joellyn and

Bobbi that everyone, including us, had been reluctant to believe.

Bobbi's expression wasn't particularly triumphant as she waited for her daughters to untangle themselves from my skirt so she could take them home.

There had been no ambiguity in Martin Buxton's conclusions, and none in what the children had told him. They had done the first half of what they promised to do—they had told the court psychiatrist. But when the report came back so decisively favorable to us, Annamay demanded the right to get another expert. The good Judge Coburn, to our intense disappointment, agreed.

Dr. Robert Gould, the second expert for the defense, had signed an affidavit recommending custody be awarded to Bobbi and Joellyn without having met either them or the girls. After Coburn gave his approval for another expert, Gould finally interviewed the four of them, but his post-interview conclusion merely confirmed his pre-interview affidavit. He also listened to the tapes. "They've been brainwashed," he said, accounting for Amy's and Jennifer's strong statements to him about their desire to live with us.

After examining Dr. Gould's deposition, Paul had insisted on another expert for us. "You don't have any choice. They have Gould, Green, Kaszerman, and Seidman. All you have is Buxton. I'm going before Coburn day after tomorrow and I need a name." He paused. "And the interviews have to be conducted within a week."

"Paul. Tomorrow's Christmas. Where am I going to find somebody now?" Even Stan thought this assignment difficult.

"Sorry, Stan. There's no choice." He was more upset than he let on; for once he didn't use his speaker phone.

A psychiatrist friend of a psychiatrist friend gave us two possibilities. Stan called them both, leaving word with their respective answering services. We didn't have much hope.

That year we were having a New England Christmas in Vermont. The three girls were with us, and my sisters, Lacey, with her family, and Liz. It was the best Christmas I could ever remember, with my whole family together, as well as a blessed interlude in the ever-growing craziness of the custody fight. Stan and I found much appreciated solace, and sympathy from both my parents.

It was nearly eleven o'clock on Christmas Eve when the phone rang, and everyone was in the midst of ribbons and wrappings, eggnog and cheer. It was Dr. Bertrand New. He listened to a capsule of the case, and agreed to take it on provided we understood at the outset that if he found Amy and Jennifer were better off where they were, he would recommend they stay.

As had Dr. Buxton, Dr. New interviewed not only Bobbi, Joellyn, and the children, but Stan, Leslie, and myself. And when he was deposed by Annamay, he was almost as strong in his conclusions as Dr. Buxton. We dared to breathe just a drop easier. He had listened to several "selected" tapes, recommended by Annamay as most damning, but they didn't change his opinion. In fact, they supported it because he felt they showed the strength of the bond between the children and us.

"Don't kid yourself," said Captain Paul. "Now you're going in only a little bit behind, instead of a lot. You've got two shrinks; they've got two shrinks. They've got Kaszerman. And you're trying to go against everyone's natural instinct, which is that mothers are terrific, no matter what. We've got a shot now, but that's all."

The last big question to settle before the trial began was the tapes. The defense wanted the judge to hear the tapes, proof, they thought, that Stan had "brainwashed" Amy and Jennifer into saying they wanted to live with him. Paul wanted to keep the tapes out of evidence, but decided at the last moment to withdraw the motion he had prepared to suppress them.

"If we win, it might make Gould worthless as an expert because he partially based his conclusions on them. Then they would be able to get another expert. New heard them too, so his testimony might be knocked out also. And I don't want to make this a constitutional issue, whether or not a parent can tape calls without her children's knowledge and consent. We'd end up in the Supreme Court.

"But the real reason I think we shouldn't proceed is that Coburn wants to hear them. For whatever reason he can think of, he'll overrule me. What do you think?"

Stan and I both agreed. After all, it was his show. Besides, we didn't think we could conceivably have said anything that was so terrible, and nothing we probably wouldn't say again given the same circumstances.

The Friday before the trial was to begin, Stan picked up the girls as usual for the weekend. They were crying.

"Joellyn put her hand under my chin, and pushed my head back till it hurt," Amy sputtered.

"And she grabbed my face and squished it," Jennifer related wide-eyed. "It hurt. I don't ever want to go back there again."

Saturday she locked herself in the bathroom, letting me in only after much cajoling. Her face was tear-streaked, and the smudges of weariness under her eyes stood out against her pale complexion.

"I've been talking to my grave," she told me. "I want to die." She confided to me tearfully about the night when she had sneaked down to the kitchen in Camden and taken a knife out of the drawer.

"I held it to my tummy, but I couldn't do anything. I knew you and Daddy would be too sad."

So instead of the actual trial beginning, Judge Coburn heard another motion requesting immediate transfer of custody. Once again Paul warned us it was a futile effort.

"He'll never do it. Don't get your hopes up." But we couldn't help ourselves. How could a wise judge send them back to Camden?

The mini-trial took three days, and the children spent the intervening nights with their guardian ad litem. The days were spent with me in the big green waiting room of the county courthouse.

Each child finally had about thirty minutes with Judge Coburn. When Amy came out she said, "I did good." Jenny shook her head. "I did good too, but not good enough. He didn't believe me. I could tell."

Amy stood on one side of him, and Jenny on the other, high up on the bench when he made his pronouncement.

"I've decided that you should go back home with your mom." He was talking to them, but he didn't look at their faces, didn't see the shock and agony that crumpled Jennifer, the fear and defeat that washed over Amy.

We were allowed to take them out to dinner, he added.

Jennifer rushed sobbing to her father, around Bobbi. Amy went to him too, more slowly, carefully avoiding Roberta.

"Go back to your mother, Amy. Say hello to her." It was Judge Coburn speaking. Amy turned and went back, woodenly obedient, so that Bobbi could give her an equally wooden hug.

Stan and Amy went to get the car, and I waited, holding Jenny in my arms, rocking her as the tears wracked her little body. I sat on the steps right outside Coburn's office willing that he hear the effect of his decision, and imagine that it was his own nine-year-old daughter who was so unhappy.

28

Despite the fact that the three days we spent fighting for temporary custody didn't achieve the desired result, it had given Judge Coburn an opportunity to get a feel for all the players in our drama, and unusually in this kind of an action, to listen to much of the evidence that would be presented in court, having already met and talked to the children.

The sequence of trial events was: plaintiff fact case; defendant fact case; court experts; plaintiff experts; defense experts; and finally, rebuttal. Then the judge would meet with Amy and Jennifer *in camera*, privately in his chambers.

Right from the beginning we were fighting two different cases. All we wanted to do was provide Amy and Jennifer with a forum where they could speak their piece. Bobbi and Joellyn were ignoring the myriad of factors that over the years had created the children's distress, fixating on their desire to prove that they led a "traditional" life, and tried to impart "traditional" values to their children.

Stan and I occupied the same seats for the entire course of the trial, usually just the two of us front row center in what seemed like a theater of the bizarre. The rest of the courtroom was filled with what felt like fifty but was actually closer to ten supporters of Bobbi and Joellyn, most of whom disappeared when it was time for the defendant's case. Several reporters from area newspapers attended on a daily basis.

Stan was the first witness. Paul took a day and a half to question him; Annamay four to cross-examine. Judge Coburn kept taking potshots at Stan's attempts to overexplain and overdetail.

"When you ask Mr. Silverzweig what time it is," he said wryly at one point, "he tells you how to make a clock." The judge seemed oblivious to the fact that Mrs. Sheppard always had one more question, always wanted one more answer.

Paul questioned Stan casually, leaning against the empty jury box or the window sill; sometimes he sat sprawled at the attorney's table the way he did in his office. In her turn, Annamay stalked the room, holding her right side with her left hand constantly as if she were in sustained and terrible pain.

Her questions were often double-negatived and often incomprehensible. At Stan's puzzled expressions she would pause and glance at the judge and then at Paul, who likely as not was on his feet with an objection. Biting hard on a pencil, Annamay would say, "That wasn't a very good question, was it?" (She must have, by the end of the trial, chewed the erasers off a dozen gross of pencils.)

Paul would agree with her assessment, and the judge would overrule the objection. "You're right, Mr. Rowe, but I'm going to let it in anyway." Then Judge Coburn would say to Annamay, "What you really mean is . . ." Her eyes lighting up, she would scurry off to ask the judge's question, which Stan was obliged to answer.

Sometimes Annamay helped us. "She might as well give you a crib sheet," Stan laughed, when he clued me in.

Along with one of her voluminous questions, she would often present her copy of the piece of evidence she was using to make her point. Invariably there would be sufficient penciled notes in the margin so that we could figure out what was coming and what was to follow.

She also had a helpful tendency to ask questions of Paul, and occasionally Stan or me, during the recesses. More than once that prepared us for what might otherwise have been a surprise.

Because of the interruptions, objections, other cases on Coburn's calendar, recesses, and interminable colloquies, it took Stan and me five weeks to get through our testimonies, even though I spent only a little more than two days on the stand.

Judge Coburn chastised me for my "inappropriate behavior and bad taste" in signing two of more than forty-eight of Bobbi's support and alimony checks. (Paul consoled me by telling me of a client who had had alimony checks imprinted with a photograph of him and his second wife waving from a California beach. "*That's* bad taste," he teased.)

And Coburn rebuked me for not answering Annamay's questions as directly as he thought I could. He raised his voice and it came down to me from the bench like God to Moses, and his eyes crackled, making me tremble even more.

In her best lawyer fashion, Annamay would purse her face and punch with her voice, trying to make me say something I didn't want to say, or contradict myself. Her prim and mousy manner belied her force and formidability, and it took a tremendous amount of willpower not to let her convince me that black was white.

Most of testifying was painful, remembering things I'd rather forget, things that had created such resentment in our early together years. The saddest moments came when I talked about Leslie, how hurt and rejected she felt by the deterioration of her relationship with her mother. Bobbi got up in the middle and left the courtroom.

Leslie was called upon to testify next, an ordeal that lasted on and off for five days, a few hours each day, which makes the experience worse, not better. And if there was one witness Annamay tried to get, it was Leslie. The object of the exercise, as we saw it, was to make her seem malicious, conniving, lying, hysterical, revengeful, and materialistic.

Perhaps Annamay was only doing her job. In Paul's mind, Leslie was the most critical witness in the trial. She was the only person in the world who could with any degree of objectivity compare the two households in which she had lived, and describe the environment that she perceived in Bobbi's home which had made her leave.

Leslie's believability would be paramount in Coburn's mind as he drew his conclusions and made his decision, Paul felt. We didn't tell her that beforehand, because we didn't want to make her any more nervous than she already was. She was terrified and desolate, because her testifying in a crowded open courtroom would transform the betrayal of Bobbi that she had felt only in her mind into the real thing. It is to Leslie's credit that she survived, and with a great deal of dignity.

The first forty minutes of her cross-examination were filled with "I can't remember"; "I don't know"; "I can't answer that." She was drawing a complete blank, saying nothing rather than make a mistake. Coburn thought she was stonewalling, and criticized her severely for it.

He called a recess when he saw her start to cry, and I followed her into the ladies' room.

"I hate him, I hate him. I really can't remember. He's so mean. How can anyone so mean be a judge?" It was hard to reassure her when I was having the same thoughts myself.

Annamay played to all of Leslie's insecurities, to the feeling Leslie harbored that sometime between infancy and puberty she had done something so dreadful to her mother that Bobbi hated her. Annamay tried to convince Leslie that she was the one who had created the breach between herself and Bobbi and it was therefore her responsibility to heal it. Leslie argued with Annamay, plainly but politely.

"Why should it be me? I write to her, and she doesn't answer. She doesn't call me, or come to see me. Why don't you ask her why *she* doesn't reach out to *me?* What else can I do?" Leslie's eyes were wet but she wasn't crying. Her face was flushed with emotion.

Annamay bit down hard for a moment on her pencil's eraser, appraising Leslie thoughtfully. "Leslie, you and I ought to get together over lunch someday, and I'll *tell* you what you should do." She waved away Paul's objection at her gratuitous remark with a brief apology.

We'll never really know if Judge Coburn believed the facts that Leslie offered about her life in Camden. But no one sitting in that courtroom, not the judge or the lawyers, not Stan or I, not Roberta or Joellyn, or the people whom they brought with them every day to intimidate Leslie—not one person there could doubt that she cared about her mother, but felt through and through that her mother didn't give a damn about her.

Leslie was finally done, having suffered from enormous pressure and ridiculing laughter from Bobbi's friends in the courtroom, some of whom were people whom she too had counted among her friends. She had withstood a far more pressing cross-examination on the facts than either Stan or I, and she left the stand drained and pale, but proud of herself. As we prepared to leave for the day, Bobbi pushed me aside roughly and faced her daughter.

"I do love you. I've always loved you. And don't you ever forget it." She emphasized each word with a stubby forefinger, and turned and walked away without waiting for a response. That was six months ago as I write this, and she hasn't spoken to Leslie since.

We had one more fact witness, Sara Stone. Sara was really a witness for the children. Sara and Adam, still living in their smokehouse, had stayed in close contact with Stan and me over the years, and all three girls had often confided in her. Amy and Jenny had asked Sara six months before to mail letters to the judge for them, letters they had written because they saw the court process as taking too long.

Then the plaintiff rested, and the Camdenites got their shot at us.

By time we'd been in court on and off for more than six weeks. We'd practically given up working, rarely knowing until a day or two in advance what the court schedule was going to be. We also didn't have the energy to work. The weeks in court, on the heels of the months of preparation and waiting, had sapped us of energy, passion, and patience; we had very little left for each other, let alone our clients.

As I think back, the days melt into each other, drab pools of gray winter skies and slushy streets. Even when the sky was blue, the ground dry, and the daffodils sprinkling the gardens of Morris County. Beyond custody, the strategy, the outcome, the day's events, the events of yesterday and tomorrow, there was little conversation between us.

It took an hour for Stan and me to drive to Morristown from New York, and more often than not we'd drive in uncompanionable silence. One morning he admitted something I had always suspected, and he had always denied.

"You were right, Marila, all those years when you told me you had to go through this thing whether you wanted to or not."

"What made you come to that conclusion?" I looked up from the notes of Bobbi's testimony that we were going to review with Paul.

"Next to marrying you, this is the most important thing I've ever done in my life. Win, lose, or draw, I had to give those kids a chance to get out of there if they wanted to. If you had stopped me—and you could have—things would never have been the same between us. I always would have been resentful."

The brightness in each of those long court days for me was Paul. The three of us met over breakfast to plan the day in a coffee shop near the courthouse, and he usually greeted me with a sleep-crusted "Hello, Mary," and grinned a crooked grin. For lunch there were two options, a luncheonette with a big cook, or a pub where all the waitresses had big boobs. Paul invariably chose the latter, and by the time the trial was half over they were holding a table for us every day.

Paul is a brilliant lawyer, sometimes arrogant, usually sensitive. He always seemed to know when to smile, tease, counsel, or command, telling us in various ways what to say, when to say it, and how to say it. He knew what points to press, and which

283

ones to pass by because they weren't important enough in the larger picture, or he sensed Coburn didn't want to deal with a particular issue. He also became our very good friend.

"The thing that really pisses me off is that I can't win this case for you," Paul said sadly over an after-court Bombay martini. Then he laughed. "Even though I'm so good." Once again serious, he added, "All I can do is make sure you don't lose it. We shouldn't lose. But we might." If he made any mistakes, we still don't know what they are.

Another resource that I depended on during those difficult days was my mother. She came down from Vermont to spend the first week of the trial with us, and tired as I was at the end of each day, I seemed to need the hours that we spent talking into the early morning. And many was the day during court when I would slip out the back door, having had more than I could take for the moment, and go to the old wooden phone booth in the foyer to call her. No matter when I called, no matter what I asked of her, she was always there. So was my father, and Stan felt especially grateful for the many times Papa listened to him, counseled and commiserated, supporting him through some very difficult days in a way that I couldn't.

Judge Coburn was fascinated by the tape recordings Bobbi had made. It was our own private Watergate, complete with erasures, gaps, and a few extraneous conversations which were hilarious.

Bobbi stated two motives for taping her children's phone calls. One was to have a record that the girls called on a regular basis as required by the court order signed in September, and the other was to ensure that Stan didn't abuse the girls verbally as she said she had heard, and a baby-sitter who also had eavesdropped on one of his conversations claimed. So Bobbi bought an adapter at Radio Shack for $3.95 that enabled her to record any incoming or outgoing call once the receiver had been picked up.

The judge used special audio equipment so he could listen to the tapes carefully, examining them as closely as I'm sure he would have had they been submitted as evidence against him when he was an attorney, or before he would have submitted them as evidence himself.

"You know," he said, "I probably know more about these two homes than anyone else. It isn't just from the conversations that take place on the telephone, either. Those tapes are in evidence, and *everything* that's on them is in evidence." We all realized that he had heard things that no one else had. His equipment picked up background sound, as important to him as the content of each conversation.

As expected, Bobbi's testimony was largely the opposite of Stan's, although, unlike him, she often contradicted herself or the evidence, or had no explanation at all. Take P-19, for instance.

Plaintiff's exhibit P-19 was the yellow piece of lined paper Amy had written on in the night, a spontaneous expression of her feelings, and a recounting of happenings. Part of its significance was that it reinforced the impact of the letter Amy had written to the judge, a letter scoffed at by the defense as implausible and prompted by Stan.

Roberta could think of no reason for anything that Amy had written; in fact, she didn't believe that Amy had done it at all. "Amy doesn't print," she said.

Judge Coburn took the sheet of yellow foolscap from Paul after he had finished his cross-examination on it, and examined it carefully for several minutes. Then he stepped down from the bench and stood by Bobbi at the witness stand.

" 'My mother said I was an asshole,' " Coburn read. "Did you say that?"

"No, I've never said that."

" 'She said I was going to lose out on going to live with my dad.' Did you say that?"

"No."

" 'She called her lawyer at nine thirty-five.' Did you speak to Mrs. Sheppard that night?"

"No, I don't think so. I don't remember."

" 'She said she got what she wanted, she got Leslie on tape. Did you say that?"

"No, that's not true. I didn't mean to tape Leslie. I just forgot to turn the machine off after Amy and Jenny had spoken to her."

He read on and on, every statement and comment that Amy had scrawled. "She called my dad a liar." "They are going to try and shoot my dad down." "Joellyn slapped me across the face. I hate Joellyn." Bobbi didn't have an explanation for even one of the twenty or so remarks.

Except for the tapes submitted as evidence by the defense, P-19 was probably the single most important piece of evidence in the trial. Amy had written it, it turned out, on the night in December that Bobbi had talked to Leslie for the first time since August. That summer call had ended with heated words on both sides and with Leslie nearly putting her fist through a window in rage.

The night that Leslie was taped, Amy and Jennifer had phoned Cutler and gotten Leslie instead of us. After about fifteen minutes of nonsensical sisterly chatter, Bobbi asked Joellyn's daughter to arrange for Bobbi to speak to Leslie. They exchanged brief pleasantries, ending on a note that left Leslie optimistic that her relationship with her mother might take a turn for the better.

Once Leslie discovered that conversation was to be admitted as evidence in the trial, her hopes were shattered.

"I *knew* she must have had a reason to talk to me like that. It just wouldn't be like her to start talking to me nicely in the middle of this mess."

During her testimony, Bobbi dismissed Leslie's testimony and her years of unhappiness perfunctorily.

She recalled her daughter's complaining that "Nobody cared about me" over trivial things like her hair, or not getting enough attention when she thought she had done something special. Bobbi said she just didn't think any of this was important.

One day Bobbi made me laugh, when she surreptitiously made faces at Judge Coburn and Paul, looking as if she'd slipped a set of Halloween fangs into her mouth. She also made me cry, the day she told the court that Leslie, Amy, and Jenny had all lied, making up everything they had said.

The only person she defended was Joellyn. Never, Bobbi said, in over five years had Joellyn been wrong and one of her daughters been right in a confrontation. Even when Paul showed her the Polaroid pictures that Stan had taken of Amy's bruised arm she stood fast in her belief that Joellyn hadn't done it.

Joellyn, in her turn as a defense witness, painted a portrait of a wonderful loving home where there were rarely arguments or problems once she had helped all the girls, particularly Leslie, work out the trauma of having me for a stepmother. They were just one big happy extended family, with all of her and Bobbi's friends a constant part of it.

Joellyn described her interactions with Amy, Leslie, and Jennifer in glowing terms. "Why, until this started, I had a better relationship with them than their father did," she concluded.

Paul only caught her offstride once, when he asked how she felt about her own children's becoming homosexual. As far as her daughter was concerned, it didn't matter either way.

"And your son? Is it okay if he's homosexual?"

She thought about it for a moment. "No," she said, to everyone's amazement at her double standard. "I prefer that he be heterosexual."

The defense had fifteen witnesses, all of whom were devoted in varying degrees to depicting Bobbi as a saint, Camden as a model home, and Leslie as an ogre who never fit into the family anyway.

Paul decimated the eavesdropping baby-sitter, who had been Leslie's best friend in Camden. Beyond that he barely questioned anybody, except Amy's school principal, Mr. Johnson.

Mr. Johnson had been called to attest to how well Amy was doing in Admiral Perry School, so well in fact that he was going to "mainstream" her from the special-ed school into a private girls' school, although he was recommending she be left back a grade.

He took exception to a letter Stan had written complaining

of many incidents in the lunchroom and on the bus where Amy was hit, or teased, and called "whitey," "honkey," and "faggot."

Johnson insisted such things happened all the time. "It doesn't mean anything."

Judge Coburn finally called a halt to the parade of witnesses. It had been nine weeks since the trial started, and he wanted to wind it down.

"Unless you have any more fact witnesses who are more than just corroborative, Mrs. Sheppard, I think we should schedule the experts next week. Then I can see Amy and Jennifer, and we'll be done." Annamay had been prepared to call most of the forty-three original affidavit writers plus a few more.

As soon as we knew the end was at hand, things moved very fast. Like Sisyphus, we'd been pushing the huge boulder up the mountain, and now it was about to tumble down the other side, gaining momentum.

Dr. Buxton, as the court's expert, was scheduled first, and though his report had been so one-sidedly in favor of our obtaining custody, in the interim he had listened to the tapes. Paul had no idea whether they had changed his opinion.

"Dr. Buxton is here to testify today if either of you choose to call him as your witness. Mrs. Sheppard?" Judge Coburn asked.

"No, your honor." She looked grim.

"Mr. Rowe?"

"Yes, your honor, I will."

Dr. Buxton was sworn in and took his seat on the witness stand.

After establishing his credentials as a board-certified child psychiatrist (the only subspecialty recognized in psychiatry) and a professor of child psychiatry at the New Jersey Medical College, Dr. Buxton reiterated the findings he had made several months previously. It was definitely in the best interests of Amy and Jennifer to be removed from the environment in which they were living.

He described his comprehensive interviewing procedure, including two interviews with Amy and Jennifer.

"I always have each parent bring the children involved, because very often a child will express a preference to be with whomever they are with at the time. These children were unusual in that they were strong in their desire to live with their father, even when their mother brought them to see me."

In his report he had referred to "lists" that Amy had brought, and was questioned about that.

"It's never happened to me before that a child would actually write down things she wanted to remember. The first time Amy just read from a piece of paper that she took out of her pocket. The second time she gave it to me when she was done." Paul placed the piece of paper into evidence.

P-107. Among Amy's notes were sprinkled the usual names by which Stan was referred to in Camden. Plus one singularly brutal one: "They called my dad a spayed dog."

As for the tapes, Dr. Buxton found they expressed a warm and loving relationship between Stan and his children. He also felt that more than anything they demonstrated the strong desire of the girls to live with us.

"There was one conversation where Amy wanted to be Dracula for Halloween, but Mr. Silverzweig didn't approve," Buxton recalled. Most children would have told their father they wouldn't come at all if they couldn't have their own way. But upset as Amy was, that thought had never even occurred to her.

The issue of brainwashing he considered nonexistent. "Children really can't be talked into doing something that they aren't already inclined to do, especially with the limited contact that a noncustodial parent has." He felt the parent *having* custody is the one who primarily influences a child's opinion. Children would have to have an extremely strong drive and be very unhappy to withstand the pressure that can be placed on them at home when they want to live with their other parent.

One colloquy that had taken place early in the trial was over the issue of whether or not the children's verbal expressions were hearsay if they were not direct statements made in the presence of one of the parties in the litigation. (I was considered a party because I was married to Stan, and the judge ruled that Joellyn was a party by virtue of her long-standing relationship with Bobbi, and their open admission that they had "a lifelong commitment to each other" and were a stable family unit.)

Annamay had objected when Leslie related what her sisters told her about how they felt and why they wanted to live with us. Coburn overruled her, based on a seldom-used exception to the hearsay rule which admits such statements if they put the party making them at risk.

Buxton reinforced Coburn's ruling by describing how openly the children had talked about Joellyn's anger, even though they knew how mad she would get when she found out what they had told him. "Children really have to be desperate to take a chance like that."

The very open homosexuality was of concern to him primarily because of the concern it was to Amy and Jennifer. Paul put into evidence the two pictures apiece that Amy and Jennifer had drawn for Dr. Buxton, starting with the outline of a blank boat. They had labeled the boats "lesbian boat," and they had drawn in flag masts bearing feminist banners.

"It's an intrusion in their lives." Dr. Buxton said it showed the frustration that they felt because their mother was more involved in a cause than she was with them.

Annamay was chewing her pencil frantically, trying to think of a way to salvage at least a little something from the testimony that was so disastrous to her client. "Dr. Buxton, if you had to choose between a foster home for these children or leaving them in their home with their mother, what would you do?"

He sat pensively, a young slender man, very decisive, very bright. "I would have to think about that. It would really depend on the foster home," he said steadily.

I guess that's why Paul says a good lawyer never asks a question when he doesn't know what the answer will be.

Dr. New, also a board-certified child psychiatrist and Chief of Child and Adolescent Psychiatry at the Westchester County Medical Center–New York Medical College, testified next. Since we had hired him, in our minds his opinion was not quite as powerful as Buxton's.

But Judge Coburn was of a different mind, and made that clear in court. "I am not giving any more weight to the court's expert than to any of the parties' experts in this case," he said after Dr. Buxton's testimony. Paul couldn't believe it, but an extensive search of the literature by one of the lawyers in his office proved the judge correct. There is no precedent in New Jersey law for granting greater credibility to an independent expert.

Dr. New's testimony was all the more important in the light of this finding, and it was essentially the same as Dr. Buxton's; he drew the same conclusions for the same reasons.

"There is something about the household that makes them uncomfortable. They are exposed to a lot of subtleties, and experiences they are not yet ready to assimilate."

Dr. New also used the word "intrusion," and at one point had a heated discussion with Annamay about "causes," whether they be political, sexual, or spiritual.

"There is a real intrusion here. It wouldn't matter what the issue." He was gentle, but firm. "She has made a choice, she has elected to commit herself to the women's movement and lesbianism to the exclusion of her children, and my interviews with all three children bear that out."

New found Bobbi's tape-recording the children's conversations to be another example of intrusion in their lives. Beyond that, he felt they were an expression of a very strong relationship between Amy, Jennifer, Stan, and myself, with the children trying to prolong the contact with us. "Perhaps Mr. and Mrs. Silverzweig didn't always use good judgment in trying to impress on the children the importance of what they would have to say to Dr. Buxton or the judge, but given the circumstances it's not surprising."

He interviewed the children only once, but had had Bobbi bring them for the same reason as Buxton. He was also surprised at the strength with which they related the urgency of the change they desired, despite the fact that they were brought by the custodial parent. "That's where the brainwashing takes place," he said. "From the inside, not the outside."

The defense didn't call the psychologist, Dr. Seidman, and didn't call the probation officer, Mrs. Kaszerman, a move which surprised us. They just called Drs. Green and Gould.

Dr. Green, who had interviewed Amy and Jennifer eight months before in the bedroom of his mother's apartment, was not a child psychiatrist, although well credentialed. He frankly admitted that his work primarily dealt with homosexuals, homosexuality, and transsexuality.

His interviews with the girls had been brief, but he had believed them when they said they wanted to stay with their mother because "they looked me in the eye." But it turned out to be a wasted day for the defense, because when Dr. Green had been given an opportunity to examine Dr. Buxton's report, he acknowledged that he would have to investigate the case further to see if his initial opinion was still merited.

Dr. Gould was not a certified child psychiatrist either, but he was all the defense had left. Unlike Drs. Buxton and New, he had not felt it necessary to interview all the parties involved.

"After I talked to Bobbi and Joellyn and the children I was ninety percent sure that custody should remain with the mother. Interviewing the father and stepmother would have made me about ninety-five percent sure."

"Why didn't you think it necessary to interview Leslie?" Paul asked.

"She was just another relative. You can talk to lots of people. Where is it supposed to end?"

Gould described at length the interviews he had with Amy and Jennifer, whom he saw on two different occasions. He catalogued the list of events, indignities, and feelings that the children had expressed to him, nearly identical to what they had told Buxton and New; but despite this he didn't feel they had given him any convincing reasons why they should live with their father. It was obvious to him, especially in light of the way he viewed the tapes, that "the children had been brainwashed."

He went on at length describing his interpretation of what he had heard on those cassettes.

"They threatened them and bribed them constantly," he said at one point.

"Why don't you give me an example?" Paul asked, knowing full well that the transcripts of the tapes would show not even one instance of that.

"Both Mr. and Mrs. Silverzweig kept telling the children repeatedly that they loved them and they wanted them to be happy. The implication was that if the children didn't state a preference in their favor, they would withdraw that love."

One of his interviews with Amy and Jenny was conducted in the presence of Bobbi and Joellyn, with Jennifer being held for at least a portion of it on Bobbi's lap. Jenny and Amy both reiterated even in that situation their desire to live with us, although when Joellyn began asking Jenny about wanting to commit suicide Jennifer refused to talk.

It was a stress interview, Dr. Gould explained to Paul.

It was of no great moment to him that Amy had been beaten with a belt. "Unfortunately, you see a lot of that. I saw no need to go into it."

Paul questioned Gould as to the opposite conclusions that Drs. Buxton and New had drawn from the same information provided by Amy and Jennifer.

"All I can say is that the children fooled them," responded the last expert for the defense.

Judge Coburn conducted his interviews with Amy and Jennifer on a Saturday, in his chambers. It had finally come—their long-awaited chance to talk fully to the judge.

They were awake at dawn after a sleepless night, nervous, excited, and relieved. They dressed carefully in sherbet-colored denim dresses, and were so exhausted from being up most of the night that they slept all the way to court.

In their single turns and together they spent about three hours with Judge Coburn, three hours while we paced and drank coffee and smoked a rarely purchased pack of cigarettes.

It had been cold and cloudy when we arrived, a raw mist in the air. When we left the sun was bursting through and patches of blue were spreading across the sky.

Paul walked us out. He and Annamay had been listening on earphones in the courtroom.

"They did it. They really did it." He just shook his head. "They corroborated eighty percent of what you and Leslie said. I don't see how we can lose now. And if we do, you *have* to appeal. But they did it!" He looked as pleased as he deserved to look.

It took more than two months for the case to be resolved.

While we were waiting for the decision, Stan and I began to work furiously, trying to rebuild the business that had trickled nearly to a standstill, trying to get back on our feet financially. The final bills weren't in, but we knew they would top six figures. Without a decimal point.

Moreover, Paul assured us constantly that if we won custody, Judge Coburn would award liberal visitation to Bobbi. And if we lost, God forbid, we didn't want Amy and Jennifer to think we had abandoned them. We decided sadly that there was no way our lovely life, half in Maine, half in New York, was going to work. Cutler was too far, and what the girls needed was a house, not a city apartment. Home, for most of the year, would have to be New Jersey.

And in the end, Judge Coburn didn't hand down a decision at all. When Paul notified him that we had decided to move back to New Jersey, the judge called both lawyers into his chambers for a lengthy conference and pressed them to come to an agreement, the terms of which he for the most part outlined.

Paul reported back to us by telephone. "He said your move to Jersey is a godsend." He paused for effect.

"Why?" Stan and I asked in unison.

"It means he can do what he really wants to do."

"And what's that?"

"Nothing. He wants you and Bobbi to agree to joint custody."

"What?" This time we shrieked in unison. And Stan added,

"I don't get it. Why doesn't he just go and do what the facts indicate?"

"I'm not sure," Paul said. "I suspect he's still reluctant to admit there's such a thing as an unfit mother. And we've also heard him say a few times in court that the best decisions are those that don't satisfy anybody completely, that force all the people involved to compromise. He might have other reasons, too. But he must think this would be better for the girls."

No winners, no losers.

"What would our agreeing to this mean?" All that we knew about joint custody was bad, but we had to face the issue; this was Coburn's ball game.

"Actually, from what he's indicated, the kids *would* live with you and go to school where you lived," Paul said. "And you would make all the custodial decisions."

"That doesn't sound like joint custody to me," Stan said. "Why doesn't he just give me custody?"

"He said he would definitely transfer custody if there was no agreement, and based on the facts he'd have no choice. But as I said, it goes against the grain for him. And I suspect that if you push him to this, he'll make you pay for it. All kinds of expenses, transportation, things like that. He very much wants you to agree to settle."

"I don't want to."

"Neither do I," said Paul, "but I'm not sure if it's just my need for blood and a clean win, or if his reasoning is really sound."

Bobbi agreed, at least in principle, immediately. For her it was better than losing outright. The three of us thought about it and talked about it all that week, trying to find a reason to say no.

The only rationale we came up with that Coburn might listen to was from the experts. Paul called Buxton and Stan called New, and explained the situation. Once again, independently, they concurred. Joint custody could work if there was a good relationship between the parties. But given the animosity between Stan and

Roberta, and the children's strong desire to be free of their home environment, neither Buxton nor New felt joint custody would be in the best interests of the children.

It didn't fly with Coburn. "I want him to agree," he told Paul.

"I don't think we really have a choice, Stan," Paul said finally. "But I'll write the ticket, so don't worry. We'll do the best we can. And if they give us a hard time, we'll just throw it back to Coburn."

Paul drafted an agreement, and sent it to Annamay. The edited version she returned was totally unacceptable; she had left only one major clause intact, the one transferring custody of Leslie to her father.

The next go-round was a three-hour session among Coburn, Annamay, and Paul, with the judge seeing them separately and together, as he had Amy and Jennifer. Annamay was about to leave for France, and Coburn was insistent that this be decided before she departed.

It was. And the terms were substantially those that Paul had anticipated, with the agreement basically a reversal of the original custodial arrangements. The children had their legal residency with Stan and visitation with Roberta—only this time it was called joint custody.

The outcome is that we have all three girls back together again, with us, and that's all that really counts. It doesn't matter what it's called. And Amy and Jenny perceive it as a victory.

"We won, we won!" they danced around shouting after a Saturday-morning telephone call to Judge Coburn in which he told them the news. They called everyone they could think of to share their joy, and went around for weeks writing "We Won" on posters they would hang up, and on the sides of dusty cars.

When the euphoria wears off, they'll meet the same struggles that Leslie had to face, and we'll do the best we can to help them through the difficult times. I asked them once if they were angry at us because of what we'd put them through, misleading them that it wouldn't be as difficult as it turned out to be.

"Oh, no, Mommy," said Jennifer, hugging me, peace in her

face already. "We asked you to, and it wasn't so bad."

"Are you kidding, Mom?" Amy's grown about eight inches and gained twenty pounds since we started the suit, more woman now than child. "We won, didn't we? It was worth it!" She flashed her wonderful smile.

29

It's over now, the grueling experience behind us, and we can get on with a normal life, whatever that is for us. We've moved to a suburban community in New Jersey, to a split-level cape with a two-car garage, and traded in the four-wheel-drive jeep that served us so well in the snows of Maine for a Chevy station wagon, complete with roof rack; we'll go home to Cutler in the summers.

The girls are all enrolled in school. Leslie will have three years in a high school that will challenge her intellectually and socially, and we are certain she will be up to it. Amy will start the sixth grade in the Middle School, escaping, to her relief, the shame she felt at having to be left back. She'll be in a small class where she can get individual attention in the areas she needs it, and be mainstreamed into the regular classes when she doesn't. Jennifer will attend the Lower School and come home for lunch like the rest of her classmates.

I'm still numb.

I know we had to do it. And knowing we had no choice, we found the strength to get through the ugly vicious year.

I didn't want to do it. I didn't want the past to be raked up, accusations to be made, mud to be slung. I wanted things to be as neat and orderly as possible. I didn't want the pain for us or the children.

I often wished that Leslie, Amy, and Jennifer could have been happier with Bobbi, and enjoyed the benefits of two homes where they felt loved. I didn't want them to need me as deeply as they did.

And even now I sometimes still wish none of this had ever happened. I wish I were living in a cottage in the English country-side, roses and ivy rambling over the fence, dew on the flowers in the garden. (Funny. The image that I conjure up is of that night garden in Jockey Hollow, where I first thought Stan might kiss me.)

Being a stepmother is unique and difficult. I don't always know how to deal with the out-of-the-ordinary problems. The phantoms of the past are always with us. And of course I still frequently feel used, abused, put-upon, overworked, and taken for granted.

But I also know I wouldn't want to be without my three chicka-dees. They have added an unmatchable dimension to my life in their own special ways, and the sweet trusting faces, the confidences they share, the handmade cards for Mother's Day, and the memory of a half-empty box of bath cubes for Christmas are all treasures I couldn't bear to part with.

I guess I'm really not so different from other mothers after all.